NINE INNINGS

'85

Also by Daniel Okrent
The Ultimate Baseball Book,
edited with Harris Lewine

Daniel Okrent

NINE INNINGS

Ticknor & Fields • New York • 1985

Library of Congress Cataloging in Publication Data

Okrent, Daniel.
Nine innings.

Includes index.
1. Baseball. I. Title.
GV867.O57 1985   796.357'2   84–26687
ISBN 0–89919–334–X

Printed in the United States of America

V 10 9 8 7 6 5 4 3 2 1

Portions of Chapters 3 and 7 originally appeared, in
somewhat different form, in *Inside Sports* magazine.

*For Harry Okrent and John Lazear Okrent,
and in memory of John Cushman*

This ball — this symbol; is it worth a man's life?
— Branch Rickey

ACKNOWLEDGMENTS

Work on this book began in 1980, when I first traveled to Milwaukee to discuss my plans with Bud Selig, the president of the Milwaukee Brewers, and Harry Dalton, his executive vice president and general manager. My intention was to write about a game in the 1981 season, and to spend the months leading up to that game reporting on the events, people, and issues which would likely have a bearing on it. But 1981 was riven by an unprecedented midseason strike by members of the Major League Baseball Players Association, and on the advice of my publishers I postponed until 1982 the selection of a game that would serve as the book's focus while continuing to gather the material that would constitute the digressions from my narrative. So much of baseball's shape *is* digressive that this turned out to be a fortunate delay.

Over the course of two years of research, during which the Brewers played under the leadership of three different managers, I received the patient help of many people in the Milwaukee organization. Among these, I wish to thank Bud Selig; Harry Dalton; Tom Skibosh, the Brewers' publicity director; managers George Bamberger, Harvey Kuenn, and, especially, Bob Rodgers; and Tommy Ferguson, who served as Milwaukee's unflappable, generous, and superbly helpful traveling secretary until early 1983.

Tom Flaherty of the *Milwaukee Journal* and Vic Feuerherd of the *Milwaukee Sentinel* were my companions on road trips, colleagues in the press box, and ever-helpful advisers. This book will probably be less interesting to Tom and Vic than to anyone else, for they live with, think about, and write daily about most of the matters addressed here. If the book is interesting to others, Tom and Vic deserve much of the credit, and absolutely none of the blame if it is not.

Longer-standing debts of gratitude must be paid to Bob Fishel of the American League office, Joe Durso of the *New York Times,* and Jerome Holtzman of the *Chicago Tribune,* all of whom — entirely unwittingly — played roles in getting me involved in baseball writing in the first place. Bob Creamer and Steve Wulf of *Sports Illustrated,* and John Walsh of *Inside Sports,* provided professional support and encouragement; John, not incidentally, also provided the magazine assignments (and the much-appreciated expense money) that paid for my attendance at the baseball winter meetings in Dallas and in Hollywood, Florida, and at the Brewers' spring training in Sun City, Arizona. Several people in baseball who asked that they not be mentioned in the book were even more generous than they were self-effacing (or, in a handful of cases, justifiably fearful of the reproach of others).

I also owe deep thanks to Liz Darhansoff, who was endlessly supportive; to Michael Stevens, who made me welcome in Milwaukee; to Tony Lake, who offered a valuable set of fan's notes; to Bill James, who will immediately recognize in my work the influence of his thinking, even if not the clarity of his prose; and to all the Rotissarians, but especially among them Lee Eisenberg, who pushed me, and the tall tactician, Cork Smith. Friend, confidant, confessor, drill sergeant, editor, Cork would make a great manager.

Virtually as common as acknowledgments in which the writer thanks his wife are acknowledgments in which the writer first points out how common it is for writers to thank their wives. Thus may I appear to be unoriginal. In fact, though, no one else is married to Becky, and no one else could ever know how extraordinarily fortunate I am.

D.O.
Worthington, Massachusetts

NINE INNINGS

PROLOGUE

Most days, Harry Gill was the first one at the park. He was the superintendent of grounds and maintenance, responsible for the playing field. His turf was composed of Kentucky bluegrass, half an inch long in the infield, an inch and a half in the outfield. The bluegrass grew out of eighteen inches of clay soil, and the clay rested atop a grid of tiles that directed excess water out of the park. The infield skin was a mix of sand and clay loam, with about five or six tons of Turface mixed in each year. Turface was a ceramic-like, heat-treated clay that absorbed about a hundred times its weight in moisture. It was a reddish substance, and it looked good on television.

Along the third and first base lines, Harry Gill had contrived to keep all but six inches of the six-foot-wide dirt basepaths outside the chalk foul lines. Milwaukee's players bunted well, and the less naked the clay in fair territory, the less likely their bunts would roll foul. In front of the pitcher's mound, bare spots showed where batting practice pitchers who needed ten feet of cheating distance wore out the bluegrass. The grass in front of second base was all right now, not as it was when the crowd at a Rolling Stones concert had compacted it down four inches. Concerts were always a problem; Gill had to gas nitrogen underneath the grass after each one to get it green again.

The area around first base was also a problem, as it was in every ball park. The constant traffic up the line from home plate was murderous on the grass and took its toll on the clay around the bag. At least Harry Gill could these days give the first base area its fair share of water. It was different a few years back, when George Scott played the position for Milwaukee. Scott liked a clean bounce. When the slightest hint of wetness set in around first, Scott would seek out Gill.

"We ain't growing parsnips here," Scott would say. "We're playing baseball."

1

	1	2	3	4	5	6	7	8	9	R	H	E
Baltimore										0	0	0
Milwaukee										0	0	0

On the morning of June 10, 1982, beneath the stands of Milwaukee County Stadium, equipment manager Bob Sullivan and his assistants placed clean uniforms in the clubhouse lockers. Above each locker a shelf contained gloves, caps, spare shoes. These shelves were further individualized by other items: containers of Super Acerola, jojoba oil, mink oil, Desenex, Aqua Velva, Nivea cream; pouches of Levi Garrett and Skoal; cans of Foot Guard. Gorman Thomas, the center fielder, arrived early for the afternoon's game. Thomas was always the first one there, arriving as many as five hours before game time. On June 10, as on virtually every other game day, he sat in front of his locker drinking coffee, greeting (or pointedly not greeting) his various teammates as they wandered in. They were a reasonable cross section of professional athletes. The youngest was a lithe, 24-year-old Puerto Rican named Eddie Romero, a reserve infielder whose very membership on the team was all but unknown to any but the Brewers' most ardent fans. The eldest was a tall, elegantly mustachioed relief pitcher named Roland Glen Fingers, 35. Fingers, who was born in Ohio and raised in California, had in his thirteen seasons in the major leagues distinguished himself as had very few others in baseball's entire history. Their 23 teammates stood on a line between Romero and Fingers, spaced along it by age, talent, wealth, renown.

Somewhere near the middle of this line was Bob McClure, today's starting pitcher. McClure didn't arrive in the clubhouse beneath the stands until very late in the morning of June 10, barely two hours before game time. He had lingered over the carbohydrate-heavy breakfast he always ate before day games. Now, he spoke with his catcher, Charlie Moore, as he dressed, then quickly went out on the field. "Once I've talked to the catcher," McClure said, "once that input is lodged in my melon, I have to go out on the field and be part of what's going on. I can't stand the clubhouse. You can only sign so many autographs and read so many letters before you get bored stiff. I have to be out on the field, shagging flies, hanging around the cage, talking with the players. That's relaxing."

Up in the stands, as McClure and his teammates and the members of the visiting Baltimore Orioles stretched and ran and threw and socialized and started batting practice on the field below, the day's crew of ushers waited for the gates to open. It was a lovely, sunny Thursday. The Orioles and the Brewers were scheduled to play at 1:30 in the afternoon. Allan H. Selig, the president of the Milwaukee Brewers Baseball Club, Inc., arrived at his unprepossessing office in the bowels of County Stadium just before noon. By then, the rest of the front office staff had been at work for nearly three hours. In the publicity department, Tom Skibosh and Mario Ziino entered statistical data from the previous night's game into large ledger books. In the ticket office, armed guards stood by to protect the stacks of bills that would be collected in the hours leading up to game time. Bruce Manno and Dan Duquette, in the farm department, read the game reports the minor league managers had phoned in the night before. Harry Dalton, the general manager, was on the phone. At the reception desk, Betty Grant told callers that, yes, it was a day game today. The Milwaukee newspapers sat on Grant's large desk. There were no sports sections left.

Bud Selig had always loved baseball. He had been the chief executive of a major league club for thirteen years. Baseball "is not a toy," he said. "It is not a hobby. When we were starting out here, Walter O'Malley said to me — I'll never forget it — that baseball was his only business. It can't be tinkered with."

By and large, Bud Selig abided by O'Malley's dictum. Although Selig was also the president of his family's auto dealership and often found himself of a morning reviewing inventory sheets and sales reports at the showroom, it wasn't auto business that had him arriving late for work on June 10. When things were going bad for the Brewers, Selig could all too easily sink into despair, chewing up his insides with as much energy as he chewed the little cigars that were usually clutched between his teeth. Things were definitely not going well for Selig's Brewers these days. In April they had been one of the favorites to win the American League's Eastern Division championship, and now they were in fourth place. The Orioles, their primary rivals for the championship, had the night before won their third straight game in Milwaukee. Bud Selig had allocated many millions of his partners' dollars to build a contending team. He had, wisely, placed those dollars in the hands of Harry Dalton, a widely admired executive who had, it seemed, deployed the money well. He had seen Dalton barely a week earlier resort to the most expedient of solutions in any attempt to turn a team around: Dalton had fired the manager, Bob Rodgers, who had led the Brewers to the best record in the American League just one season earlier. For a moment, the team had appeared to come alive, winning four in a row under the new manager, Harvey Kuenn. But Baltimore today stood 27 outs from a sweep of the series — a sweep in the Brewers' home park — and Bud Selig had simply stayed in bed until the last possible moment.

For his part, Bob Rodgers was in no hurry to get to work either. He had just returned home to Yorba Linda, California, having left Milwaukee after cleaning out his small apartment at the Astor Hotel. Throughout his baseball career, Rodgers had spent the off-seasons as a glue salesman, representing a firm that manufactured industrial adhesives. He said he understood why Dalton had fired him — the moment came for all managers — but he was nonetheless embittered by what he deemed the selfishness and obstinacy of some of the team's players. He was happy enough that he had his glue-selling job to turn to, but he had spent a lifetime in baseball and was now suddenly on the outside.

Rodgers was a tall man, broad in the shoulders, blessed with bright eyes and a movie star's face. He wore cowboy boots, well-cut sport coats, open-collared shirts. Expectedly, his baseball friends called him "Buck." He had chewed tobacco all of his adult life, yet always took care to use whitening drops on his teeth to combat the inevitable staining. *Playgirl* magazine had once featured Rodgers in an article on baseball's sexiest men. Pete Vuckovich, when he was still working for Rodgers, once noticed the older man off in the distance. Vuckovich, a pitcher, had just been making some uncomplimentary comments about Rodgers' professional capabilities. "He sure is good-looking, though," Vuckovich said.

Vuckovich, a pitcher of frightening mien, immense strength, and wildly unpredictable behavior, was rather mild in his criticism of Rodgers, complaining mostly that the manager was too quick to pull a starting pitcher from a baseball game. "He doesn't know as much about pitching as he thinks he does," Vuckovich said. "He's never been out there."

Rodgers had, indeed, never been out there, out on the small rise in the middle of the baseball diamond. Rodgers was, as the spectacularly bent digits on his right hand revealed, a catcher. In fact, in a nine-year major league career, he had spent only one game at any position but catcher. He was proud of that career, even if it was more distinguished by his indefatigability — in 1962 he caught 150 games, just 5 games off the American League record — than by his offensive statistics. He was particularly proud because the career almost didn't happen. He was foundering in the Detroit Tigers' minor league system, making no progress, when he finally decided, still only 22 but a five-year veteran of professional baseball, to find another career. Then the American League of Professional Baseball Clubs, the unincorporated association that controls half of major league baseball, decided to expand. The eight members of the league voted to increase their number by 25 percent in 1961. The new teams needed players, of course, and the established clubs arranged to provide some of the least accomplished in their own organizations. Bob Rodgers was the twelfth player picked by Gene Autry's Los Angeles Angels. "Autry saved me from having to find a real job," Rodgers often said.

The first major league manager Rodgers played for was Bill Rigney. Rigney had distinguished himself as one of the particularly combative, and especially cagy, members of the New York Giants teams of the late 1940s and early 1950s. He was as cerebral as he was bumptious, and he put the two qualities together to become a manager of considerable accomplishment. With the Angels, he often found his catcher, Bob Rodgers, and his shortstop, Jim Fregosi, challenging him after a game: " 'Why'd you do that? What were you thinking? What did you know?' Bob and Jimmy were always asking me things. It never stopped. You could tell these two were thinking, and they wanted to learn things," Rigney remembered. "Hell, if you had to pick future managers on that team, you wouldn't have had to look very far." Rigney, for his part, had learned his managing from Leo Durocher, who had learned from Miller Huggins in the 1920s. Rodgers' managerial bloodlines, at least, were superb.

It took Rodgers, the catcher, nineteen years from his first season at Rigney's elbow to become a major league manager. After his retirement as a player, in 1969, he became a coach with the Minnesota Twins — a pitching coach. He managed in the minor leagues for two seasons, coached the San Francisco Giants' pitchers in 1976 — working for his old mentor, Rigney, who was doing his last turn as a manager that season — and came to Milwaukee as third base coach in 1978. In the beginning of the 1980 season, Rodgers was made acting manager of the club while George Bamberger recuperated from heart surgery. At season's end, he formally took over the team when Bamberger announced his retirement.

"There's a lot a manager can do," Rodgers said one day in 1981. "But on this team there's not much: you can pinch hit for [second baseman Jim] Gantner when there's a lefty pitching, and you can rest your regulars every so often. You can talk to your pitchers and catchers, and make sure they don't throw the change-up to a Doug Flynn–type hitter." Flynn was a weak-hitting second baseman for the Texas Rangers. "Other than that, you just got to let 'em play ball." The Milwaukee Brewers played ball in 1982 for Bob Rodgers until June 2, when Dalton fired him. He was replaced "on an interim basis" by hitting coach Harvey Kuenn, a former major league shortstop and outfielder who, in the preceding five years, had undergone quadruple-bypass surgery, lost fifty pounds from a mysterious stomach ailment, and had had a leg amputated because of life-threatening blood clots. Kuenn was 51.

Bob McClure, the left-handed pitcher, looked at Charlie Moore, the catcher. He had thrown in the bullpen, and he had come to the center of the diamond and thrown his eight warmup pitches. Now he would start the game.

After nearly four years of erratic performance in the Milwaukee bullpen — one press box joker called McClure and his right-handed relief partner Bill Castro "Ethyl and Premium" — McClure had been placed in the team's starting rotation in September of 1980 by George Bamberger. "I always thought of myself as a starter," said McClure, who never pitched in relief until the day he reached the major leagues. "But no one else ever did. I guess there wasn't anybody else to be the relief man here, and because my arm was pretty trouble free, the job fell to me.

"In fact," McClure remembered, "when Bambi did tell me I was going to start, I thought he was joking." But McClure won four of his five starts that September, and when the newly installed Rodgers assembled his starting rotation out of the available arms in the winter of 1981, McClure had a place in it. Then, what appeared to be tendinitis assaulted his previously "trouble free" arm (it was later diagnosed as a rotator cuff tear), and McClure was fundamentally useless for the 1981 season. His return to health toward its close was one of the primary reasons Rodgers and his colleagues in the Milwaukee front office were confident entering 1982.

Baltimore's first batter was Lenn Sakata, a Hawaii-born nisei who had reached the major leagues in the Milwaukee organization. An excellent second baseman who could also play shortstop, he was nonetheless deemed enough of an offensive liability that he was shipped to Baltimore for John Flinn, a pitcher of little consequence who was unable to stick in either city. Sakata was one of the shortest players in the majors, listed in the Baltimore press guide as 5'9" but at least a full inch shorter. He was also distinguished as one of the first major leaguers to turn to the Nautilus machine as a strength builder; standing next to a taller teammate, like the elongated pitcher Jim Palmer, Sakata's overdeveloped chest and shoulders gave him the appearance of a midget wrestler.

On the mound, Bob McClure stared in at Moore, his catcher, then pivoted on his left foot, swinging his right leg back and around, twisting his body so far that Sakata could see the numbers on the back of McClure's uniform. Then, spinning forward, he released the first pitch with his wrist stiff, the edge of his hand slicing perpendicularly through the air. The ball tumbled straight ahead, then suddenly dipped when it came near the plate as the topspin imparted by McClure's release made itself felt. He had devised his spinning motion at the urging of Bob Rodgers and pitching coach Cal McLish, who noted that McClure's pitches sank more readily when his arm dragged and that his arm would drag more if he adopted the whirling delivery. But on this pitch the ball dropped a millisecond too late; ball one, high.

McClure missing with his curveball was good news to Baltimore, for without an effective curve, McClure was rarely an effective pitcher. Sakata waited on the next pitch, this time a fastball, also out of the strike zone. He looked toward Cal Ripken, his third base coach, received no intelligence from the sequence of gestures Ripken offered, and swung ineffectively at the next pitch, a fastball. He fouled off another fastball, and McClure had managed to restore a bare edge over the batter, the count 2 and 2. It is called an "even" count, but there is nothing even about it: there is still room for the pitcher to err, none for the batter. And the pitcher holds both a weapon in his hand and the power of commission in his head. It was up to McClure to execute; Sakata could only react.

At 2 and 2, Paul Molitor, Milwaukee's third baseman, backed up some five feet, no longer guarding against the bunt down the third base line. Then, another fastball, another foul. McClure peered at his catcher, Moore. To Molitor's left, Robin Yount, the Brewer shortstop, saw Moore signal for a curve, then shouted a "Hum-now!" at McClure: it was more than encouragement; it was a signal to Molitor, out of view of Moore's signals, that a curve was coming. McClure pivoted, kicked, spun, threw; as he released the pitch, Molitor leaned slightly toward the third base line, prepared for Sakata to get around more quickly on a slow pitch and, perhaps, pull it down the line. Sakata watched it go by: 3 and 2.

In their broadcast booth, Bob Uecker and his partner, a young man named Dwayne Mosley, were talking about Uecker's military career when McClure threw the seventh pitch of the afternoon. It was a change-up, the second off-speed pitch in a row. Sakata immediately judged its speed and its trajectory, and brought his arms around in front of him, fully extended. Uecker interrupted his armed services reverie to watch the ball land ten rows up in the left field bleachers. As Sakata circled the bases, and as the boos began to well up from the grandstand, Uecker told his listeners, "Lenny Sakata leads off the Oriole first inning with his second home run of the year, and the Brewers play from behind again today."

The team Bob Rodgers took north in April of 1982 had been expected to contend for a pennant, yet the only contention in the season's first two months had been in the clubhouse, on the plane, in the dugout. For their first eleven years in Milwaukee, the Brewers were either tolerated in their early mediocrity or honored in their subsequent competence. In the past two seasons, though, the city and the Milwaukee organization for the first time realistically expected the Brewers to win a pennant. A strike in 1981 gave the team half of a half of a pennant, capturing as they did the Eastern Division championship in the second half of the season and subsequently losing in the first round of that season's two-tiered playoffs to the New York Yankees. This year, the same team, which had compiled the division's best record overall in 1981, was back, intact; alone among the 26 major league teams, Milwaukee had acquired no new personnel over the winter. McClure was healthy, which was seen to be an advantage; Larry Hisle, a prodigious power hitter who missed almost all of 1980 and 1981 with a shoulder injury, was expected back, too.

In spring training, Rodgers admitted he felt pressure, though one never would have guessed it by observing his public behavior or by listening to the statements he made to the press. He was, publicly, a cocky man, articulate, witty, always in control. He was even bold enough to stop, without club approval, taking ten minutes daily to record the "Buck Rodgers Show," a pregame interview that provided the manager with the opportunity to speak directly to the fans and provided radio station WISN with more programming around which to sell commercial time. The station, badly bruised financially by the 1981 strike, had cut Rodgers' daily fee from $75 to $50. The manager of the team with the best 1981 record in the American League East didn't need that sort of insult.

Nonetheless, those close to Rodgers knew that even the euphoric moment in October of 1981 when Rollie Fingers, the extraordinary relief pitcher whose season earned him the Most Valuable Player award, caught a leaping Ted Simmons in his arms — even that moment was slightly sour for Rodgers. Three times during the 1981 season — a lot for even a full season, let alone a strike-diminished one — there had been urgent team meetings in the Brewer clubhouse. The first occurred in May, when Dalton, the general manager, who was distinctly unhappy with the team's performance in the early going, gave a school principal talk to his errant wards. Eyes were averted around the room as Dalton evenly and forthrightly lectured the team, not naming names but citing possible miscreants with an apparently effective "you know who you are": you who aren't running out ground balls, who're burning the late night candles, who're more concerned about your personal statistics than the welfare of the team.

Dalton's talk either had some real effect or happened to coincide with fortuitous lunar movements that got the Brewers on their feet. The next meeting occurred in August, and this one was players only: griping about the manager and his use of certain players had begun to corrode the team's unity, and Sal Bando — the team's captain, its senior man, without question its most dignified and respectworthy member — called the players together. Air was cleared anew, and the team was back on track.

The last meeting, though, was the one whose provenance most affected Bob Rodgers. Several players had, not for attribution, told the *Milwaukee Journal*'s Tom Flaherty — he had known most of them as rookies, and they trusted him — that the team's problem was its manager. They accused Rodgers of remoteness, poor communication, lack of faith, inconsistency, overmanaging, and a variety of other sins. When the story broke, Rodgers called a meeting. He confronted twenty-five blank faces, none of which would admit culpability, and stared them down. Some players said they had renewed respect for Rodgers. Some went to him, privately, to assure him they weren't the ones who had gone to Flaherty. Among these last, Rodgers felt, at least two were indeed Flaherty's sources. And if he had any villain at all to choose, it was Simmons, whose joyous leap into Fingers' arms that fall day in Detroit marked the first time in his twelve years in the big leagues Simmons had won anything, even half of a half of a pennant.

Withal, Rodgers in spring training in '82 appeared confident, but felt no comfort in it. He knew he had detractors and enemies on the team, and that these men — catcher Simmons, pitcher Mike Caldwell, outfielder Gorman Thomas, Pete Vuckovich — were among the most vocal and visible players he had. He knew, too, that he couldn't expect soft treatment from the press: the time was past when he could go to a writer like the *Boston Globe*'s Peter Gammons, who in his influential column the previous September had written that the Brewers' managerial problems were "like a yellow cloud" over the team; he couldn't go to Gammons, as he had in 1981, and say, "Come on, please give me a break. I'm a rookie manager."

"The Brewers play from behind again today." Uecker's eulogy upon Lenn Sakata's lead-off home run rang an accompaniment to Bob McClure's, as he distractedly picked dirt out of his cleats on the mound. The three straight losses Milwaukee had endured at Baltimore's hands had begun to unsettle the Era of Good Feeling ushered into the Milwaukee clubhouse with Kuenn's replacement of Rodgers. The "yellow cloud" had exited with the rookie manager, who licked his wounds at home in Orange County while his sluggish team suddenly awakened — at least until the Baltimore series — under Harvey Kuenn's leadership.

In the Milwaukee dugout, Kuenn chewed the enormous wad of tobacco that was his constant ball park companion (out in society, he favored equally gargantuan cigars). His bright blue-gray eyes watched McClure, and then moved to take in the second batter, Cal Ripken Jr. Ripken's father, Cal Sr., was the Baltimore third base coach, a quiet, stolid man who was in 1982 daily able to live through the deeds of his son the major league career he himself had never enjoyed. Kuenn thought Cal Sr. was probably enjoying himself too much this week; the younger Ripken had used Milwaukee's pitchers to end a batting slump. The day before, Kuenn and Pat Dobson, the Brewers' acting pitching coach, surveyed the wreckage Ripken *fils* had made of Milwaukee pitching in the first two days of the series. They discerned that Ripken had been confronting fastballs on the outside half of the plate as a land developer confronts a bankrupt farm. Kuenn and Dobson agreed that the coach should instruct Milwaukee's pitchers to come in tight on Ripken, with breaking pitches as well as with fastballs. In Wednesday's game, Ripken had hit a home run off left-hander Randy Lerch, whose control was erratic. But in the first inning today, McClure and his catcher Moore were literalists: six pitches, all of them on the inside half of the plate, culminated in a fastball that spun the hitter around and sent Moore in pursuit of a harmless pop foul, the first out of the game.

The inning's third batter was Dan Ford, a big, balding black man whose stance was one of contemporary baseball's great improbabilities. Ford stood nearly perpendicular to the normal right-hander's stance, his back almost square to the pitcher; had he worn an advertisement on the back of his jersey, pitchers all over the American League would have bought the product. At the peak of McClure's whirling motion, *his* back presented to the batter, Ford and McClure made a comic tableau, two duelers still pacing off steps with their weapons in the air. In center field, Gorman Thomas stood like a man waiting impatiently in line at a bank, his gloved hand on his left hip, his left leg straight, his right indolently bent. Robin Yount, at shortstop, placed one foot twelve inches ahead of the other, his body crouched, his arms poised like a wrestler's. Jim Gantner, the second baseman, bent over, his glove grazing the infield dirt.

As McClure began his spin toward Ford, Thomas's bulky body began to stir, moving almost imperceptibly toward left field. Gantner crouched yet further. And Yount brought his feet square with each other, creating movement that would spring into muscular activity as Ford wrapped his bat around the flight of McClure's fastball and sent the pitch on a windblown arc into short left field. Yount altered his forward-leaning course, dashed back on the ball, and leapt for it an instant too late. It grazed off his fingertips and fell lazily to the grass.

The next batter, Eddie Murray, singled rather more assertively down the left field line, Ford pulled into second, and Kuenn turned to Dobson, his pitching coach. Dobson picked up the dugout telephone. Bullpen coach Larry Haney answered at the other end. Haney told Jim Slaton to begin to warm up. McClure labored successfully to keep Baltimore's Benny Ayala and Gary Roenicke off base and to keep Slaton, his teammate, in the bullpen. Sammy Stewart, the Baltimore pitcher, thus began his day's work with a 1-0 lead.

	1	*2*	*3*	*4*	*5*	*6*	*7*	*8*	*9*	*R*	*H*	*E*
Baltimore	1									1	3	0
Milwaukee										0	0	0

If McClure was a particularly unimposing figure — less than 6 feet tall, only 170 pounds, curly hair closely cropped to a smallish head — then his opposite number with the Orioles was, indeed, opposite. Sammy Stewart was a hulking fellow from Swannanoa, North Carolina, up in the Blue Ridge. He looked like a farmer's hardest working boy, 210 pounds gathered mostly in his broad shoulders and powerful, heavy legs. He stood 6'3", and the slow, easy, tossing-stones-in-a-river manner of his eight warmup pitches added further to his rural mien. He had bushy, unruly hair, a drooping mustache, and, in 1981's truncated season, the best earned run average in the league. This last still hadn't earned Stewart a regular spot in Baltimore's estimable starting rotation; his manager, Earl Weaver, picked spots for him, and today's was ideal: Stewart had, in his career, held Milwaukee hitters to a .146 batting average. He began his work now with three of his teammates having just completed 27 consecutive innings in Milwaukee without the intrusion of a relief pitcher.

Milwaukee's first batter was Paul Molitor, the third baseman. He was an elegant young man with deep, startling eyes, broad shoulders, and incongruously bowed legs. As the Brewers' leadoff batter, and as the only man on the team capable of stealing bases at a remotely healthy rate, Molitor was critical to the Milwaukee offense — mostly because his game was antithetical to the one the team played as a whole. Cecil Cooper, the professorial first baseman and unquestionably Milwaukee's — perhaps all of baseball's — best overall hitter, nicknamed Molitor "the Igniter" for his role on offense. And today the third baseman began Milwaukee's first offensive turn with a single to center field on a 1-1 pitch from Sammy Stewart. The gloomy quiet of the first half of the first inning gave way to a stirring in the Milwaukee stands as Molitor stood on first base, removed his batting gloves, and took his lead.

It was Kuenn's laissez-faire position to give Molitor the "green light": the freedom to decide on his own whether or not to steal. The other Brewer who usually had the green light was Robin Yount, who didn't have Molitor's speed but in whose "baseball sense" Kuenn had great faith. Occasionally, Kuenn would have Harry Warner, the third base coach, send a sign to the baserunner telling him specifically *not* to steal, but certainly in a situation such as this one, Molitor was free to go.

Yount came to the plate. He was an extraordinary athlete, equally as gifted as Molitor, with unerring instincts and uncompromisable skills. But whereas Molitor was a thinker, Yount relied utterly on instinct, and his manager and coaches ceded judgment to those instincts. In fact, worried that the knowledge that Molitor would be running might disrupt Yount's natural behavior at the plate, Kuenn specifically wanted his shortstop *not* to know when Molitor might be going.

Yount held his bat away from his shoulder at a 45-degree angle, his muscles held in tension preparatory to beginning the fluid series of crack-the-whip arcs that constituted his swing, beginning with the movement of his feet, migrating upward through the knees, hips, shoulders, arms, and wrists. Stewart stood motionless in the peculiar position he used with men on base: unlike most pitchers, who brought their hands down to a stop at abdomen level when pitching from the stretch, Stewart brought his arms to the position he might assume if he were playing a cornet. With his elbows apart, his hands joined about ten inches in front of his chin, Stewart turned and threw toward first. Molitor stepped back to the bag.

Yount, who had not hit safely in 14 tries against Stewart, was impassive. The first pitch, a fastball called for a strike, revealed at least a glimpse of Stewart's capabilities this day, and in combination with the pickoff throw had given Molitor a sense of his chance to run. As the pitcher, working quickly, lifted his cornet to his lips once more, Yount flexed his bat ever so slightly. Stewart, absolutely still, jerked his left leg upward with the crispness of a performing Lipizzaner, pulled back his right arm, and the pitch came. Yount always concentrated on the first moment of a pitch's flight, intuitively triangulating its perceived course from that briefest clue, and now, discerning a slider, he executed a swing that intersected the plane of the ball's movement at knee level, on the outside half of the plate. But Yount's instinctive calculations were infinitesimally off, and the ball looped languorously out to left field, where it was gathered in by Benny Ayala.

The next batter was Don Money, playing first for Cooper, who was protecting a slight hamstring pull on the orders of Dr. Paul Jacobs, the Milwaukee team physician. Money had been playing professional baseball for eighteen years, fourteen of them in the major leagues, nine of those with Milwaukee. He had done everything but pitch and catch. He was somewhat infirm now, his lean body ravaged by the endless ailments of a long career. He particularly loathed the ceaseless travel, the drain of sitting in airports and riding midnight buses (superstitious, Money always took the right-hand window seat in the third row, up with the coaches and writers). He much preferred his farm in southern New Jersey, except there he couldn't play major league baseball — something he did with surpassing professionalism. He was a great sign stealer, a still-powerful hitter, a useful, if slew-footed, man afield. More, as his physical skills waned, he learned to accept his fifth-wheel role on the team with equanimity.

While Sammy Stewart, on the mound, went through the muscular exertions required by one throw to first, two called strikes, and three balls, at the plate Don Money barely moved. On Stewart's seventh sweep of the arm, Money — who stood still as a statue, without so much as a hemidemisemiquaver in his bat as he waited for a pitch — threw his bat off his shoulder and sent the ball, aided by the day's healthy wind, into the first row of seats in left field. Molitor preceded Money across home plate and it was 2–1. The Brewers no longer had to play from behind.

Ben Oglivie, the next batter, had single-swing capabilities far beyond Don Money's. Oglivie was a whip-lean, finely conditioned left-handed hitter of Panamanian birth and Bronx upbringing. He had been in the major leagues just over ten years, but until 1978 he played only for men who saw him as a part-timer. He had considerable natural speed but could slide barely better than the average high school athlete. His immense wrist strength made him capable, despite his spare 170 pounds, of propelling home runs out of any American League park, but Oglivie had been perceived as overmatched by left-handed pitchers. Though his unorthodox outfield style — he seemed all arms and abrupt movements — had earned him the nickname "Spiderman," he had worked on his fielding ceaselessly, and had become adept in the outfield. (He still *looked* funny. Bob Rodgers said, "He just doesn't always wait for the ball to come down — he goes up and gets it.") Though Oglivie had pursued a college education in whichever American League city he happened to light — he had matriculated at Northeastern University in Boston, Wayne State University in Detroit, the Milwaukee branch of the University of Wisconsin — there were people in baseball who thought him less intelligent than most ball players. He read indiscriminately and voraciously: Thoreau, Rousseau, electronics manuals, Dale Carnegie. He either chose not to discuss his reading with teammates or couldn't find a teammate with whom he *could* discuss it.

The American League's perception of Ben Oglivie changed in 1979. After a creditable 1978 season, playing mostly against right-handed pitchers, Oglivie found himself in the lineup full time when his teammate, Larry Hisle, suffered a crippling shoulder injury. He proceeded to demonstrate consistency as well as power, and by 1980 had become widely recognized as one of the most threatening hitters in the league. His fellow Panamanian Rod Carew, of the California Angels, said that Oglivie was the one batter in the league he feared while holding a runner on first base. In the line of Oglivie's furious, flailing, pull-hitter's swing, anyone on the right side of the diamond had reason to tremble.

But, these last few weeks, Oglivie's bat had been quiet. The week before, in Oakland, he had tried to come out of his slump by spurning his power and attempting instead to poke hits down the left field line. It was a tactic worth pursuing: most teams lined up against Oglivie in a defense resembling the one the old St. Louis manager Eddie Dyer threw at Ted Williams in the 1946 World Series.

Williams, of course, was a vain hitter, and he read Dyer's shift as a challenge: if he couldn't get his hits in right field, he didn't want them. (Still, while suffering through a dismal Series that year, Williams at one point fooled St. Louis with an adept bunt that, despite his lack of speed, he beat out for a hit. It so shocked all who knew Williams' arrogance that one Boston newspaper headlined "Ted Bunts!" as if V-E Day had just been announced.) But Oglivie, if anything, lacked confidence, and he came to see the inside-out hit to left as his salvation.

In early June 1982, though, it hadn't sufficed, and on the tenth Oglivie determined that patience, rather than cunning, was the best way to emerge from a prolonged slump. As the Baltimore defense lined up — third baseman Ripken was nearly 25 feet away from the left field line, and the entire outfield was canted heavily toward right — Oglivie watched six consecutive pitches go by. Stewart managed to get only two of them across the plate, and Oglivie was on with an uncharacteristic walk.

Though Oglivie did not score before the inning expired — following Gorman Thomas's fly ball to Benny Ayala in left and Roy Howell's amiable ground ball to first — his walk was immensely significant: a free swinger, generally loath to let conceivably hittable pitches pass, Oglivie was obviously in a mood today to confound whatever pitching strategies the Orioles had devised for him. He was a complex and unknowable man, to his teammates and to his employers. The more he could be the same way to his professional opponents, the better he would do against them.

2

	1	2	3	4	5	6	7	8	9	R	H	E
Baltimore	1									1	3	0
Milwaukee	2									2	2	0

For Harry Dalton, a game against the Orioles was always a special event. Dalton had emerged from West Springfield, Massachusetts, Amherst College, and the air force to take his first baseball job, in 1954, with Baltimore, in the first year the former St. Louis Browns played in that city. He had turned down a sportswriting job with the *Springfield Daily News,* for whom he had worked in college, to take care of the paperwork piling up on the desk of Jim McLaughlin, who ran the Baltimore farm department. Dalton was paid $47 a week.

He progressed with reasonable rapidity in the Baltimore organization, eventually taking charge of the farm system and the scouting operations until one day in December 1965, when Lee MacPhail, the Baltimore general manager, walked into Dalton's office with three pieces of news. First, MacPhail said, he was leaving the Orioles to join the commissioner's office as assistant to General William Eckert, the improbable new commissioner (called "the Unknown Soldier" when his appointment was announced) who knew nothing about baseball administration. Second, MacPhail had virtually completed arrangements with the Cincinnati Reds on a trade that would send Baltimore pitchers Milt Pappas and Jack Baldschun, and outfielder Dick Simpson, to the Reds for outfielder Frank Robinson. And, third, Dalton was the new general manager. (Dalton's first act, Lee MacPhail was surprised to note, was to try to get another player from Cincinnati in the Robinson deal.) Dalton, at age 37, took over an already healthy organization, saw it enhanced by the addition of one of the game's finest players, and proceeded to preside over four American League pennants and two World Championships in his six years on the job. In 1972, Dalton left Baltimore for six years as head of baseball operations with the California Angels, and he moved on to Milwaukee before the 1978 season.

When Dalton was with California, the Angels didn't do terribly well, and the consequent pain reached beyond a simple bruise to his pride. Dalton's wife, Pat, remembered when the newspapers in Southern California were being particularly vicious toward her husband, and how she would on occasion cross the street rather than have to face certain people in the community. Late in Dalton's tenure there, club owner Gene Autry, a former singing cowboy who had achieved immense wealth as owner of a chain of radio stations, brought in Emil "Buzzie" Bavasi as a special assistant, in the process publicly undercutting Dalton's authority. And Bavasi himself, a lifelong baseball man who had worked for such imposing and disparate figures as Branch Rickey, Walter O'Malley, and Ray Kroc, the man behind McDonald's, had not survived those jobs by being an inept office politician.

In Baltimore, it had all been very different. Dalton's career started in the sort of mentor-protégé relationship that provided nurture as well as education, and had proceeded in stately increments until he was at the very pinnacle of his profession. He was an engaging, generally good-natured man, and he attracted men of similar spirit and profound loyalty. In the late 1950s, he had spent springs with the Baltimore minor leaguers in converted army barracks in Thomasville, Georgia, devising a systemwide training and instructional program, and he did it alongside two washed-up minor leaguers named Earl Weaver and George Bamberger. When he first had a chance to hire his own manager in Baltimore — it was 1968 — Dalton picked the unknown Weaver. When he went to Milwaukee, he similarly knighted Bamberger for *his* first big league managerial job. When he became Baltimore general manager, Dalton needed an experienced and knowledgeable hand who knew the arcane nooks and crannies of baseball administration, and reached to hire Walter Shannon, who had spent a career with the St. Louis Cardinals and was more than twenty years Dalton's senior, as assistant general manager. Sixteen years after that, Shannon, in his middle seventies, was Milwaukee's — Dalton's — assistant GM.

In December 1981, baseball's winter meetings were set amid the bizarre 1950s garishness of the Diplomat Hotel in Hollywood, Florida. On the convention's penultimate evening, the Milwaukee organization people convened for their annual winter meetings dinner. At two elongated tables in the Gold Coast restaurant, within a raised voice's range of similar groups from the Chicago White Sox and the Minnesota Twins, the Milwaukeeans drank and dined. Bud Selig was the host, of course, and three reporters, semiofficial members of the Milwaukee family, were there. So were Tom Skibosh, the club's public relations director, and Bob Rodgers, and Dee Fondy, a special assistant to Dalton who was the one survivor from the regime that preceded Dalton on the baseball side of Milwaukee's front office. But, otherwise, there were so many Baltimore roots at the Brewer tables that it could have been a meeting of the Oriole Alumni Association: Walter Youse, 67, East Coast scouting director, who first worked with Dalton in 1956; Ray Poitevint, director of scouting and player procurement, associated with Dalton since 1959; Julio Blanco-Herrera, Latin American scouting director, who first worked with Dalton as an emigré from the Cuban revolution more than twenty years earlier; and Walter Shannon.

Shannon, though stooped with his years, and perhaps not quite so willing as he once had been to drive 150 miles into the Louisiana bayous to see a high school pitcher, was nonetheless an energetic man who sparkled with enthusiasm and quick wit. His wife, Tommye, a former radio and big band singer, sat with him in the Gold Coast. A strolling musician, summoned to the White Sox table, sang a heavily accented "Chicago"; grabbed as he walked by the Milwaukee delegation, he countered, at Selig's request, with the "Beer Barrel Polka." Then Tommye Shannon, inexcusably elegant, quieted the guitarist, stepped over to Dalton, and sang, a cappella, a lyric that centered on the words "This time we almost made it." The song's text evoked the Brewers' hairbreadth loss of the Eastern Division championship the year before; Tommye's voice was emotional, sad yet inspiriting. The raucous restaurant quieted down, and Twins and White Sox and vacationing dentists stopped to watch the old Baltimoreans, all of them shamelessly in love with one another.

At the far end of the double table sat Ray Poitevint. If Shannon was number one in service to Dalton, Poitevint was number one in authority. He spoke Japanese; he could get by in Spanish; he was a ferocious contract negotiator, a careful and firm administrator.

He was a 50-year-old Californian who graduated from high school at 16, signed with the Cleveland Indians, and was nearly blinded when he was hit in the temple by a line drive. He tried to come back from the injury, but eventually quit and enrolled in a pre-law program at UCLA. In the meantime, he remained involved in youth baseball as a coach, and in 1959 became a part-time scout for Baltimore. A few years later, he resigned from his position as the sales manager of an institutional food company, took a substantial salary cut, and went to work for the Orioles — and Harry Dalton — full time. Poitevint often acknowledged that he would like someday to be a general manager, but just as often, this evening especially, he said he simply wanted to work wherever Harry Dalton worked. "If Harry left tomorrow," Poitevint had said before, "we'd all probably go with him. Our loyalty is to Harry Dalton, and if Harry Dalton is working for Milwaukee, then we're going to work to make Milwaukee the best damn club in baseball."

Together they were called, of course, the Dalton Gang: the reference was too tempting for sportswriters to ignore. Dalton even posed for a cover photograph in the *Milwaukee Journal*'s Sunday magazine in gunfighter's garb, smoking pistol pointed at the reader. Those on the outside, save Dee Fondy, whom Dalton had taken very much into his inner circle, were somewhat resentful of how you were either in the Dalton Gang or you weren't. And none of those on the outside had any idea what it meant to Dalton and his gangsters to beat Baltimore.

Harry Dalton watched the June 10 game from his enclosed box on the press level, two boxes up the first base line from Selig (in between, Marie Selig, Bud's 78-year-old mother, sat intently in the box she occupied at every home game). Eddie Wellskopf, the press room attendant, came by periodically to bring Dalton coffee or soda; Dalton had given up beer ten weeks earlier, one hung-over spring training morning. The telephone next to Dalton rang often, with news from the trainer's room, or from a scout on the road in Montreal or Wichita or the Dominican Republic. Dalton kept score on a handout scorecard. He couldn't remember when he didn't.

Baltimore's leadoff batter in the second inning was Ken Singleton. He had arrived in Baltimore from the Montreal Expos two years after Dalton had left, coming in one of the best trades Baltimore made in the post-Dalton era. The Montreal-bound players were

Rich Coggins and Dave McNally, who between them played another 115 games in the major leagues before their careers ended, Coggins' because the capability simply wasn't there, and McNally's because he chose instead to challenge the game's reserve clause and create a baseball revolution.

The switch-hitting Singleton was having trouble in 1982, but for nearly a decade had consistently hit as well as any other player in the game. He failed to win batting championships only because he was so painfully slow, one of the slowest men, along with Don Money, in the major leagues (Singleton, said one Baltimore writer in the Milwaukee press box, "couldn't tag up from third on a fly to Green Bay").

Defenses always ganged up on Singleton, because they knew they could get away with it. Both Robin Yount, the shortstop, and Jim Gantner, the second baseman, played on the outfield grass when Singleton batted, increasing the time available to get to a ball — and thus their range — almost exponentially. Pitchers, too, in 1982 got an edge on Singleton; plagued by a lingering injury to his right elbow, he was no longer as readily able to hit the high pitch that he so loved when batting right-handed. McClure, who was more likely to get in trouble high than low, with the occasional nonbreaking curve or too fat change-up, had latitude this time. He threw a fastball, inside, around the letters; a slider away from the batter that Singleton could not handle; a curve, inside, for the second ball; then three fastballs high. The third was the kind of pitch that Singleton, when healthy, would drive out of the park in right center field. Today, he was unhealthy, and managed a line drive in that direction, but with neither the height nor the velocity that he could generate when fit. As Singleton began his swing, Jim Gantner, picking up the flight of the pitch and the arc of Singleton's bat, broke for the first base line, out across the grass, and gathered Singleton's drive to his chest as if it were a football precisely thrown to a running back on a screen pass. Dalton marked a 4 on his scorecard.

Singleton was followed by Rick Dempsey, the Baltimore catcher. Dempsey was a right-handed hitter who, in frustration, had briefly tried switch hitting in an effort to make himself into something of an offensive threat. Dempsey had become a major leaguer not because of his hitting prowess — or even potential — but because he had an arm of unerring accuracy and admirable strength, and because he knew, simply, how to catch.

There was little for Dempsey to betray at the plate, however. He stood slightly closed, his front foot closer to the inside of the plate than his trailing foot, his bat held upright in the classic position taught by Ted Williams, and contrary to the flattened angle favored by the Chicago White Sox batting coach, Charley Lau. The Lau method, which seeks to enhance contact as it diminishes power somewhat, had invaded batter's boxes for more than a decade, beginning in fact when the former catcher was a coach with the Orioles.

As he moved from job to job, Lau eventually joined Chicago as the highest paid coach in baseball, a batting theoretician who had a zealot's belief in his own views, a self-confidence that struck other baseball men dumb, and an unprecedented six-year contract worth more than half a million dollars. He had been with the Orioles for only one year, in 1969. Though the proximate cause of his dismissal was an insistence that he be paid $40,000 a year — this was more than a decade before the average major league coach was earning $25,000 a year — there were some people in the club's management who felt Lau really lost his job when he determinedly refused to drink the beer provided, and brewed, by Jerold Hoffberger, then the Baltimore owner and the president of National Brewing Company. If there were a batter who would seem to benefit from Lau's approach, it was Rick Dempsey, who had a little power and less consistency. Yet Earl Weaver wanted home runs from his catcher, and the upright bat was a more likely provider of the big bang that Weaver craved.

McClure worked Dempsey in the classic manner that baseball wisdom demanded of a lefty pitching to a low-average, moderate-power righty: don't give the fastball. He began with a curve for a strike, and followed that with a slider, just low, for ball one. A fastball, next, was perfectly planned for the off-balance Dempsey. It came in across the outside edge of the plate — the conventional misnomer, "corner," is particularly inapt for a straight fastball — and Dempsey fouled it back. Ball two was a slider, low, and then Dempsey fouled off another curve into the seats along the first base line, where Charlie Moore, McClure's catcher, dove into the lap of a fan in vain pursuit of the ball.

Moore was, in a game populated by not a few boors and juveniles, a gracious man. He was nobly so whenever he committed one of the blunders that seemed to punctuate his career. Frequently, his mental lapses had cost Milwaukee victories: two years before, in a critical game against New York, in the eleventh inning Moore took a throw from an infielder and stepped on home, thinking he had made a forced play when none was in effect and a tag-out was necessary. This blunder cost Milwaukee the game, yet Moore later stood stoically by his locker, waiting for the last reporter from the dinkiest paper to ask the predictable question for the fiftieth time. He was equally gracious the time he was playing in the outfield and a ball was hit over his head: Moore, still a catcher in overdrive, threw off his cap before chasing after it. In 1980, Moore was actually caught in a rundown between first base and the Milwaukee dugout, as a result of a sequence of events that defy description. Yet Moore never shrank from *trying* to explain to credulous writers what it was that found him again and again in such peculiar circumstances.

On June 10, 1982, having failed to capture Rick Dempsey's pop foul as it veered into the box seats, Charlie Moore pulled himself out of the fan's lap, touched the man's shoulder, apologized, asked after his health, and returned to his position. The count on Dempsey was 2 and 2.

Dempsey had seen one fastball and, having been unable to get around on it, needed to be primed for another. Thus did Moore call confidently for a curveball. McClure wound, turned, spun, threw, and sent a curve whirling end over end. Although it began its break shortly after leaving the pitcher's hand (as do all curveballs), the telescopic effect of a batter looking down a figurative tunnel at a small object made it appear to dive about ten feet in front of the plate. With two strikes on him, Dempsey brought his bat around in hope of contact, and caught an excellent pitch right on the fat. He had watched the pitch come swooping in to the lower inside quadrant of his strike zone, then watched it sail majestically into the left field seats.

In the dugout, Harvey Kuenn and Pat Dobson were surprised. It was a good call by Moore, and a good pitch by McClure. Dempsey's swing was better. Neither the manager nor the coach was dismayed, for McClure had been beaten on his best pitch. It was a tie game, and it was early.

*

Up in front of the press box, on an open-air terrace for photographers and for those writers and club officials who preferred the sun, Sal Bando took a seat. Bando was serene in his retirement. After seventeen years of playing professional baseball, fourteen of them in the major leagues, with three World Series rings earned in Oakland and a substantial fortune amassed through the wise application of both his baseball salary and his substantial intelligence, the 38-year-old third baseman had finally entered civilian life. During the 1981 season, as a little-used utility player, Bando had occasionally got angry, his pride wounded by Bob Rodgers' seeming determination to bury him. He complained that Rodgers said nothing to him about his status, and had come to wonder why the club had prevailed upon him to postpone his planned retirement a year. In Sun City in 1981, Brewer officials had watched the newly acquired Roy Howell play third base and began to wonder about the wisdom of the scouts who urged that the club sign the free agent from Toronto; Bando was persuaded to stick around for one more season. But one evening in May of 1981, after Bando had sat inactive on the bench for the season's first month, he said, "I don't know about this organization. I'm puzzled, dismayed and disappointed. They said they wanted me to stay active this year because I'm swinging a good bat and could help, but I haven't hit yet, and now, if I did, after all this sitting I probably couldn't do it well. It can't go on like this." From Bando, these were shocking words. He was the team captain, a local hero, the rare player who was a favorite among his teammates, the press, and the ball club's management. He had been loyally devoted to the Brewers' organization ever since he had escaped the repressive atmosphere fostered by the Louis XIV of the Oakland A's, Charles O. Finley. When he signed with Milwaukee in November of 1976, Bando was asked if he found it hard to leave the A's, the team he had helped to win three championships. Bando answered with a question: "Was it hard leaving the *Titanic?*" Coming to Milwaukee, he had sought logic, decency, stability, and consistency.

Later, though, because of Bob Rodgers' use of him, Bando had begun to despair and felt that, perhaps, a certain dehumanization was inevitable in baseball, even in the best of organizations. Rodgers firmly maintained an announced "open door" policy but made the miscalculation of never inviting anyone through it — not even Bando, the team captain. Dalton never interfered with a manager's tactics, and Bando wasn't one to go crying upstairs in any case. He knew for certain that 1981 would be his last year, and he was glad that when he finally was called upon at season's end (Howell's egregious fielding and Don Money's various physical ailments had forced Bando into the lineup), he acquitted himself well. He finished the year as a regular, and his career ended satisfactorily. Best of all, it had finally ended. Even as he played daily in the heat of a pennant race, Bando recognized his time had come. "Pitches I used to crush I'd foul back; hits I used to shoot right past the third baseman were being caught," he said. "It hurt me a little, but it didn't surprise me. And then, I knew baseball for what it was — my occupation, not my life. I could adjust." Bando had become a successful businessman in his latter years as a ball player and had also signed a television contract as an occasional color commentator. He had also accepted a job with the Brewers after the 1981 season, becoming "special assistant" to Dalton, charged with occasional scouting and instructional duties. But on June 2, when Bob Rodgers was fired, Bando declined, and declined again a week later, Bud Selig's urging that he become the manager.

"I didn't need the job," Bando said on June 10, in his folding chair on the press terrace, "and I can't tell you how nice it is to be home with my family." He looked down at the field. "It's amazing how I don't miss it at all."

Harvey Kuenn didn't require any persuasion to accept the managerial job when Dalton offered it to him. After his playing career ended, in 1966, Kuenn was a sportscaster briefly, then sold television time and printing before Milwaukee general manager Frank Lane invited him in 1971 to join the club as a coach. He admitted to some disappointment when he was passed over for the managerial job after Del Crandall was fired in 1975 — he had managed the last game of that season as an "interim manager" — but his gratitude to Selig was nonetheless profound and unwavering. Throughout his extraordinary series of illnesses and incapacitations, he had been kept on the payroll, and even when he was out of the hospital, but unable to travel with the team, no one complained that the club might be better served by a full-time hitting coach.

When Dalton offered him Rodgers' job — again on an "interim basis"; the general manager told reporters, "That could mean one week, or a whole season, or for several years" — Kuenn accepted immediately.

27

He called a meeting that first day, and he might have expected the reception he got. The team, soured from too many personality conflicts between the proud Rodgers and the most stubborn of the players, was thrilled. Kuenn told the players, "Have fun." And he removed the proscription, installed first by George Bamberger and then reaffirmed by Rodgers, against the players' drinking at hotel bars on the road, a privilege previously reserved for the manager, his coaches, and the reporters. The theory — Earl Weaver subscribed to it, too — was that the manager shouldn't have to worry about the players' behavior, and that they especially ought to be away from the observant eyes of the press. Others maintained that managers who invoked the rule also wanted to make sure the players didn't see how they behaved after a few drinks.

From his seat near the home plate end of the dugout, with his coaches gathered around him, Kuenn watched McClure pitch to Baltimore second baseman Rich Dauer. Dauer was a contact hitter, a player who rarely struck out, rarely hit home runs, and generally acquitted himself at bat with more consistency than flair. He stood in a slightly unorthodox position, toward the back of the batter's box, his hips pulled back away from the pitcher, front leg extended, rear leg bent. McClure gave him a fastball, inside, then a change-up that Moore later described as "over the fat of the plate." Dauer proceeded to send the pitch into the same general area of the left field bleachers where Dempsey had just deposited McClure's earlier offering.

Kuenn was concerned now. Dempsey had got to his pitcher on a good pitch, and on a good sequence of pitches; Sakata, though, and now Dauer — they didn't hit home runs off pitchers who have their best ammunition. Jim Slaton was summoned to get up again in the bullpen.

All of the Baltimore batters had now seen McClure, and he had seen them. Lenn Sakata came up to the plate again, his muscular arms popping out of the sleeves of his small-man's shirt. Burned on his curve and his change, McClure gave him nothing but fastballs, and Sakata lined out to Oglivie in left. Four out of five pitches to Cal Ripken were fastballs, too, culminating in a foul out to Yount, but Kuenn was not sanguine. "Pitchers get too fearful of being hurt on pitches that aren't working well," Kuenn said, "but they've got to get away from using the same pitch over and over." He had Dobson talk to McClure after the inning's last out, to tell him not to be afraid to use his curve. Without it, McClure surely wouldn't last.

	1	2	3	4	5	6	7	8	9	R	H	E
Baltimore	1	2								3	5	0
Milwaukee	2									2	2	0

Sammy Stewart was working fast, his Prussian delivery clicking along in orderly cadence. Charlie Moore, the first batter he faced in the bottom of the second inning, stood away from the plate, relaxed, almost casual, his bat held loose and rather flat. Cal Ripken was playing even with third base, while on the other side of the infield Eddie Murray stood back from the base line, but moved nearly imperceptibly toward it with each pitch. Stewart pumped a called strike over the outside part of the plate, then threw low for a ball. Moore stepped back, checked where the fielders were positioned, and stepped back in. A second ball, on a curve, swooped by. The next pitch, a slider outside, suited Moore perfectly, precisely because of its distance off the plate, and he sent it zooming down the first base line, where it nearly upended Milwaukee coach Ron Hansen. Murray took another step to his left. Baltimore was working Moore outside, apparently by design.

And thus did Stewart's next pitch come in outside, and thus, also as if by design, Moore fell for the bait. It was a difficult ball to hit, no matter how tantalizing, and Moore reached for it rather reluctantly, forced to follow through on an involuntary commitment his muscles had made. His bat caught the ball about a foot off the ground and propelled it on a short loop into center field. Gary Roenicke charged in for it, sliding in on his knees at the last instant. But the ball came in slightly higher than Roenicke had expected it to, laden as it was with the backspin imparted by Moore's choppy swing, and Roenicke helplessly watched it flop out of his mispositioned glove.

In the press box, sitting next to Milwaukee public relations director Tom Skibosh, Pancho Palesse looked up at the television monitor on the wall and saw a replay of Roenicke's effort. As in most cities, the Milwaukee baseball writers, and their employers, had determined that it was a conflict of interest for writers to be official scorers, and Palesse was one of two moonlighters who performed the job at County Stadium, for $50 a game. He was, admirably, somewhat tougher on the home team than a compromised writer might be, and he judged Roenicke's play — Moore's crypto-hit — an error. When the flashing "E" appeared on the big scoreboard in right field, heads popped out of the Milwaukee dugout, and several Brewer players did what glaring they could at the part of the press box in which they figured the scorer would be sitting. It was a mild reaction, in contrast to the evening before, when Moore sent a line drive deep to right field and Baltimore's Jim Dwyer apparently lost it in the lights. Then, mere glares were insufficient. Twice Skibosh's telephone rang, and Jim Gantner and one other player lit into the PR man with strings of indelicacies. Skibosh hadn't scored the play an error, but he had hired Palesse, who had. (Though paid by the league, scorers are procured by the home team.)

Kuenn was dismayed by the Wednesday night call on Moore, yet even more so by his players' rather bumptious effort (in his view) to vent their frustrations or (in Skibosh's) to intimidate the scorer. Kuenn worried that scorers' calls were a distraction, and he was further concerned that overtly responding to such calls made the players look bad in the eyes of the press. For his part, Moore, ever understanding, jokingly said to the *Milwaukee Sentinel*'s Vic Feuerherd after the game, "Tell me, Vic, am I fucking the scorer's wife?"

On June 10, another tick taken off his batting average by Palesse's judgment of Roenicke's misplay, Moore was nonetheless happily on first as Marshall Edwards came to bat. Edwards was 29, one of three Edwards brothers to play in the major leagues. However, among the three, not one had ever been a regular. Dave, the youngest, had been a part-time outfielder with Minnesota and San Diego, and Mike, Marshall's twin, had played the infield for Oakland before leaving the major leagues in 1980. Marshall, for his part, was initially signed by the Baltimore Orioles in 1974, by Ray Poitevint. Left unprotected by the Baltimore organization in 1977, Edwards was drafted by Milwaukee, newly under the control of the Dalton Gang, its player procurement efforts directed by Poitevint.

He was an extremely fast man, slight of stature, who attended his first big league camp with Milwaukee in 1981. There, he captivated reporters and Brewer coaches with his perpetual smile and uncomplaining enthusiasm, and made quite a show on the field as well, slapping singles to the opposite field, stealing bases, covering ground in the outfield, throwing creditably. (The coaches had improved Edwards' arm by showing how he had been throwing sliders from the outfield and by teaching him to adjust his grip as he prepared to throw, placing his fingers across the seams, to impart a more nearly vertical rotation on release.) But when one of the enthusiastic writers conveyed his excitement about Edwards to Alan Hendricks, a Houston-based player agent who represented nearly 70 professional ball players, Hendricks was uninterested: "I don't trust his genes," he said.

In the two seasons that followed Hendricks' instant judgment, Edwards had not, indeed, demonstrated that his talents were substantially different from his brothers'. And his limitless eagerness to please, to make his mark in the minds of the Milwaukee front office, manager, and coaches, made him appear, paradoxically, almost hopeless. In the environs of a big league team, where one encounters in most cases 25 young men who have been honored and pampered all their lives, who have had the doors of life held open for them since their early teens, one is struck by the self-possession of the clubhouse. There is a big league way of walking, a slow sort of rolling strut that announces, "I've made it, man; I'm cool." Players chew their gum or their tobacco with an affected nonchalance. They speak (most of them) when spoken to, but often enough a visitor from the outside world could walk through a major league clubhouse and feel ghostlike. Certainly, with Milwaukee, there were exceptions; while he was active, Sal Bando was especially cordial and civil, as was Charlie Moore. But more often outsiders are perceived as nuisances to be abided by the ever-so-detached denizens of the clubhouse. Marshall Edwards, on the other hand, had a look of perpetual eagerness on his face; when he first joined the club, one almost expected him to pull out an autograph book when one of the established players, or even one of the writers for the two Milwaukee dailies, passed his locker. Edwards never complained that he wasn't in the lineup enough, and when a coach or a more established player offered advice, he'd listen with his eyes wide open, head nodding in constant agreement. He tried so hard to do well, and to be good, that he could, on the road, be more likely than not found in front of a mirror in his hotel room, practicing his swing, working on the advice he had just received from one or another of his colleagues.

No one could have gainsaid Edwards' attitude, but in subtle ways it left him defenseless before those who would judge a player — not altogether unreasonably — on his major league comportment. When in April 1982 Bob Rodgers told Edwards, who had spent most of 1981 with the Brewers as a pinch runner and reserve outfielder, that he was being sent down to Milwaukee's Triple A ball club in Vancouver, the player cried. Rodgers virtually cried himself, and thought it was far and away the toughest cut he had ever made (Rodgers recalled Edwards from Vancouver shortly into the new season). When Dalton spoke of Edwards, he'd chuckle in an affectionate way, as if to say "Good old Marsh, he's quite a guy." They were positive reactions, but there was a condescension, an unwillingness to accept Edwards as a full-fledged major leaguer, in both men.

Kuenn was not utterly free from a patronizing attitude toward Edwards, but at least he had had, in his role as hitting coach, a pedagogic relationship with the player, and could think of him as a man with a certain set of skills in need of certain refinements. More than anything else, Kuenn had worked with Edwards on a physical disadvantage that was a clear product of nerves, of the anxiety of overeagerness. Edwards, a left-handed hitter, would choke up on the bat several inches when at the plate; subconsciously, though, as the pitcher began rocking into his motion, Edwards' hands would twist and twitch on the bat, his top hand eventually moving up so that a two-inch gap would open between his hands by the time his swing would begin. Kuenn saw nothing inherently wrong in such a grip, no matter how unconventional; after all, Ty Cobb had used a spread-hand grip throughout his major league career (although Cobb, ever calculating, would often move his top hand down before swinging if he wanted to pull the ball to right field, or move the bottom hand up if he wished a short swing, to drop the ball in left). What disturbed Kuenn about Edwards' unorthodoxy was that it was unintentional. Until Kuenn could prove it to Edwards by placing a ring of tape on his bat handle during batting practice, Edwards did not even believe his hands were actually moving.

But even more than the master-student relationship, what enabled Kuenn to regard Edwards as an integral part of the team was need. Charlie Moore had become the regular right fielder, but Kuenn's desire to rest Ted Simmons occasionally, or to let him play a game or two as DH, or to keep Moore ready should Simmons be injured, periodically pushed Moore behind the plate and Edwards into right. Edwards was also the reserve center fielder. He wouldn't play regularly, but he had to remain capable of playing should the need arise. He was a member of a class of players, almost interchangeable, who occupied the bottom rungs of every team's roster. Every club has at least one Marshall Edwards; every club *needs* one.

The one sort of swing that did not suffer because of Edwards' spreading hands was, of course, the bunt, and Edwards was the best left-handed bunter on the team (Molitor was the ablest from the right side). His quickness to first also made him a likely candidate to bunt, and so, now, in the bottom of the second, did the presence of the speedy Moore on first base. Too, it was a close ball game, which increased the likelihood of a bunt, and Baltimore's infielders crept in as Edwards took his place in the batter's box. Kuenn, though, felt that his team did not need to play for one run, not so early in the game, not here at home, and especially with Stewart, who fielded his position well, on the mound. There are pitchers to bunt against, and Kuenn would as soon wait for them. When he played with Detroit in the 1950s, other teams would bunt on his teammate Jim Bunning as if there were no other way to hit him. Indeed, there *were* few other ways to hit the accomplished Bunning, but a bunt on the third base side of the mound was particularly appealing to Tiger opponents, as Bunning's ferocious delivery inevitably found him ten feet toward first by the time he completed it.

So Kuenn left Edwards on his own, and Moore as well. As the catcher took a few steps off first, Edwards, standing up in the batter's box, his front foot next to the middle of the plate, lost control of his hands. First the fingers on his top hand opened and closed; then his lower wrist began to twist back and forth; finally, as the gap between his hands opened up, he whipped his bat around, flailed at a high fastball — the bad pitch that is most tantalizing to the undisciplined hitter — and vainly took off for first as the ball settled in Gary Roenicke's glove in center field.

Ron Hansen greeted Moore as the catcher retreated to first after the catch. Hansen had been the Milwaukee first base coach for not quite two seasons, having returned to baseball after a wrenching seven years away as an insurance claims adjuster in the Baltimore area.

Hansen was tall, rangy, in his forties, a modest and quiet former shortstop who had seen his fairly distinguished thirteen years in the major leagues rendered historically invisible behind his feat of a single day: on July 30, 1968, while playing for the Washington Senators, Hansen caught a sharp line drive off the bat of Cleveland's José Azcue, ran to second to double off Dave Nelson, and greeted a stunned Russ Snyder, who was on his way down from first, with a tag-out. It was the first unassisted triple play in the major leagues in more than forty years.

Now, as a first base coach, Hansen had the job that Earl Weaver, who wore his first major league uniform in the same position for Baltimore in 1967, described as "the best job in the game. You don't have to think, like a third base coach, and you don't have to work, like a bullpen coach. You just stand there and pat guys on the ass after they get hits."

There is, of course, more to it than that. Hansen needed to be sure baserunners correctly read the signals from Harry Warner, the third base coach, and he had to be alert to the hidden messages between pitcher and first baseman when a pickoff play was on. Against Baltimore, he'd try to read the signs Dempsey was giving to the pitcher when the catcher's legs opened too wide for proper security. An attentive runner on second can often break the catcher-pitcher code and flash a signal to his teammate at bat; but coaches, and runners at the corners, only glimpse signs when the catcher absentmindedly spreads his knees in the crouch, as Dempsey often did, especially in the late stages of a game. Teams will often use more elaborate tactics to steal catchers' signs. The New York Giants in the 1950s placed a spy with binoculars in the outfield scoreboard. The spy would pick up a catcher's sign, cover an open slot in the scoreboard if a breaking pitch were called, and leave it open for a fastball. Don Lee, who pitched for the Angels in the '60s, had such extraordinary eyesight he was able to read catchers' signs from the left center field bullpen in Cleveland's Municipal Stadium. Lee would stand casually with his left arm on the bullpen fence to signal a fastball, his right arm up for a curve. But Ron Hansen's primary role on the club wasn't performed from the coaching box, even when he could peer in and steal one of Dempsey's signs. Like all coaches, he served to help out in practice (the infielders were his particular responsibility), to be a conduit between manager and players, and, always, to do the manager's bidding.

When Dalton fired Rodgers in Seattle nine days earlier, Milwaukee reporters immediately began their private and public speculation about whom Dalton would name to the position. The popular choice, George Bamberger, the avuncular ex-manager who had led the franchise to its first on-the-field success from 1978–80, was unavailable. He had been plucked from a brief retirement with an immense contract to manage the New York Mets, and would perhaps have been passed over even if he had expressed interest in returning. Dalton and Selig, who had kept Bamberger in the organization as a special adviser after he stepped down as manager, had taken his professed wish to retire at face value, and both were hurt and dismayed when he soon thereafter took the New York position. Few other candidates stood out, and Kuenn's appointment was seen as "interim" in the strictest sense: given his medical history, it appeared doubtful Kuenn would serve more than the two or three days necessary for Dalton to find a replacement. Two days after Kuenn's appointment, Dalton said, "I guess I've put up a 'Help Wanted' sign of a kind; I've got one call already." The vastly experienced — and controversial — Alvin Dark, for one, sent a telegram of application to one Brewer official; the job appeared open. What was clear, though, was that none of the other Milwaukee coaches was a real possibility. Hansen was a reticent man, and he had never managed, not even in the winter leagues. Harry Warner held his job in the third base coach's box primarily because he was an old minor league buddy of Rodgers'. Larry Haney, the bullpen coach, an ex-catcher who drove a UPS truck in the off-season, also had no managerial experience, and Calvin McLish, the pitching coach, for whom Dobson was substituting, had recently been stricken by myasthenia gravis, a potentially crippling disease.

They were, collectively, in most ways typical of a major league coaching staff. They were the manager's handmaidens, drinking buddies, drill sergeants. Coaches know to subordinate their own personalities to that of the manager. They are rarely outspoken, and rarely last in their jobs if they are. The more generous-spirited players — with Milwaukee, Gorman Thomas, Paul Molitor, Pete Vuckovich — granted credit and gratitude freely, and the coaches were inevitably thrilled to hear it had been given. Mostly, though, they were apart, attached to the manager, part of his court. Milwaukee's coaches, like all coaches, contented themselves with the feel of a uniform on their backs and the esprit of the baseball life itself —

especially the endless talk, talk of baseball days past, of moments and experiences shared, of players they played with and against.

Lubricated at countless hotel bars, the talk is always good, richly textured, even if at its heart repetitious. Inevitably, sitting in on coaches' conversations, one found not mere themes but specific stories recurring and recurring. Foremost among these were tales of Steve Dalkowski, a star-crossed pitcher in the Baltimore organization who never could control what all who knew (or claimed to know) him considered the fastest fastball ever. Then there were the accounts of "the Luplow Catch." This last was always called that — never "the catch I saw Luplow make" — and it came up whenever conversations got around to great fielding plays. In 1963, Al Luplow, a journeyman outfielder then with the Cleveland Indians, leaped over the Fenway Park bullpen fence on the dead run and stole a home run from Boston's Dick Williams. After two decades of the story's circulation, it finally came to appear as if hundreds of future coaches, scouts, managers, and broadcasters had somehow found themselves in Fenway that day, and the Luplow Catch had become as essential a point of reference for baseball hands as Easter Sunday 1916 at the Dublin post office had become for Irish patriots.

Among the Milwaukee coaches of recent vintage, the most distinctive, and "managerial," were Rodgers himself, who had coached third before he replaced Bamberger, and Frank Howard. Howard, who had been with the club for four years, was clearly hurt when he was passed over for Rodgers, and soon enough found his way to temporarily greener diamonds when he was made manager of the San Diego Padres in 1981 (he did not last into a second season). Yet his was certainly a colorful (and immense: 6'7", more than 300 pounds) presence when he was with Milwaukee. He had the spirit of a football cheerleader, constantly exhorting players, his fellow coaches, loitering sportswriters, and anyone else within earshot. Howard trotted virtually wherever he went at the ball park, resembling nothing so much as a runaway skyscraper. Among other responsibilities, he took it upon himself to protect the ball club's financial condition by making certain that the old, game-used balls that were employed for batting and infield practice weren't needlessly wasted. Howard took this duty so seriously that once, hitting grounders to Don Money at third base, he offered up a baseball so aged, so infirm, so green with the patina of overuse, that Money, upon fielding it, examined it with a screwed-up face and tossed it into the stands. The fan who greedily retrieved it was even more offended than Money, and threw the offending ball back on the field. Charlie Silvera, Yogi Berra's backup with the Yankees in the 1950s, performed a similar duty at the Oakland A's spring training camp in 1982. Silvera would walk along the foul lines, depositing stray batting practice balls in a shopping cart he pushed before him. In the bleachers, kids would importune him for a free ball. "When they say 'Gimme a ball,'" Silvera said, "I tell them to say 'please.' Then they say *'Please* gimme a ball.' Then I say no. Each one of those balls is a three-dollar bill. I learned that from Frankie Crosetti." Silvera called Crosetti, who coached with the Yankees for twenty-one years after completing his seventeen-year career as their shortstop, "the greatest ball man I've ever known."

With Howard gone, there was much less color, not to mention bulk, on the Milwaukee coaching staff. McLish was the most experienced among them, and certainly the most coachlike, in the traditional baseball sense. He was born Calvin Coolidge Julius Caesar Tuskahoma McLish in 1925 in Anadarko, Oklahoma. Save for a year in military service, he had, with his seven weeks in Sun City in 1982, spent his last 39 Marches in a spring training camp. In uniform, he was inscrutable: he'd sit quietly on the bench, arms folded, back hunched, his cap pulled tight on his head, and watch a pregame practice with an impassiveness broken only by the streams of tobacco juice he'd use to punctuate the passage of time. The pitchers loved him, because he was loyal to them and because he could genuinely help them. He suggested to a struggling Pete Vuckovich, early in 1981, the pitcher's first season in Milwaukee, that he go to a no-windup delivery, even with no one on base, and it immediately turned Vuckovich's year around. The pitchers also cherished McLish's induplicable and invariable instructions when he'd come out to the mound in the middle of a particularly dicey inning: "If you're gonna th'ow the bawl," he'd twang, "th'ow the fuckin' bawl!"

Off the field, McLish was entirely different. He was a stylish dresser, a witty joker, and an exceedingly opinionated man. Many coaches open up in hotel bars in a way they never would at the ball park, with two unwritten but indelible dicta hovering over their behavior. At the ball park, in uniform, coaches are, by definition, subordinate to the manager, whose job it is to talk to reporters, to make decisions, and to have errands for coaches to run. In the hotel bar, where loquaciousness comes not solely from the liberating effects of alcohol but equally from the need to have — and to voice — opinions of their own, the second rule protects the coaches: whatever is said, or seen, in the hotel bar is utterly and irrevocably off the record. Managers, too, use this rule to their advantage, and it is not uncommon to hear a man who has made excuses for one of his ball players two hours earlier savage him at the bar. It is even more common to see informed opinions about, say, the mechanics of a particular pitcher's delivery appear in the newspaper under the name of a baseball writer — even though these were the barroom judgments of a pitching coach.

McLish, generally, was circumspect about his pitchers, less so about other members of the team and other players in the league. But he would get particularly inflamed in defense of one of his friends or favorites. One night in 1981 he and Harry Warner were sitting in a bar in Seattle with a few writers and broadcasters. As the talk turned to managers, the name of Gene Mauch, who had just been appointed to run the California Angels, came up. McLish had been Mauch's pitching coach with the Montreal Expos, and he felt Mauch knew more about baseball, and managing a ball club, than any man alive. So McLish remembered with bitterness Mauch's firing in Montreal, and the appointment of his successor. "Do you know who they named?" McLish demanded, his voice saturated with sarcasm. "Karl Kuehl! A minor leaguer! A fuckin' minor leaguer!" Warner, who spent thirty-four years in minor league uniforms, on minor league buses, and in minor league hotels, as player and as manager, squirmed uncomfortably, but quietly. McLish was the senior man.

Then, too, McLish was a major leaguer. He had first entered the big leagues in the Brooklyn Dodgers organization but had attained major league prominence with the Cleveland Indians in the 1950s. He also earned some notoriety when, pitching in Venezuela one winter early in his career, he removed his glove, dropped it on the mound behind him, and threw his next pitch lefty.

The opposing team squawked, the umpires fulminated, and McLish was instructed that his effort was illegal. It wasn't, of course, but its conclusion ended the experiment that might have produced the first switch pitcher.

McLish was not in uniform on June 10 because he had recently begun to suffer from a series of symptoms — dizziness, exhaustion, general weariness — that had tentatively been diagnosed as myasthenia. He had for several weeks been unable to travel with the team, and although Dalton was not ready to replace him, the general manager had elevated Pat Dobson, a minor league instructor, to serve as interim pitching coach. Dobson was as modern as McLish was not. He was articulate, enthusiastic, earnest. He pitched in the major leagues for eleven years, achieving true distinction only in 1971, when he was one of four pitchers on his team each to win 20 games. That was in Baltimore; that's where Harry Dalton had got to know him.

For their part, the Baltimore Orioles had only their third pitching coach in the club's twenty-eight-year history, dating back to 1954. (The New York Yankees, by contrast, had had 16 in their 6 most recent seasons.) Harry Brecheen served for nearly a decade and a half. (George Bamberger remembered watching Brecheen working with a young pitcher, explaining various aspects of the art in great and complex detail, then asking his pupil, "You got that?" The pitcher, Bamberger recalled, nodded earnestly, eager to show comprehension — and then, when Brecheen left to minister to someone else, the pitcher turned to Bamberger and asked, "What'd he say?" Such was, Bamberger insisted, the burden of *all* pitching coaches.) In 1968 Brecheen was replaced by Bamberger, who presided over Baltimore's pitchers until he took Dalton's underground railway to Milwaukee in 1978, the first Baltimorean hired by the new general manager. Bamberger in turn was replaced by Ray Miller.

Miller's nickname was "Rabbit," a distortion of "Rapid," as in "Rapid Ray" Miller, as in "Rapid Robert" Feller: perhaps the nickname had been altered when it was finally and firmly established that Miller's fastball, no matter how potent it was, would never get him to the big leagues, let alone to the heights attained by Feller. He was an affable, glib young man who contrasted sharply with George Bamberger, his grandfatherly predecessor. Yet Baltimore pitching continued to be the best in the league after Bamberger's departure, and it was clear either that Miller was able or that maybe, after all the years Baltimore pitching had been so dominant, Earl Weaver knew more about pitching than he let on — or more, at least, than Mike Cuellar, a former Oriole pitcher of great skill and guile, gave Weaver credit for: "All Earl knows about pitching," Cuellar said, "is that he couldn't hit it." The most common disparagement of Weaver's abilities inevitably summoned forth his own failure to reach the major leagues as a player. After being accused by Weaver of ordering his Yankees to throw at Baltimore batters in 1978, Billy Martin said, "What does Weaver know about throwing at guys? He never played in the big leagues. He must have read about it in *The Lou Gehrig Story.*" Even Weaver knew to belittle his own playing abilities, so confident a manager he was: "The best part of my game," the former minor league second baseman said, "was the base on balls."

Weaver, for all his visibility as the preeminent manager of his era, rarely strained to take credit for his teams' success, for such credit came to him without his bidding for it. Not only was he a proven winner; he was great copy. He was as demonstrative a manager as there was in the game, a pestiferous and tireless umpire baiter, a man utterly comfortable in the spotlight. He put his genuinely creative turn of mind to work as a quotable anecdotist and an admirable strategist. (The Orioles won a game in 1980, against the Chicago White Sox, on a prearranged maneuver — Baltimore players called it "the famous play" — that had a runner on first take a long lead, fall down to attract a throw from the inexperienced pitcher on the mound, and enable the runner from third to steal home with the winning run.) He was famous for his one-sided feuds with his players; they would fulminate about one slight or another, or second-guess his decisions, or fume about his alleged misuse of them; once, Rick Dempsey even threatened him in the middle of a game. For his part, Weaver would offer to the press a pithy put-down of the player in question, then put the same fellow in the lineup the next day. He'd stride grumpily through the clubhouse after a loss, and the players would tease him with a chorus of honking sounds. After Sammy Stewart heard the honking choir for the first time, he told Thomas Boswell, of the *Washington Post,* "Here was this manager you'd heard about all your life chewin' us out and these guys were making fun of him. I thought, 'It's kinda dark in here and you don't have to move your mouth to make that sound, so I guess I can do it too.' "

Weaver professed not to care whether his players liked him or treated him with respect. One believed him, for Weaver avoided them at all costs. At times this caused him a bit of heartache. In a voluble moment on a 1980 road trip, he told some writers he had "saved" Terry Crowley, an aging pinch hitter who appeared in games about twice a week, "from a job in a paint factory." Reporter Dan Shaughnessy put this in the *Washington Star,* and at 3 A.M. was awakened in his hotel room by a call from Weaver. Back home in Maryland, a friend of Crowley's had read Shaughnessy's report and had called Crowley to tell the player about it. A bruised Crowley called Weaver, Weaver tried to soothe him, and then the manager called Shaughnessy. He wasn't angry with the writer — he just wanted his help in trying to revive Crowley's spirits.

It was rare, though, that Weaver troubled himself about a player's feelings. He asked them to put out on the field, nothing more, and offered no special treatment in return. Not once in his entire managerial career did Weaver fine a player, and he never rebuked a player for criticizing him in public. He went his own way, and he allowed — forced, actually — his players to go theirs. Not only did Weaver ban the Orioles from the hotel bar on the road, but the day was rare when he so much as bothered to speak to many of his players. It had not always been that way, but ever since one of the players he truly loved, Paul Blair, with whom Weaver socialized and played golf, criticized him with especial vituperation after the outfielder was traded away, Weaver had simply vowed he wouldn't get close to his players again.

Instead, Weaver ran his club by presiding over the most baroque lineup card in major league history, an ever-changing document that he would alter from day to day, depending on conditions as varied as the opposing pitcher, the ball park, the weather, and some inner astrology that had enabled Baltimore, year by year, to be the most consistently competitive team in baseball. To be sure, Weaver believed in identifying his four best arms and using them day after day, altering his rotation only in extreme circumstances. But beyond the realm of pitching (where he depended heavily on Bamberger and, later, Ray Miller), Weaver used his roster as a complex tool with a score of delicate parts. Any one of three or four people might put in a day in left field, and the batting order would bend and flutter constantly, all of this while the Baltimore pitching rotation changed as rarely as Weaver's socks (preposterously superstitious, the manager changed these only when his team lost). Weaver clearly felt that finding four good arms was hard enough, and if you had them, you should stick with them. It was a theory that certainly had much to do with the four Baltimore pitchers who won 20 games each in 1971, and it also enabled Baltimore to boast, almost unfailingly, at least one 20-game winner annually. Over the past few years, Weaver had determinedly given the ball, day in and day out, to Scott McGregor, Mike Flanagan, Dennis Martinez, and Jim Palmer (except in 1980, when Palmer was ailing and a journeyman named Steve Stone suddenly attained satori with his curveball, winning 25 games and the Cy Young award).

In 1981, though, a variety of physical problems, and the intrusion of the players' strike, disrupted the predictable flow of Baltimore starters to the mound, and Sammy Stewart made his talents known. Stewart had been floating in the foggy world of the long-relief man, unable to insinuate himself into the Gang of Four who regularly pitched for Weaver, when 1981 saw his apotheosis. Used unpredictably and inconsistently, he nonetheless pitched often enough and well enough to lead the league in earned run average. Thus, when Stone abruptly retired in 1982 rather than futilely attempt to come back from a serious arm injury, and when Mike Flanagan was unable to pitch with consistency in the early going, Stewart briefly entered the Oriole rotation. And on June 10 he was poised to complete his team's four-game sweep of Milwaukee.

Charlie Moore stood on first as Marshall Edwards retreated to the dugout following his fly ball to center. Jim Gantner, a rural Wisconsin boy, came to the plate. The left-handed-hitting Gantner was called "Gumby" by his teammates, after a cartoon figure, made of chewing gum, that apparently had some currency in the late 1950s. Gantner was relatively short, and his wide blue eyes, rosy cheeks, and farmboy openness conspired to make him appear doll-like. At the plate, further compounding this deception — for Gantner was tough, a fighter, fearless — he stood very still, his backside pulled back away from the plate, those blue eyes popped open: he almost appeared apprehensive.

On Stewart's third pitch, a fastball straight across the upper part of the strike zone, Gantner reached around and looped the ball over shortstop. Gary Roenicke charged in from center, Benny Ayala from left, and they met as they came sliding in on the ball, neither of them quite able to reach it. Ayala scrambled to his feet, to look behind them for the ball, and, failing to locate it, shouted to Roenicke: the offending presence rested between the center fielder's knees. Moore stopped at second base and Gantner stood safely at first. (On a similar play in Texas in April, Yount, Gantner, and Kevin Bass, a rookie outfielder briefly with the Brewers, engaged in a three-man collision. After the ball was dead, Bob Rodgers and John Adam, the assistant trainer, ran to the outfield to check on the players' health. Learning that Yount's knee had caught Bass in the groin, Rodgers said, "Don't rub it — we're on TV.")

There was one out when Paul Molitor came to the plate. Milwaukee was one run behind. The big bats studded through the Brewer lineup had been silent for four days, and one, Cecil Cooper's, was immobilized, on the bench. Kuenn watched as Molitor fouled a ground ball toward the Milwaukee dugout. Molitor stood fairly far back in the box, enough to take advantage of a power-enhancing stride into the ball, enough to increase the advantage his quick reflexes already afforded him in waiting that millisecond extra and discerning the break of the pitch. He displayed an uncanny balance at the plate, his High Episcopal manner — graceful, classical, formal but for his rhythmic gum-chewing — a paradigm of a kind.

Molitor was the best contact hitter on the team, save perhaps for Cooper, and Kuenn felt he would hit as well as Cooper if he had the first baseman's patience and selectivity. Kuenn knew that Molitor had made great progress as a hitter, and was no longer the predictable first-ball hitter he was when he arrived in the major leagues, when on some days he would see only four or five pitches in an entire game. Needing to play the primary role of the leadoff hitter — to get on base ahead of the power hitters — Molitor had learned to wrest a walk from the pitcher. As a rookie, in 1978, Molitor walked only 19 times in 521 at-bats, but in half as many plate appearances in 1981, he walked 25 times.

Molitor stood in the batter's box waving his bat in arcs toward the pitcher as Stewart prepared to begin his motion. But the pitcher instead whirled toward second base and threw to Sakata, who dashed over from shortstop to field the pickoff throw. Moore was back in time. That Sakata was covering second could be expected, but it was nonetheless good news: Molitor could thus be able to pull an inside pitch into the hole left by Sakata should Moore take another big lead. Then again, that very fact might keep Stewart working outside.

Moore stepped away from second after the next pitch, a ball, and again Sakata danced over toward him. Baltimore had a play — or two or three — for such circumstances, each of them endlessly rehearsed in Miami in spring training and each of them, in Weaver's fondest hopes, usable only four or five times in a given year. Sometimes the pitcher merely looked for daylight between the runner and the shortstop. Sometimes a timed play was on, wherein a predetermined signal — the catcher literally giving the nod or the pitcher hitching his belt — started the pitcher and catcher counting, the pitcher turning to throw and the shortstop lunging for the base as the count reached three. Sometimes there was only the illusion that a play was on, which at the very least might catch Moore leaning (or even "thinking") back toward second when the pitcher released the ball toward the plate, delaying the runner's potential progress toward home a critical fraction of a second. On a single, it might save a run from scoring.

Molitor fouled a pitch back, and the count was 1 and 2. Stewart offered a curveball, tantalizing in its approach to the plate yet on its arrival far enough outside to be virtually unhittable. In command of his wishes, and his reflexes, Molitor did not swing. Now another ball, and it was a full count.

At second base, umpire Durwood Merrill moved away from the base: there would be no put-out at second on a steal now, no bang-bang call to be made. In the dugout, Kuenn touched various parts of his face with his forefinger in precise sequence; in turn, near third base, coach Harry Warner began a more exaggerated routine for Molitor's benefit, and for Moore's and Gantner's. Simultaneously, Dempsey twitched his fingers between his legs, Stewart dropped his ghostly cornet from his lips, a fastball zipped toward the plate, and Moore and Gantner began their mad dashes forward: hit-and-run.

Yet Molitor did not swing; the pitch appeared low and outside, and altogether not to his liking. The play did, at 3 and 2, allow Molitor to decide on his own whether to swing or take. Kuenn sent the runners on faith, faith in Molitor's eye, and faith in his ability to make contact. But before Molitor had dropped his bat from his shoulder, before umpire Dan Morrison's right hand was extended fully into the air for the called third strike, Dempsey exploded from his crouch and gunned the ball to Ripken at third. Moore was out, the inning over. Kuenn was disappointed, but not angry; he had counted on Molitor to use discretion and a good eye, yet on June 10 Molitor's good eye did not look through the same lens as Morrison's.

3

	1	2	3	4	5	6	7	8	9	R	H	E
Baltimore	1	2								3	5	1
Milwaukee	2	0								2	3	0

Surely it was forgivable for Paul Molitor to fail; the grand, explosive successes that made batters heroes were so stunning partly because they punctuated the steady drizzle of failed moments that so filled the offensive part of the game. "The successful hitter fails seven times out of ten" is a truism that creeps its way into every play-by-play announcer's litany, every columnist's musings. In fact, batters don't fail so much as pitchers triumph or fielders succeed, or, in fact, so much as *geometry* is victorious: decades of evolutionary modification have led to the nine men in the defensive alignment arraying themselves in such a fashion that the overwhelming majority of balls hit into play are converted into outs. That Molitor failed to make contact with Stewart's inning-ending pitch was almost incidental; it was the smooth clicking of the defensive machine — 1–2–5 in the score book — that stopped the Milwaukee offense.

Molitor's lapse was also forgivable because of his special role on the Milwaukee team. In the fans' eyes, at least, he was the blessed boy, the golden hope, the avenging angel who would lead the club to success. And the path he had followed since he joined the Brewers in 1978 — asked as he was to play five positions in five seasons, sent in one instance to dislodge Gorman Thomas from his prime-billing spot in center field — was convincing evidence that no set of circumstances would stop him.

Molitor was born with the gift of uncanny physical ability, a grace and speed and fluidity that even other athletes envied. In high school, he had captained everything — his St. Paul, Minnesota, high school could barely put an athletic team on the field without

Paul Molitor's taking the featured role. In college, at the University of Minnesota, on the other side of the river, he was an All-American shortstop. He was grateful to his coach for teaching him what didn't come naturally — how to steal home. The rest — the whistling throws from shortstop, the fleet effortlessness that got him from the right side of home plate to first base in barely 4 seconds, the swing that produced line drives to all fields (Harvey Kuenn, who was then still his batting coach, said it was, on a team known for its hitters, the one swing that never needed adjustment or doctoring, that was always exactly *right*) — these things were beyond a coach's capacity to teach. When his time came to sell his skills, Molitor was the Brewers' first-round draft choice, the third player picked in the entire country. As befit a player picked in his draft position, he skipped rookie ball and instead joined a last-place Class A club in Burlington, Iowa, in midseason; they went on to win the league championship. The next spring, he began his major league career, with all of 64 minor league games behind him, as the starting short-stop. He stole bases, he batted in runs, he became Rookie of the Year.

Molitor was a handsome, charming, intelligent, and unfailingly polite young man, and he could play ball immaculately. He was somehow different from his teammates, a generally quiet man, out of place in the roisterous life of a clubhouse whose other occupants nonetheless treasured his skills. The man who paid his salary seemed genuinely to love him. "I don't have to tell you what a remarkably fine young man Paul Molitor is," Bud Selig said. Neither did he have to tell the Milwaukee fans, particularly the young ones, who loved him just as much.

If Molitor was the dreamboat that every 17-year-old girl in greater Milwaukee pined for, then James Gorman Thomas was the hero that every 47-year-old brewery worker idolized. However, unlike the gifted Molitor, Thomas had not experienced a baseball world so perpetually bright and golden. He, too, had exceptional talents, but they were talents predicated on his ability to resolve athletic problems with the precise and considered application of his remarkable brawn. For nine years, Thomas had bounced around the Brewers' system, up and down between the major league club and various less glamorous outposts: Billings, Danville, Evansville, Spokane. He hit ferocious home runs, and he amassed equally memorable strikeouts. He, too, had begun as a shortstop; in high school, the best athlete was always the shortstop, no matter if, like Thomas, he was also the biggest kid, an intimidating 6'3" 200-pounder who loved baseball, only wishing it had some of the contact, the *crunch,* of football, at which he had also excelled. Having imperiled the lives of those who happened to sit behind first base in Clinton, Iowa, minor league infielder Gorman Thomas took his arm, his competitiveness, and his glove to the outfield. In 1978, when George Bamberger left Baltimore's coaching staff to come to Milwaukee as manager, he looked at the organization's rosters (or so went the official Milwaukee story) and noticed there was no Gorman Thomas. "Where's that big kid who loves to catch the ball?" Bamberger asked. He might have read Bud Selig's comments of a year earlier, when the Brewers' president told the Milwaukee papers, "He doesn't make contact at the plate. He is still striking out one of three times he comes to the plate. Nobody wanted him in a trade, nobody wanted him on waivers." As it happened, Thomas had found his way to temporary haven in the Texas Rangers organization through considered (but legal) manipulation of baseball's rules. Thomas had been "loaned" to Texas, and now Bamberger wanted to call in the note. Harry Dalton got him, and the manager placed him in center field.

In the ensuing three seasons, Thomas hit more home runs (115) than anyone else in baseball. He used outfield walls as if they were blocking sleds. He refined a decoy play that could freeze a baserunner, paralyze him between first and second, pull his pants down in public (he'd lope in as if to play a ball on one hop, then catch it at his shoetops and double the runner off base). Arriving first at the park almost every day, he'd strut around the batting cage half dressed in the hours before the stands were opened up to the public, pass time with opposing players, luxuriate in the life of a ball player. Luis Tiant said Thomas was so ugly he "could be anything in the jungle [he] wanted to be, but not the hunter." His uniform was always dirty, his face often unshaven. He drank beer with the fans at their tailgate parties in the County Stadium parking lot. All he needed to motivate himself, Thomas said, was to put his uniform on.

And Thomas was aware of how he was perceived by the fans. "They come to see me strike out, hit a home run, or run into a fence," he said. "I try to accommodate them at least one way every game." He also well knew his role in the clubhouse, where his alternating tough guy–prankster role made him the dominant figure, even if it had earned him from his teammates the nickname "Sybil." This was derived from the title character of Flora Schreiber's book, which had been made into a popular television miniseries. The character Sybil was a psychotic plagued by nearly a score of different personalities.

The second season Paul Molitor played professionally, 1978, the all-star Class A shortstop suddenly found himself in the big leagues because the equally gifted, equally prodigal Robin Yount, who played Molitor's position for the Brewers, chose to sit out the first chunk of the season, making noises about joining the professional golf tour, complaining that he was underappreciated. There had been talk Yount was going to be moved to the outfield, to make way for Molitor. But Yount's rebellion was as successful as it was determined, and when the shortstop came back, Molitor was moved to second base. Two years later, at the beginning of the season, Molitor was occupying Gorman Thomas's spot in center field. As that year ended, he was in right, on Thomas's flank. And in 1982 Molitor became Milwaukee's third baseman. That made five positions, as a regular, at the behest of Milwaukee's management: one could see why they loved him.

"I never found it hard changing positions," said Philadelphia first baseman Pete Rose, who played second, left, right, third, and first in his career. But Pete Rose was given 20 seasons in which to adjust to the changes and the pressures wrought by his circumnavigation of the diamond; Paul Molitor was given only 5.

Sun City, Arizona, where the Brewers train each spring, is a planned retirement community built by Del Webb, former owner of the New York Yankees. It is a desolate landscape of mile upon mile of tract homes, many with "lawns" made of gravel painted green. Rotting oranges, fallen from the citrus trees that are Sun City's only real landscaping, line the roads. The tallest building is the hospital. The desert sun beats ceaselessly on the awnings of the golf carts that putter down the streets. In this atmosphere the young men of the Brewers get ready for the season. For most of them, Sun City is part vacation, part reunion, part tedium; it passes quickly enough, though, as the anticipation of opening day looms ahead.

For Paul Molitor and Gorman Thomas in 1981, Sun City was a jousting field on which neither could win.

Molitor had hurt his rib cage swinging a bat in 1980, and the gritty little third baseman, Jim Gantner, took his place at second; with Yount, Gantner quickly became part of the league's best double-play combination. Gantner's pivots were things of beauty, if the eye was quick enough to follow them; his throws were true vectors that inevitably intersected the spot where a baserunner's eyebrows would be if he dared to come straight at Gantner to break up the double play. By December of 1980, after the Brewers had sent right fielder Sixto Lezcano, his home runs, his runs batted in, and his reluctance to make the acquaintance of outfield walls to St. Louis, Paul Molitor was informed he would be moving to center field.

Bob Rodgers had told Molitor the previous fall to bring an outfielder's glove to camp, "just in case." (An infielder's glove is generally designed to be broken in with the fingers curled down somewhat, toward the pocket; an outfielder's glove, usually larger and less flexible, is broken in with its pocket running diagonally from webbing to heel.) Then the Milwaukee papers, an effective if circuitous vehicle for Brewer management to make its thinking known to Brewer personnel, began to fill with rumors of a switch. "Ten days before the winter meetings," Molitor said, "Harry Dalton called me in and told me the rumors were true. Harry asked me if I had a preference about where I wanted to play, but I didn't really have a choice. I had to do it if I was asked to." And Molitor spent the rest of the winter of 1980–81 working on the flexibility of his throwing arm, getting ready to make the long throw from the outfield.

"It's a little demeaning to be made the scapegoat," Gorman Thomas said that spring of his being shunted to right by Molitor's shift. "I think I'm the best center fielder in the league. I may not be the best, but I approach it as if I am. In my mind, the move shouldn't have been made." He sat on the bench by his locker, silent for a moment. "I had credibility in center field, and then I was zapped to another position. I haven't lost two steps, like they're saying. I haven't lost any steps at all. But I'm an employee here, and I do what I'm told. I can swallow my pride, but I'll never really like it." Silence again. "In center field, you're the driver in a grand prix race; in right, you're a mechanic."

All spring long, Thomas made clear to anyone who asked, and anyone who didn't, his displeasure with the prospect of becoming a mechanic. "He didn't say anything to me," Molitor said, "but I could see it in his face. Gorman's a very intimidating person." Thomas never said Molitor was ill-equipped to play center; Molitor's skill, his gift, was manifest. But, Thomas thought at the time, "It'll be five or six years before Paul's totally comfortable. What I lack in speed, I make up for in experience, knowing the hitters, the pitchers, the ball parks." Speed, experience — the first Thomas would never have, the second he would always have. Thomas bore a month-long scowl on his face but worked hard at his new position, even facing the prospect of what he considered the hardest adjustment — having to field the line drive in the lights. "People don't understand how scary it is," Thomas told one who didn't understand. "It's like looking into a flashbulb" — with a sphere hurtling at you at a hundred plus miles per hour, with the game on the line, with fifty thousand people watching.

Molitor was followed that spring by a fleet of reporters. He told them that all he wanted was to be as good as he could be; he spoke engagingly of how he hoped to play center field as well as the California Angels' Freddy Lynn, and of the dozen or so outfielder's gloves he had got in the mail from sporting goods manufacturers that winter.

Out on the field, Molitor was placed in the class — student body of one — of an improbable 50-year-old professor named Sam Suplizio, a millionaire banker, developer, and Republican party loyalist who knew a few things about playing the outfield. In fact, Sam Suplizio knew — and cared — more about playing the outfield than about either politics or banking. A prospect in the Yankee system in the 1950s — his prospect, he hoped, was someday to become Mickey Mantle's backup — Suplizio had seen his career end with an act of what he called "stupid courage." He had decided to break up a double play by thrusting his right forearm at a pivot man, and found his thumb somewhere back near his elbow, his ulna and radius snapped clean. "The next spring," Suplizio remembered, "I tried again, but all I could do was throw the ball straight up in the air or straight into the ground."

Suplizio excelled at banking, prospering beyond his dreams, becoming active in politics, eventually rising to become finance chairman of the Colorado Republican party, a friend of New York congressman Jack Kemp, a key Rocky Mountain supporter of interior secretary James Watt. Yet he stayed close to the game he loved, scouting for his friend Harry Dalton at Dalton's various stops in front offices around the American League, doing some minor league instruction, constantly trying to decide whether to run for Congress or to go to yet another spring training.

The spring of 1981 saw Suplizio carrying a case stacked full with manuals on outfield play. The most important of these was Suplizio's 22-page dissertation on the art of outfielding. Molitor studied Suplizio's treatise, shagged Suplizio's flies (though generally useless, conventional time killers, fungoes are somewhat helpful in training an outfielder to go back on a ball), picked up ricochets Suplizio tossed against the outfield wall, threw letter-high to relay men stationed by Suplizio around the infield fringes. And Suplizio worked with Molitor on his throwing, getting him to cross-seam the ball as he brought it from glove to hand, to ensure a 6-12 rotation and a throw that doesn't tail away from the relay man; on his positioning, so he could break in the right direction before the batter completed his swing; on his glove work, conditioning him to catch the ball in the webbing and not in the palm, as an infielder would; and on his running, mostly on his running, despite Molitor's sizzle afoot: center fielders, Suplizio pointed out, need to run straight after the ball, shoulders square to the body, no turning of the head to follow the ball in flight. One day in Mesa, late that spring, the Brewers had just finished a game with the Cubs. Suplizio approached Molitor and said, "I finally saw the back of your head today when you were chasing that gapper. You're a major league center fielder."

If Molitor was a major league center fielder, it didn't show right away. Before April was out, he went back for a fly ball in Chicago and looked up in the air when he got to the spot where he had expected it to alight. He heard the ball land on his other side, not ten feet away. The game was lost. He heard broadcaster Mike Hegan call it an "eminently catchable ball" that night on the news. And he heard, in his mind, yet another phrase: "I was worried that people thought Gorman would have made that catch." If Thomas agreed, he didn't say so, although later, when he was back in center field, he did say, "You don't rip people for their bad play. And if you do, you'd better have a clean closet. No one does."

Soon after the Chicago fiasco, though, Molitor's native skills, and his determined application of them, indeed made him a center fielder. Suplizio was brought in to help him further, late in April, and a week later, back home in Colorado, the tutor found himself watching his pupil on a cable telecast from Anaheim. "He looked great. He went into the alleys. Only 15 percent of the season was over, and he ran down a couple in right center, and I thought, He's really got it." But in the first inning the next night, trying to beat out a roller in the infield, the pupil lunged for first base, landed on its far side, and came down as if shot. Torn ligaments in the left ankle: the bone was floating around unmoored, the leg black with hemorrhaging from knee to foot. Molitor went on the disabled list, and Thomas went back to center. "I was unhappy about the circumstances," Thomas said a few days later, "but I was glad to be back." How long did it take him to get used to being in center again? "Oh, about an inning."

Bob Rodgers, who had engineered the Gantner-Molitor-Thomas chain reaction, felt Molitor had progressed enormously. "He was already better than the average major league center fielder. He was as good overall as [Detroit's] Chet Lemon; he could come in as well as [Boston's] Rick Miller. He hadn't thrown to the wrong base; he was great going to his right; he had the best arm in our outfield." But when Molitor returned to the lineup after the strike that summer, he was used as a designated hitter. At first, he simply didn't have the mobility necessary for center; later, in the high noon of the pennant race, Rodgers decided to stick with the one who had got them there, Gorman Thomas. "You could tell in his face," Molitor said, "that Gorman felt he proved he could play center field, that he knew he was the center fielder. It wasn't anything directed at me; he has a great deal of pride." As the season came to a close, and as right field replacement Mark Brouhard himself went down to injury, Paul Molitor found himself back in the defensive lineup, this time in right. He was still limping; he was in a new position; he had to stare into the flashbulbs. He was, one of the Milwaukee coaches said, "Adequate, at best." Which is a coach's way of saying he was no good at all.

The Brewers lost to the Yankees in the divisional series and in the process lost second baseman Gantner to a knee injury, replacing him with reserve Eddie Romero. Had they beaten the Yankees in the fifth game of the series, Rodgers would have used Molitor at second in the American League playoffs.

It would have been a short stay, for before the Brewers' bags were packed for the off-season, Ron Hansen came to Molitor and asked how he felt about playing third base. Two months later, almost a year to the day after he was told he was the center fielder of the future, he learned that Hansen had acted as Rodgers' emissary. Back from his honeymoon in Hawaii, the Rookie of the Year shortstop, the All-Star (1980) second baseman, the great center field hope, learned that he was going to third the following spring.

"When Buck called me in late November, I said I had a right to think about it; I wasn't going to say yes right away. We agreed to talk again in ten days. I wanted to think about who would be affected by it, and whether it was beneficial to my career. Then, in mid-December, I agreed to move. I went to see Bud [Selig]; Bud and I could always talk. He said he'd tell Harry that this was it." Molitor said as much to the Milwaukee reporters — especially the part about Selig's implicit promise that his wandering days were over. Dalton read about it, and went across the hall to Selig's office. "Bud said he'd told Paul he'd hoped this was the last time he'd be moved, that he *wanted* it to be the last time. But we could never make such a promise." For his part, Selig said to a reporter, "I told Paul we had asked a lot of him, and that this would be the last time." And if Dalton or Rodgers came to him and told him they'd like to move Molitor again? "I wouldn't want to see that. I wouldn't be happy," Selig said.

But, to Molitor, it was a promise — because he wanted it to be a promise. "I didn't see what good it would do for me to argue," he said. "I don't want to be Mr. Agreeable for its own sake. In fact, if I had my way, I'd still be a shortstop. But so few people get any chance at all in the big leagues." Molitor was sitting by the pool in Sun City; it was spring 1982, and he had been spending his days with his new tutor, the recently retired Sal Bando. ("Sal's very complimentary, which is nice of him.") "You know," Molitor said, thinking about his odyssey from short to second to center to right to third, "the big moves, I sort of brought them on myself: I got hurt in 1980, opening the door for Gantner, and when I got hurt in 1981, Gorman was back in and I was out. If I had stayed healthy, neither thing might have happened."

But things had happened, and Molitor was the third baseman. Rodgers and Dalton figured they had solved two problems at once: they had put the team's heart, Gorman Thomas, at ease in his center field home, and they had improved a questionable spot at third by replacing the aging Don Money and the unpredictable Roy Howell with the man who could, and would, play anywhere: Paul Molitor. In Sun City in March of 1982, the reporters hovered again; Thomas was clearly a happier man, and apparently a little remorseful: he felt a need to explain his feelings of the year before. "People expected me to be pulling against him, hoping he'd fuck up. That wasn't accurate at all. But I couldn't go too much the other way. That would have been phony." Molitor's ready response to the reporters — he had first rolled it out on the winter banquet circuit — was: "Last year, I was the center fielder of the future. This year, I'm the third baseman of the future. Now I'm working on my slider, because if Rollie Fingers retires, I might be the relief pitcher of the future."

In the spring of '82, Molitor took well to the tutoring offered by Sal Bando, who had by then emigrated from the Milwaukee bench to his part-time post in the Brewer front office. Bando helped Molitor learn how to come in on a bunt or a slow roller, but most of the curriculum had to do with the mental requirements of playing the position. Early in the spring, Molitor said he expected to play a fairly deep third, that he would use his speed "to get to the ball"; Bando was soon able to show how a third baseman never gets more than one step, and that speed was surely not the secret of Brooks Robinson's success, or Graig Nettles' — or Bando's. The subtleties of positioning were the most critical part of Molitor's reeducation. Brought up in the middle of the infield, he had always enjoyed the luxury of seeing the catcher's signs and being able to lean with the pitch; even in center, he had learned from Suplizio to follow the ball from the pitcher's hand to its collision with the bat and to set his course accordingly. But in his new position, signs weren't visible, and the part of the catcher's semaphoric communication that indicated the expected *location* of a particular pitch couldn't be communicated orally by the shortstop. Besides, any third baseman who tried to follow the ball from mound to plate would soon find himself decapitated: at third, he had to focus on the batter from the moment the pitcher was ready. So, with Bando watching, Molitor took hundreds of ground balls off batting practice, and with Yount he worked out the oral signals the shortstop *can* give the third baseman — letting him know when a fastball was called by the Milwaukee catcher, when a curve, when a change.

By the time the team went north, he was ready. Although he hadn't played third since grade school, he had some especially valuable skills, most particularly a shortstop's arm and a shortstop's instincts.

Indeed, as Molitor had, as a shortstop, started on the left side of the infield, third was a natural enough position for him; in the minds of his teammates, and his employers, there was no worry at all. The men he supplanted — Don Money, who was experienced enough to cope with it, and Roy Howell, who was not — were less than thrilled, of course. Money spoke of the inevitability of his becoming a part-timer and of the obvious need to find a new position for his talented young teammate, while Howell, acknowledging Molitor's abilities, sulked and asked to be traded. (Money was used to such moves: he had himself played five positions in his career and thus had learned to accept his team's dominance over his fate. In 1981 he made the mildest of protests against his constant redeployment and his lack of playing time by taking the lineup card, writing in his name at every position, and reattaching it to its accustomed spot on the dugout wall.) Both Money and Howell, though, were generous with advice, and Molitor felt immensely less pressured than he had the year before. Save for first baseman Cecil Cooper, an unrepentant Molitorite who thought he would have been a great center fielder and was now being "penalized for his adjustability," and perhaps Money and Howell, his teammates were pleased. Left fielder Ben Oglivie, who respected both Molitor and Thomas, said, "Gorman was very unhappy last year; we all knew it. This year, things are likely to be smoother." Pete Vuckovich praised his new third baseman and then said, "Gorman Thomas should never have been moved at all. And Molitor was an All-Star second baseman." What about making room for Gantner? Vuckovich grinned. "Well, I'm not paid to make these decisions."

Those who took that responsibility felt secure in their immense faith in Molitor's skills, and in his willingness to help. "Some guys were almost forced to choose sides," Bob Rodgers said, clearly relieved there was a logical solution to the problem. Harry Dalton said, "There's nothing wrong with being able to play more than one position in the major leagues." Bud Selig said, "I can't describe my high regard for Paul." And, he said, "I guess this is a sad commentary, but it's probably true: those who behave with dignity, and who don't scream and kick — we probably ask more of them than we can of others. It shouldn't be that way."

But it was, and for Paul Molitor it appeared it always would be. A week into the 1982 season, Yount suffered a pulled hamstring in a game against the Indians, and Molitor returned whence his hegira had begun, to shortstop. The first ball hit to him went right through his legs. He stayed at short for a few games, then returned to third when Yount was healthy again.

But in Arlington, Texas, late in April, when Bob Rodgers told him he was not starting one day — it was, Rodgers said, because it was a day game after a night game — Molitor was, for once, visibly upset. "I'm an every-day player," he said. "I don't like it one bit. Let someone else sit if they want Money to get his at-bats." His anger was uncharacteristically splenetic. Who should sit, then? "Well, Gantner and Yount have got to play; Cecil's got to play . . ." Suddenly, he seemed the altar boy again, the good student, the obliging son. But then his face changed. "No, I'm the third baseman, the regular third baseman. I'm not going to be the one to sit."

When Harvey Kuenn took over the club in early June, one of the first peace missions he undertook was to assure Molitor he would remain at third, no matter what. If Thomas got hurt, reserve Marshall Edwards would go to center; if Edwards were unavailable, Ben Oglivie would move from left. If Yount got hurt, Ed Romero or Rob Picciolo, the other backup infielder, would play. But as long as Molitor's energy held up, he would be at third base every day, and if he blew a ground ball or made an errant throw — or failed to make contact on the hit-and-run — he would be forgiven.

Indeed, by the time Molitor reached his fielding position for the top of the third inning on June 10, his strikeout that had become a double play seemed forgotten as well as forgiven. Cheers cascaded from the upper deck along the left field line as he reached his position. These seats were filled with the youthful beneficiaries of a promotional campaign called the Pepsi Fan Club, guests of the soft drink bottler. Molitor was the "captain" of the club, its Designated Hero. The Brewers had, over the years, built Thursday afternoon into a successful game day by promoting it especially hard among youngsters and the elderly. Whenever Thursday was a getaway day, concluding a home stand, Bud Selig provided his team, and the fans, with an afternoon game.

Milwaukee was one of the last venues (outside of Chicago's light-less Wrigley Field) of daylight baseball during the week. Over the years, an increasing dependence on spectators unable to attend week-day games has virtually obliterated such events from the major league schedule. More recently, Saturday games have migrated to evening starting times as baseball has become, in some cities, as much social event as sporting event. This trend has been abetted by pressure from the television networks. The National Broadcasting Company, which purchased the rights to a weekly Saturday game to be able to keep its piece of the postseason playoff and World Series action, didn't want to sully its Saturday evening schedule with baseball (which rarely draws a sizable audience). Sending out its nationwide broadcasts on Saturday afternoons, NBC brings as much pressure as possible on the league offices to move non-network Saturday games to the evening, the better to avoid having to go up against local broadcasts in the afternoon. Even Sunday night games, officially discouraged by the American League, have become popular, especially in cities — Arlington, Texas, for one — where daytime temperatures make afternoon starting times an imposition on the comfort of the players and the paying customers.

But it is still the broadcasters who wield the most persuasively powerful stick. Broadcast revenues — radio, television, pay televi-sion — made possible the enormous increase in salaries that were visited on the game in the late 1970s. Broadcast exposure has built loyalty among fans, too, and broadcast sponsors shape marketing campaigns around their baseball activities. (Actually, it isn't limited to broadcast sponsors. After Cecil Cooper began calling the Kuenn-led Brewers "Harvey's Wallbangers," Brewer marketing vice presi-dent Dick Hackett moved to protect the name legally, working with the importers of Galliano, the liqueur used in the similarly named cocktail.)

Apart from the Pepsi Fan Club dates, the Brewers had 11 games on the 1982 home schedule for which tickets were subsidized by, or gifts given away by, commercial sponsors. Sports bags, baseball caps, bats, seat cushions, and socks were given to fans, underwritten by corporate marketers. Foremost Card Service Cushion Night forced Harry Gill to add staff to his stadium crew for the day, to retrieve the cushions inevitably thrown onto the field during the game. This wasn't a problem, though, on Gimbels Diamond Night, when ten quarter-carat diamonds were given to lottery-selected fans.

What Milwaukee did not have in 1982 was the sort of promotional event — beer night, disco night, and the like — that would run counter to the family entertainment aura that Selig and Hackett sought to create. (A nickel-a-beer night in Cleveland some years back had culminated in a riot and forfeiture of the game by the home team.) Hackett had got rid of the egregious top-of-the-dugout cheerleaders, Bonnie and Bernie Brewer, but otherwise his sideshows were determinedly middle of the road. The grounds crew even wore yellow and blue lederhosen. The team's logo — writer Roy Blount Jr. said, accurately, that it resembled the bottom of a dog's foot — was chosen in a fan competition. Hackett felt that tireless and consistent promotion was, along with a winning ball club, the surest way to get fans into the seats. And Selig knew that fans in those seats were the only means by which the Brewers could produce the income to remain remotely competitive, operating as they did in the smallest broadcast market in baseball.

The broadcast market was small, to be sure, but it had been rendered even less profitable than it might have been by Selig's mismanagement of the sale of radio and television rights each year. Through the 1980 season, radio had never brought in as much as $1 million a year to the Brewers, this in an era when clubs in the largest markets were bringing in $6 million annually from local broadcast.

But, in 1981, rights had finally been pulled away from WTMJ, the radio station owned by the same firm that owned the city's two newspapers, and sold at auction to WISN, owned by the Hearst Corporation. WISN was run by a short, slender, chain-smoking man named John Hinkle, who was determined to make his station number one in the Milwaukee market. WISN had an "adult contemporary" format — not especially complementary to baseball programming — but Hinkle forged ahead.

To cover and justify the expenditure of $1.2 million for the rights to Brewer games and the attendant sales commissions he'd be paying, Hinkle and his colleagues assembled a Brewer "network" of 51 stations. At a promotional meeting in January of 1981 in the Brewers' home clubhouse beneath the stands, station operators from all over Wisconsin and the Upper Peninsula of Michigan gathered to learn how the network would operate. They heard Hinkle speak, and broadcaster Bob Uecker, and they met Selig and Dalton and Bob Rodgers.

The largest of the network stations was in Madison; some, from northern Wisconsin and Upper Michigan, were 10-watters that could barely be heard around the block. Yeι what all the stations had in common was that they did not have to pay WISN — or the Brewers — for the rights to broadcast the games. They simply got some three hours or so of programming virtually nightly, and the right to sell a portion of the regular advertising spots built into a ball game and its attendant pre- and postgame shows. Hinkle's salesmen also sold, on a contingency basis, 90 seconds of ad spots for every pitching change (the advertiser set up a "bank account" for such spots, its principal drawn down every time a pitcher faltered). Such marketing made National League games, where there was much pinch hitting for pitchers, more valuable to an energetic broadcasting salesman. Extra-inning slots were apportioned to the various contract advertisers.

Within three weeks of WISN's acquisition of the rights to Brewer games, the telephone company, Pabst beer, Johnsonville Sausage, and Chevrolet had signed on for the bulk of the available contract spots. What WISN got in exchange for its rights payments, its salaries to Uecker and Dwayne Mosley (hired by the station, but only with the club's approval), and to various engineers, and its investment in telephone line fees, was numbers. The lion's share of advertising spots belonged to WISN, and the greater the listenership, the greater the time rate. By drawing in Iron Mountain and Iron River, Sparta and Rhinelander, River Falls and Rice Lake and Prairie du Chien, WISN protected and enhanced its investment, had more to sell to Pabst and Chevy and the others who signed on for the whole schedule. (The station also saved a few dollars on the salary of one evening DJ who lost his job to baseball.)

Still, John Hinkle did not expect baseball to pay for itself, and profits — not some vague sense of community service — were what motivated him to bid for the rights. What pays the bills at a radio station is morning drive time, and that was where Hinkle saw WISN leaping to the front in the Milwaukee market. For what he foresaw was hundreds of thousands of Milwaukeeans listening to the ball game on the bedside radio and waking the following day to the voices of WISN's morning personalities. Getting used to WISN in the bedroom, they would stay with it, Hinkle reasoned, at the breakfast table and in the car on the way to work.

It was the first time Hinkle had ever broadcast baseball. Asked
if he was a fan, he sat at his desk for a moment and sucked deeply
on a cigarette. Then, exhaling grandly, he broke into a grin and
said, "I'm going to be now."

At County Stadium, on June 10, Uecker and Mosley segued into
the top of the third after two advertisements, one in Uecker's voice,
played over the Brewer Network. Fans were still arriving at the
game, and 11 ticket sellers had been dragooned from Hackett's
office to supplement the 12 who had been scheduled for duty. Eighty
ushers were fanned out over the stadium, and 30 ticket takers
manned the gates. The Amoco Oil Company had a group of 135
employees in the lower grandstand. There were 46 spectators from
the Menominee Tribal Recreation Department, 50 Immaculate Con-
ception Holy Name altar boys, 25 Lake Mills senior citizens, 55
from "Red Carpet South's Wednesday's Youngsters and Darlene's
Darlings," 19 from the Wisconsin Veterans' Home. Three schools
in Waukesha each sent 25 children to the bleachers, and they were
greeted by Fan-o-Grams on the scoreboard. The Pepsi Fan Club
occupied 7,947 seats.

Dan Ford was Baltimore's leadoff batter in the third. In the
second, McClure had thrown his first pitch for a ball to three of
the five hitters he faced, and had gone to 2 and 0, then 3 and 1,
against Ripken, the last batter. After Dempsey homered on a curve,
and Dauer on a change-up, McClure had begun to lean more on
his fastball, but it had proved errant. Now, facing Ford, he stayed
with the fastball, trying mightily to keep from throwing strikes
over the outside part of the plate, where Ford thrived. With his
peculiar, closed stance, Ford was an opposite-field hitter who hated
the inside pitch, and it was the pitcher's task to throw him strikes
inside consistently. Rollie Fingers said of Ford, "He thinks we owe
it to him not to pitch inside," and McClure noted how Ford glared
at him when he threw inside pitches, as if to imply that the pitcher
was somehow breaking a rule.

The first fastball McClure threw was high and tight, and Ford
flinched away from it. Two more fastballs inside followed, and Ford
fouled off both, pulling away from each pitch on his swing. At 1
and 2, properly set up by Moore and McClure, Ford next saw an
outside pitch — but it was fully eight inches off the plate, and Ford

did not take the bait. Six inches closer and he would, with two strikes on him, have had to bite; seven inches closer, and Ford would have had nearly his perfect pitch.

Finally, at 2 and 2, McClure threw another fastball, this one high and toward the inside part of the strike zone. Ford uncoiled from his back-to-the-pitcher stance and sent a line drive toward Marshall Edwards in right.

Although playing center field generally calls for great speed, to cover the immensity of the territory, right and left fields in some ways demand more skill: playing hits off the wall in the corner is an unpredictable business, and at night line drives emerge from the stadium lights. The greatest challenge at the wing positions, though, is in discerning the path of the ball's flight. Where balls hit to center have more of an end-over-end rotation, and thus stay up in the air longer and sail in a truer arc, hits to right and left never fly straight. A left-handed hitter hits slices to left field and hooks to right; a righty does precisely the opposite. In each case, the ball veers toward the foul line, sometimes sharply. On any ball hit between the fielder and the line, it is the fielder's task to *race* the ball toward the line, as it were, to overtake it as it spins away from him.

As Ford's bat met McClure's pitch, Marshall Edwards broke immediately and instinctively on a diagonal, toward the point where the foul line met the fence. Bob Rodgers thought Edwards had the skills — speed, good hands — to be an excellent outfielder but that he was somehow uncomfortable, and appeared almost to run in place, if he were approaching a wall or another fielder in pursuit of the same hit. As Rodgers put it, "Marshall would be an all-star in a cow pasture or a parking lot," where walls wouldn't intimidate him, but his hesitant style in a stadium stunted his development. Kuenn, somewhat more diplomatically, called Edwards "a cautious outfielder."

Edwards' reaction on Ford's drive was totally consistent with his managers' views, and after four steps backward he abruptly reversed course, suddenly aware that the ball had not been hit so hard as it had first appeared to be. Edwards raced in, and caught the ball at his knees.

Eddie Murray, who came from the same Los Angeles ghetto as Edwards, followed Ford. Like Edwards, Murray was signed to his first professional contract by Ray Poitevint, who was then (1973) still in the Baltimore organization. When Dalton went to the Angels after the 1972 season, he sought to bring Poitevint with him. However, Baltimore's invocation of the antitampering rule — the same stricture that prevents one club from offering a job to another's manager without permission — stranded Poitevint temporarily with the Orioles.

Poitevint's Baltimore responsibility was what has been known in baseball for decades as "free agent" talent — not the tempting major leaguers available to the highest bidder since the collapse of the reserve rule in 1976 but the high school and college boys whose discovery and education is the game's R&D. Poitevint was one of the best men in this trade, working primarily in the lush fields of California and leading occasional raiding parties in Latin America, where he had an extensive network of productive contacts.

Poitevint first saw Eddie Murray when he was a right-handed pitcher and first baseman at Locke High School in Los Angeles; in his senior year, he shared a three-headed captaincy with Ozzie Smith, the extraordinary National League shortstop, and Darrell Jackson, who by 1982 had been pitching for the Minnesota Twins for five years. Murray was one of twelve children. All four of his brothers played professional baseball.

Murray was, for Poitevint, an extremely difficult young man to sign. Not only did his talent justify a substantial dollar commitment, but he came into the negotiations with the counsel of a family already made skeptical of big league blandishments made to his older brothers (apart from Eddie, only the youngest, Rich, would reach the majors). Years later, Poitevint idly related the story of the Murray signing to Dick Young of the *New York Daily News,* in whose subsequent column Poitevint's words were made to seem arrogant and, to Murray's mind, disrespectful of the Murray family.

If Murray was stung by the apparent insult, Poitevint was injured by the vehemence of the player's public response. Lawsuits were threatened over vague allegations; Murray made it clear that Ray Poitevint was his mortal enemy.

On June 10, Poitevint was in Milwaukee County Stadium watching a Milwaukee team that didn't contain a single player he had drafted into the Brewer system (his first draft class was picked in 1979, and its shiniest prospects had just reached the Triple A level by 1982); across the field, though, Eddie Murray, the Nicaraguan pitcher Dennis Martinez (Poitevint had "opened up" Nicaragua to the major leagues with the signing of Martinez in 1973), and Rich Dauer were all men Poitevint had known well in their teens. Before game time, Poitevint, who was in town to prepare for the 1982 draft of amateur talent, wanted to go over to the Baltimore clubhouse to say hello to his old protégés, but the public ill will that Murray bore him at the time of Young's article had seared him. He didn't want to bother Murray or to provoke his ire, so Poitevint didn't feel comfortable going to greet him. He did want to say hello to Dauer and Martinez, but was even less comfortable about the prospect of appearing pointedly to ignore Murray. So Poitevint had his pregame lunch in the Brewer staff and guest dining room with a few other Milwaukee scouts and watched his old Orioles from a distance.

Murray was a switch hitter, although he was strictly a right-hander until his third season in professional baseball, only two years before he reached the majors. (Ted Simmons, the Milwaukee catcher, had been switch hitting since he was a child; it began, Simmons said, as "sort of an outdoor parlor game," and was more typical of the experience of most switch hitters.) Among switch hitters of even two decades' experience, Murray was the rare and brilliant gem who had explosive power batting either right-handed or left-handed. Even from the second deck, Murray was an imposing presence; from the pitcher's perspective, he was a simmering vol-cano. He stood forward in the box, his legs spread wide, his powerful body pulled over in a crouch, his bat stretched back as far as it would reach, the overall prospect full of threat and menace. He was 26 years old. Behind him on June 10 crouched Charlie Moore, 28, his basic sunniness obscured by his mask, his pads, his assumption of the ungainly crouch devised (to the rue of all catchers since) by Jimmy Archer of the Chicago Cubs in 1909. Sixty-five feet from Moore, Bob McClure, 29, waited.

It was an encounter played out scores of times daily in the major leagues. "It is the hitter's job," Pete Vuckovich liked to say, "to take the food out of the mouths of my children," and the pitcher's job (with the catcher's collaboration) to "keep him from doing it." Equally common was the hyperbolic view Vuckovich espoused: a young man making (in Vuckovich's case) nearly $600,000 annu-ally, reducing his daily considerations to life-and-death matters relat-ing to the nourishment of urchins. At another level, it was a small moment in the midst of a barely larger one: 25 men (among them, only 2 who had native connection to the state of Wisconsin, let alone the city under whose name they played) attempting to touch their feet safely on a pentagonal piece of rubber more times than their opponents.

Yet the three spots along the line defined by McClure, Murray, and Moore were representative of something truly larger. The very nature of their encounter was symbolic of their respective careers, a tiny view into a large picture that showed that McClure and Moore were, in greater schemes, nobodies; Murray was much, much more. Moore was a superb athlete in Birmingham, Alabama, a strong and swift youth who played shortstop as well as catcher, who made his scholastic mark in basketball, and was accomplished enough in football to be offered a scholarship to Auburn University. McClure, too, excelled in all three sports, in Pacifica, California, and he was honored (as we honor only the deft, the fleet, the strong: our athletes) by friends and family and neighbors. They were exceptionally talented, for only a tiny fraction of the millions of American (and Latin American and Canadian) boys who play baseball get as far as a professional contract (in a city the size of, say, Detroit, perhaps 5 high school graduates annually are offered money to play baseball). Of those who begin in the lowest minor leagues, 1 of 20 will play so much as a day in the majors. Of those who reach the majors, a distinct minority — worth remembering when one shudders at the size of the salaries paid ball players — will survive as long as Moore or McClure.

But Murray — he was among the elect of the elect. Though they needn't have thought of it, Moore and, especially, McClure knew this in the third inning on June 10. Ted Williams' judgment that the most difficult act in sports is hitting a hurled sphere was the most quoted of all baseball dicta. (It was also the most self-serving, not unlike, say, a banker's asserting that the creation of wealth is immoral and the storage of it somehow uplifting.) Writers often point out that hitting is something that will make you famous, even if you fail the hoary seven times out of ten. This sort of thinking creates a cozy protection for the self-esteem of hitters, especially hitters as accomplished as Murray. If Murray failed to reach base, McClure had merely extended his tenuous time on the mound; if Murray succeeded, it was because he was a great hitter with a greater grasp of his art than McClure had of his. Were it the ninth inning, the balance might shift somewhat toward the pitcher, the hitter forced to perform his task in the face of a discernible finish line. Here in the third, though, all pressure was on McClure, none on Murray.

Either McClure had been unable to throw his curve and change for strikes (he had managed only 4 in 14 efforts so far) or he threw them so fat (twice) that they were turned into home runs. Against Murray, who was a great breaking ball hitter, McClure was at a critical juncture in his day's work. Were his off-speed pitches — his strong suit — working today, he likely would have used them against Murray. The hoariest of pitching doctrines holds that one pitch "strength to strength": faced with a batter who loves high sliders, say, the pitcher whose best pitch is a high slider would still throw it. It seems a foolhardy idea, predicated on blind *macho,* but in most cases it is as strategically sound as it is noble. At the tactic's heart is an expression of self-confidence, of true belief: you may be good, but I'm better; beat me if you dare. The pitcher who thinks, "I *can't* beat you," usually takes his self-doubt with him to the showers. In the Murray-McClure confrontation, hissing cats at 20 paces, McClure backed down. He threw nothing but fastballs.

The first one was high. George Bamberger, in three years in Milwaukee, had convinced his pitchers there was nothing more horrible than a walk ("I hate those fuckin' walks," Bamberger said. "There's no fuckin' defense for a walk") and nothing nearly that bad except a first pitch that was a ball. McClure's second fastball was intentionally directed toward the far side of the plate, but so errantly wide that Moore had to lurch to catch it. The balance of the at-bat tilted yet further in Murray's favor.

Now, at 2 and 0, his fastball missing as much as his curve, McClure's arsenal of body, and of spirit, was depleted. At 2 and 0, McClure needed a strike, or Murray would be able either to jump on a fat 3 and 0 pitch, which *had* to be a fastball down the middle, or to arrive at first without lifting his bat off his shoulder should the 3-0 pitch be errant. Three-and-o was, for a pitcher, in ways more fretful than 4-0: the latter was, at worst, one base. So now, at 2 and 0, McClure spun on his left foot, his fingers clutching the ball in the fastball grip, and sent a pitch plateward, too straight, too true, and Murray lined it on a blur past Molitor at third. McClure said in the spring he didn't need to be told by his catcher whether his fastball was working or not. "I can tell," he said, "by the line drives whizzing past me." Now, he watched Ben Oglivie in left chase down Murray's single, the residue of his last fastball.

Harvey Kuenn rose from the dugout. As he used his greatest relief pitcher's aid — his slow, wooden-legged limp to the mound, enabling the man on call to throw perhaps two or three extra pitches before emerging from the bullpen — Kuenn knew McClure had faced his last batter. McClure had thrown 57 pitches, and only one man was out in the third; 5 of his last 8 pitches were balls; 2 of the others were hit hard. He handed the ball to Kuenn, who offered a word or two of succor, and walked head down to the dugout. There, he picked his warmup jacket off the top of the bench, placed his glove under his arm, and walked into the runway that leads to the clubhouse. He neither spoke to nor acknowledged any of his teammates on the bench; neither did they say anything to him.

Jim Slaton walked in from the bullpen with his warmup jacket over his shoulder. He had already been summoned to his feet twice in the game; the last call had occurred in the second inning, when it first began to be clear to Kuenn and Dobson, not that McClure didn't have his curve and his change, but that McClure had lost confidence in the pitches. During the home half of the second, Kuenn implemented the formal chain of command and had Dobson tell McClure that he couldn't stop Baltimore without the two off-speed pitches. But McClure was down on himself, and though his catcher, Moore, may have tried to cajole and wheedle the pitcher into varying his pitches, McClure nonetheless stuck with his fast-ball — and had lost control of the game because of it. The Milwaukee pitchers all liked Moore, but it was generally less likely that he could get them to perform up to their capacities than could Ted Simmons, who usually caught, or young Ned Yost, who did occasional fill-in duty as the third catcher. Both Simmons and Yost were kick-ass catchers, assertive types, likely to browbeat or even intimidate a pitcher who has lost confidence or concentration. All catchers have the responsibility of keeping the pitcher's mind on the game — or, alternatively, keeping it *out,* and doing all the pitcher's thinking for him. Some catchers also keep an eye on the pitcher's motion, seeking as the game proceeds to detect small changes that signal fatigue, or even mental exhaustion. Pitchers respond in different fashion to their catchers' involvement; Pete Vuckovich, especially, didn't want to hear about his delivery. "The catcher should be looking for the *ball,*" Vuckovich said, "not for the motion. If he's looking at my dick, he's going to get a ball in the face."

Ted Simmons was not playing today. Kuenn felt it wise to rest him occasionally, and, not incidentally, Simmons had been failing miserably against Baltimore pitching. The catcher had come to Milwaukee at the beginning of 1981, in a headline-making trade with the St. Louis Cardinals. Outfielder Sixto Lezcano, pitchers Lary Sorensen and Dave LaPoint, and a minor league outfielder from Nicaragua named David Green had been sent to St. Louis for Simmons, Vuckovich, and Rollie Fingers. His arrival in Milwaukee heralded loudly and insistently by the Brewers, Simmons proceeded in 1981 to perform dismally, and early 1982 was a bare improvement. When Kuenn took control of the team in Seattle, he sat down immediately with Simmons, who had been Bob Rodgers' primary *bête noire,* and told him how he planned to use him. Throughout Simmons' woeful 1981 season, and in the first two months of 1982, the catcher had felt that no matter how adrift he might seem at the plate, he would come around and hit as he had throughout his career. To do it, though, Simmons felt he needed the support and confidence of his manager; as it was, Simmons was being booed, the first Brewer in recent memory to be booed by the home fans.

The support Simmons sought was never really forthcoming from Bob Rodgers, and Rodgers was puzzled that Simmons actually thought the manager's personal feelings made a difference. Rodgers saw Simmons' complaint as excuse-making; Simmons saw Rodgers' manipulation of him in the lineup — catching him, sitting him, playing him at DH, sitting him again — as nearly a calculated effort to make certain his hitting would never get back on track. Rodgers felt he had given Simmons every chance: in one memorable game in '81, against Toronto, the manager had given the sluggish Simmons the hit-away sign with two out in the seventh inning, the count 3 and 0, the score tied, and the bases loaded. It was, Rodgers divined, the way to help Simmons break loose, and the pale, wispy pop-up that ended the inning was, to Rodgers, evidence that perhaps he never would.

Despite Simmons' notable self-esteem, his perception of Rodgers' attitude made his fundamental disdain for the manager grow into open dislike and hostility: it was, to Simmons, an insult, a challenge to his own record of success that translated, in practice, to a wish that Rodgers apparently wanted to be fulfilled. Though Rodgers was proud, somewhat vain about his position and his authority, it was unlikely he wanted Simmons, so critical to his team's success, to fail; rather, he had been approaching the conclusion that Simmons was beyond redemption, that after just 140 American League games, he simply could no longer hit.

Rodgers was not alone in his doubt. There were others in the Milwaukee brain trust who felt that the monumental trade Dalton had engineered in December 1980 was not quite the brilliant stroke it had once appeared. True, Fingers and Vuckovich had outperformed anyone's highest expectations. But Simmons, who was the most expensive player in the Milwaukee lineup, had not been idly given away by St. Louis's Whitey Herzog. Though it was a rare player who lost his offensive skills virtually overnight, if anyone were to do it, it would be someone physically like Simmons: squat, heavily muscled, thick in the legs and hips, his was not the model athlete's body, and the aging process works more quickly on this body type than on any other. Too, Simmons, who had always been one of the slowest runners in baseball, was never going to be able to break a slump with a leg hit or a bunt; indeed, he was the worst bunter on the team, throughout his career so blissfully confident in his hitting ability that he had never bothered to cultivate the delicate skills of the bunter. And to compound such a dispassionate analysis of Simmons' shortcomings, there was self-doubt of another kind among those who feared Simmons was over the hill: Whitey Herzog was as astute a judge of talent as there was in baseball, and after serving as Simmons' manager for four months in 1980, perhaps he had seen something that convinced him that the celebrated Simmons was about to begin a steep and irreversible decline. Herzog also didn't consider Simmons a winning ball player, despite his prowess at bat. In fact, Milwaukee hadn't sought Simmons in the big trade; Herzog had offered him up, and made his inclusion in the trade an ironclad condition.

When Kuenn took over from Rodgers, though, he opted for a clean slate with the disappointing catcher. Simmons, too, saw the change in managers as an opportunity to start anew and to proceed with his livelihood unhindered by the arrows of doubt he had fielded continually from Rodgers. He moved off the plate a bit and began to use a longer bat in his effort to break his dreadful slump. When the two men sat down to talk the first week of June, Simmons promised Kuenn cooperation, and told the new manager that he was ready to sit, or DH, whenever Kuenn wished: he wanted only to know in advance what the manager's wishes were. He was rested on June 10, having gone 0 for 11 over the first three Baltimore games.

Yount had muttered throughout the '81 season that Rodgers' constant manipulation of the lineup card, moving him up and down in the batting order, hurt his game. And Jim Slaton, who had first played for Milwaukee in 1971 and had been with the team ever since, save for a season in exile in Detroit, and who was an agreeable, uncomplaining man who had weathered far worse times than these (until 1979 he had never played on a team that had finished higher than fifth place) — even Slaton had become unhappy, feeling he had been left dangling on the end of Rodgers' strategic string.

But Slaton was the model of equanimity. Though one of only two unmarried Brewers, he nonetheless fit in well in the team's social life. In the clubhouse, he would sit in his corner, near the other pitchers, with a towel around his waist and his powerful chest exposed, a constant, benign smile on his face. He was notably unrowdy, and he spoke with a slow Southern California drawl, quietly and evenly. Though he had been a starting pitcher since converting from catching and playing the infield as a high school senior, he reacted favorably to Rodgers' desire to move him into the bullpen at the beginning of the 1982 season: with the release of Reggie Cleveland, a pitcher who had served the team as a middle reliever and occasional starter, and with the return to health of McClure, Slaton could move out of the rotation and into the bullpen in a way that would clearly help the team. Rodgers saw in Slaton the so-called rubber arm, a man who could pitch one inning on Tuesday, six on Thursday, and then come in to face a batter or three on Saturday.

Slaton agreed, but by the end of April he had learned that Rodgers also planned, on occasion, to use him in the rotation, spotting him as a starter when an extra righty was needed against a particular team, or when one of the regulars was ailing or failing. Slaton, uncharacteristically, was unhappy: give me a job, he said, and let me keep it. Unlike Yount or Molitor or Simmons, who seemed most to dislike the surprises offered by Rodgers, insisting they needed to know before arriving at the park if they might be sitting down or hitting in a strange spot in the order, Slaton simply didn't like the policy: it wasn't the surprises that concerned him but rather the strain on his arm that would, he feared, inevitably result from the constant tinkering with his role on the pitching staff.

Slaton had, in 1981, suffered a tear in the rotator cuff, that complex of muscles that sheathes the arm's connection with the shoulder. This is the most discussed baseball injury of the age, largely because it has a name (although Bob Rodgers, generally articulate and precise in his speech, persisted in calling it a "rotor cuff"). Freddie Frederico, the Brewers' trainer, said he had seen scores of torn cuffs over his lengthy career. "But until recently," he said, "we just called it a dead arm." Dr. Frank Jobe, the Southern California orthopedist who first identified the torn rotator cuff, was also the first doctor to define its surgical treatment, a complex piece of cutting, trimming, and sewing that is designed to restore pain-free mobility to the area. The problem was that no pitcher had ever returned to successful major league form after Jobe's surgery; the pain-free mobility seemed confined to those who would use their arms for changing light bulbs, carrying groceries, and casting for bass. Jobe may have sought grander results, but what he achieved had everything to do with life after baseball and very little to do with continuing in the game — at least not for pitchers.

Slaton had managed to come back because the tear was relatively slight, and because he was able to sit for almost the entire 1980 season without pitching, allowing the natural healing process to restore full use of the arm. Now, though he didn't baby it, he worried about it, and feared the complicating effects of starting, relieving, relieving, starting.

Worse, today Slaton had been up twice in the bullpen, down, then quickly up again to enter the game on the short notice precipitated by McClure's mishandling of Eddie Murray. Relievers dislike nothing so much as the heating up, cooling off, heating up caused by preparation and re-preparation in the bullpen. Rollie Fingers, who had enjoyed the longest successful career of any non-knuckleballing relief pitcher in baseball history (knuckleball pitchers barely use their arms, so overwork is hardly a fearful prospect), attributed his longevity to managers who never got him up more than once a game and to his own ability to coast in the bullpen until the manager began his walk to the mound, whereupon Fingers would bring himself to the boil by throwing six or seven very hard pitches in rapid succession. With the eight further warmups allotted him when he reached the mound, Fingers could be quickly ready.

"Warming up" is no metaphor; the process involves the heating of the arm by inducing a heightened blood flow throughout its length. Though scientifically inclined pitchers like Tom Seaver (certainly the only pitcher who ever wrote a master's thesis on the effects of artificial turf on baseball) attributed long-term success to their understanding of a long and complex sequence of muscular exertions, notably beginning in the legs, it is the arm that bears the strain. Legs get the arm going in motion, through an interconnected series of thrusts, counterthrusts, and arclike movements, but all the power generated in the legs and torso ends up concentrated in the swift movement of the arm. At the same time, for the arm to direct the ball properly, to catapult it forward with all that collected force, and to make it dip in one direction or another through a final wrenching of the forearm and wrist at the conclusion of the motion, it needs to maintain elasticity. Elasticity is, indeed, the product not just of constant exercise and manipulation but also of "warmth." The ever-quickening movements exerted by a pitcher in his warmups break open capillaries, flood the arm with the glow of enhanced blood flow, and serve to stretch it into a more elastic configuration. Indeed, the enormous bags and pools of ice to which a pitcher subjects his arm after a game serve specifically to halt this capillary action, to stop the hundreds of little hemorrhages that have given the arm its elasticity, and to allow it to "heal" for normal use when the game is over. Lary Sorensen, a pitcher who went to St. Louis in the Simmons trade, was not even remotely hard-throwing but said his healing process was such that for two days after a start, his wife knew if she touched his arm it would make him scream with pain.

If Slaton was able to recover so well from his rotator cuff injury, it was because he took at their word the doctors who told him not to pick up a baseball for several months, and because he was blessed with a delivery of classic proportion. When pitchers and coaches speak of "mechanics," they use the term as pianists use "technique" — the sequence of actions that make a pitcher (or pianist) able to repeat an act over and over to attain the same desired results. The pitcher who is mechanically sound has an unvarying motion, and one whose components are as much arm-preserving as they are speed- or movement-enhancing.

Occasionally, a freak such as Juan Marichal, who arched his back impossibly in the years he pitched for the Giants, or Pete

Vuckovich, whose various pitches came from as many as four different attitudes of arm and body (as, in fact, did Marichal's), can triumph over the doctrine of mechanics. In both cases — that of Marichal, who had extraordinary movement and speed, and Vuckovich, who did not — the pitcher was able to derive his success from the very fact of random mechanics. Batters in wait for a pitcher to begin his motion invariably focus on the spot — the release point — where they first expect the ball to appear; it was useless with Vuckovich, who would throw one pitch in a sequence from 12 o'clock, the next from 9, the next from around 10:30, and the last with what he called the "Chinese fade-away," his right arm swooping down from 1 o'clock to 7 o'clock as he fell off the mound straight toward first base. Vuckovich reasoned that if his arm began dropping down in his delivery late in the game, batters wouldn't know if he were tiring or intentionally varying his delivery. (Bob Shaw, a former major league pitcher and pitching coach who wrote a definitive book on pitching, acknowledged that Vuckovich's method worked for him, but that "nine out of ten guys who've had a hole in their ass are better off throwing from one position.") Ted Simmons, Vuckovich's closest friend on the team, said that the pitcher's calculatedly bizarre mound behavior — crossing his eyes as he stared in for the sign, jerking his head violently toward the runner on first as he pitched from the stretch — helped him much as his strange delivery did. "Sometimes," Simmons said, "the batter thinks, 'What is this guy, some kind of an idiot?' It can't hurt, you know." Vuckovich's mound personality was at one with his off-the-field personality, too: if considered looniness won ball games, the eccentric Vuckovich would be forever a success. He spoke like Professor Irwin Corey, the double-talking monologist. He dressed preposterously, and his comportment led to such endeavors as picking fights with vending machines (one such struggle in May 1982 resulted in an injured foot that cost him three starts). The Milwaukee public relations department's "Story Ideas Information Sheet," studded with statistics and human interest angles for other ball players, said of Vuckovich with admirable succinctness, "One of the game's most interesting interviews."

Jim Slaton — mechanically, emotionally, personally — was as orthodox as Pete Vuckovich was not. His mechanics alone had allowed him to extend his career, after a serious injury, into its eleventh major league season (the average pitcher lasts fewer than three).

Now, as umpire Don Morrison stood to the side, picking up the pace and parabolas of Slaton's warmups and registering them in his head for the ball-and-strike calls to follow, Slaton threw eight pitches to Charlie Moore. On each, he began by swinging his hands up in front of him, bringing them down to his chest as the left leg pulled up into a tuck near his waist, then stretching his arm back as the leg snaked forward, action-reaction, energy conserved. As the arm came forward, Slaton brought his body down so that his right knee virtually scraped the ground, the right arm slingshot came forward, and the left leg served as a fulcrum, absorbing his weight and his thrust and enabling him to conclude his delivery facing the plate and whatever the batter might send back to him. If his right leg did not dip down quite so far, his shoulder would be too high at release, and the ball would sail high in the strike zone. If his arm came over at an angle 1 degree off, the pitch would sail directly at the batter or out of his (and the catcher's) reach. These were the bases of sound pitching, which enabled Jim Slaton even to consider doing it professionally; the speed and force he acquired in the process of delivery, and the spin he was able to impart to the ball with the final movement of his wrist and fingers, were the elements that enabled him to do it in the big leagues.

In the dugout, Kuenn and Dobson watched Slaton's warmups and saw that there was nothing awry. Although Dobson had been filling in for McLish for only a short while, it was his job to know each pitcher's delivery as if it were a signature and he an expert in forgery: one *t* miscrossed would immediately reveal itself, and it would be Dobson's duty to let pitcher, catcher, and manager know. But today Slaton had it just right, a classical motion that made him a pleasure to watch. Kuenn, satisfied, hoped that Slaton would keep Milwaukee in the game for five innings — until that moment when Fingers would come in and close things down. Five innings would likely make Slaton unusable until Sunday, but Kuenn knew that any more than two from Fingers would likely shelve his ace for a few days, too. Kuenn agreed with Dalton that, especially after three straight losses to the Orioles, this game — a "double game," as Dalton called it, where a victory both helped your team and hurt a potential pennant opponent, where a loss would set you four games back for the series and a victory enable you to salvage two — this game mattered more than most. It would be nice to save Fingers, but Kuenn would not go longer than he had to with Slaton.

Contrarily, if Slaton were ineffective, and the Orioles opened up a wide lead, Kuenn would turn to the bodies who filled the bottom spots on the pitching staff: to Jerry Augustine, Dwight Bernard, or Jamie Easterly. Their very lack of distinction forced them into unappealing roles. Though Easterly, a lefty, would occasionally be used in a crucial game where a left-handed pitcher was needed to face one batter before Fingers came in, and though Bernard would assume the right-handed short-man role if Fingers were indisposed, to these three men would also fall the role of fulfilling Milwaukee's contractual obligation: placing nine men on the field when a game was long lost. Easterly's single virtue was left-handedness. Bernard owed his spot on the roster to one of the few major league rules ownership has established in behalf of the individual player. A big league club is able to retain a minor leaguer as exclusive property for the first three years of the player's professional career. After that, the player can be protected only by his inclusion on a team's 40-man off-season roster, which finds 15 on that roster "optioned" to the minors during the regular season. A player can be thus optioned for only three further seasons and still be subject to recall by the major league club. Dwight Bernard, competing for the last roster spot in 1982, was out of options: he was either on the major league club or lost to it forever. Jerry Augustine, for his part, was still on a five-year guaranteed contract, awarded him back when he showed a great deal of promise. In Augustine, Kuenn had an inning eater, an omnivore who could occupy the mound when it was hopeless to waste a truly valuable pitcher.

It was 2:31 in the afternoon when Jim Slaton arrived on the mound. He threw his eight warmup pitches, then turned to join in a brief discussion with Yount and Gantner, who had come to the mound to go over the catcher's signals with Slaton (each Milwaukee pitcher used a basic set of signs, but there were some variations, and it was prudent to review these with the middle infielders, who positioned themselves — and the first and third basemen — on the basis of what the catcher flashed). The Brewers were trailing, 3–2. A potential run stood on first, and though it was only the third inning, Harvey Kuenn was playing it as if it were the seventh, or even the ninth.

As Slaton prepared to pitch, Earl Weaver sent the left-handed-hitting Al Bumbry up to bat for the right-handed Benny Ayala. It appeared to be his first visible managerial move of the day, but the actual insertion of Bumbry for Ayala was not the move itself; it was really the final gesture in a ritualistic sequence in which Earl Weaver had been engaging for nearly fifteen years.

Weaver's eminence as a manager derived from his unquestioned success and from his longevity; since assuming the Baltimore job in 1968, he had seen the other clubs in the American League change managers nearly eight times each (save for the Seattle and Toronto franchises, created in 1977: they'd had only three managers each). Excluding the various one-week interim bosses who finish a season for a club that has just fired the manager, the average tenure of an AL manager, excluding Weaver, was something under two years. Even back half a century, the turnover rate was nearly as high; from 1920 to 1934, AL managers served for only 2.4 years each, even though two clubs — New York and the Philadelphia A's — had only four managers between them. In fact, Weaver's accomplishment was such that in the entire history of organized baseball, only seven men had managed as many consecutive years with one club (and two of those, Cap Anson and Connie Mack, conveniently owned the clubs they managed).

If Weaver had lasted because he was good at his job (and the record clearly established he was), he was good because he could always insert an Al Bumbry for a Benny Ayala. He had other strong managerial characteristics — he hated to bunt; his teams rarely stole bases; he believed in complete games from his pitchers; he could tolerate any quirk of personality so long as the player was productive — but those were matters of decision that any manager could implement: you decided to play a game a certain way, and you went ahead and did it. But what Weaver could do that no other manager could do so well was recognize talent, and *know its limitations.*

Thus was Weaver able to institute a system of platooning complex enough to stagger even a football coach giddy over his various pass-rush specialists, special teams, nickel defenses, and the like. One could, even after only a week, examine Kuenn's managerial style and say that he had the luxury of going with a set lineup daily, making decisions only about the designated hitter and the pitchers. But if Earl Weaver had managed for Milwaukee, he would not have allowed himself that luxury; he would have assembled the team differently, collecting a variety of men who would fit the Weaver system. Employing a file case full of index cards prepared for him by the team's publicity department, each card revealing the record of any given hitter's performance against any given pitcher, Weaver could take what was fundamentally a 9- or 10-man sport and make it a 25-man sport. By doing that, he had created his own system of leverage, making each Baltimore team greater than the sum of its parts. Al Bumbry, a once speedy outfielder with a weak arm and no better than an average outfielder's bat, would have sat on the bench in Milwaukee in 1982 — assuming Milwaukee would have had him on the roster at all. To the Brewers, Bumbry would have had little or no value, but on Weaver's Orioles, he was a critical cog in the machine, one who would play in almost all of Baltimore's games in 1982. And the Orioles were none the weaker because a critical lineup spot was being consumed by a player whose capabilities would barely measure up in Milwaukee; with the Brewers, Bumbry would probably have played as often as Marshall Edwards, while being paid nearly six times as much.

The only impediment to Weaver's team-building existed in his ferociously antagonistic relationship with Jim Russo, Baltimore's chief scout. The most valuable function performed by Hank Peters, Baltimore's dry, rather colorless general manager, was probably his mediation of the running battle between the two men. Peters was able to fuse a plan of action from the seemingly disparate approaches of the mercurial Weaver and the emphatic Russo. In effect, Peters used Russo to get the best out of Weaver's imaginative mind. With Russo out scouting and appraising talent, Weaver was compelled constantly to justify the assembly of his roster. It worked marvelously. Thus on the Orioles did Weaver make his team fit his managerial style, and thus did that style make the team singular in all of baseball.

Thus, too, on June 10, did the prospect of replacing a starting outfielder with a pinch hitter in the third inning not indicate panic or disorganization in the Baltimore dugout; other managers would rarely make such a move so early, because Slaton could be replaced by a lefty in an inning or two, and they'd be stuck with the wrong platoon in the game. But Weaver could withstand such a change because the very best of his interchangeable outfield parts, an outfielder named John Lowenstein, was still on the bench, as was another left-handed outfielder, Jim Dwyer. Such manipulations were not dictated by the Orioles' deficiencies; Weaver's team, like no other in the history of baseball, was built precisely, and intentionally, to make them possible. No doubt it worked partly because Weaver had been granted de facto tenure, and could assemble a team for the long, several-season haul, while other managers were pressured to win *this* year — or they'd be gone. No doubt, too, Weaver would not have engaged in such lineup contortions if he were managing a team like Milwaukee's — but, despite the Brewers' extraordinary offensive prowess and their considerable defensive strength, it is not likely that Earl Weaver would have found himself managing a team like Milwaukee's. He relished too much using the Terry Crowleys of the baseball world.

There was one out when Bumbry took his position in the batter's box and Eddie Murray took a few steps off first. Although he was far from lead-footed, Murray had stolen only 25 bases in his five years in the major leagues. (When Murray came up to the Orioles, in 1977, Weaver was slightly disappointed in his speed, but not nearly so dismayed as Casey Stengel was when Elston Howard became the first black member of the New York Yankees in 1955. "They finally get me one," Stengel said, "and he's the only one in the world who can't run.") Don Money nonetheless moved to hold Murray on first, taking his position on the inside corner of the base, his glove held before him, his knees bent in preparation for the charge he'd have to make for a bunt. At third, Paul Molitor took three steps forward. Although Weaver, who saw most bunts as the needless wasting of a precious out, would surely never tell Bumbry to bunt, especially with one out, it was possible the batter might attempt to bunt for a base hit on his own.

Slaton needed also to consider Bumbry's options, for they would dictate his own. A high pitch was the likeliest way to discourage Bumbry from bunting, but Bumbry was a notorious high fastball hitter who liked his pitches inside, and Slaton was himself most effective in the lower half of the strike zone. Then again, a bunt might well be easily defended. Money was already playing in at first, holding Murray; Molitor was very fast coming in from third; and Slaton was the best fielding pitcher on the Brewer team. But even a successful defense against the bunt hit would probably leave a runner on second base, able to score on a single.

Bumbry, for his part, could think along with Slaton, going over all the same possibilities. He knew Slaton had a good fastball, and a hard breaking pitch, called a "slurve," which broke more than a slider but not quite so much as a curve. (Vuckovich tried to teach Jerry Augustine a subvariant, a slider thrown with a sharp turn of the wrist at release, the hand passing beneath the ball as it shot forward. It broke "bigger than a slider, but smaller than a slurve." Or so Vuckovich said.) Slaton, who knew Bumbry knew what he knew, threw a high fastball. Bumbry, appearing to commit himself early, took a swing at the ball and fouled it back. Slaton could draw little intelligence from this; he knew some batters *intentionally* made themselves look bad on certain pitches, thus hoping to make the pitcher throw the same pitch again.

The guessing game continued on the next pitch. Now Bumbry had acquired additional knowledge: he knew the speed of Slaton's fastball today; he knew the pitcher was not fearful of throwing it high; and he was able to see just how quickly Slaton, following his delivery, was in his fielding stance. The Brewers were capable of taking away the bunt, both with their fielding alignment and their choice of pitches.

Bumbry returned to the batter's box and saw Molitor tiptoe forward at third. On the mound, Slaton brought his hands down to his waist, glanced first at Moore, his catcher, and then over his shoulder at Murray. He then pulled up his left knee, drew his right arm back and threw another fastball, high, in on Al Bumbry's hands. Bumbry could only push it, perfectly placed as it was, and send a weak grounder toward Yount at shortstop. Slaton's pitch was *too* good, and Yount had to race in for the ball in the vain hope of buying time for a double play. He was able to get the ball speedily to Gantner at second, who drew his left foot away from the base as he caught Yount's throw. Saving effort, which was the same as time, Gantner kept his right foot stationary, moved his left in front of him, and threw across his body to Money. Bumbry reached first before the ball did.

Although the quick Bumbry replaced the slower Murray at first, it was a substantial net gain for Milwaukee: two outs, and a right-handed hitter coming up.

The batter was Gary Roenicke. He was part of Weaver's six-man outfield army, a right-handed hitter with power who had gained some renown because of the special batting helmet equipped with a football face mask that he wore, a device Earl Weaver thought up after Roenicke was hit in the face by a pitch from Chicago's Lerrin LaGrow in 1979. Though left-handers John Lowenstein and Jim Dwyer were available, Weaver chose to stay with Roenicke. There were four arguments in behalf of the outfielder: first, with Bumbry in the game, Roenicke could move to left, and two of the three outfield positions would thus have their best practitioners in place; second, Ford, a defensive liability, would surely come out later in the game if Baltimore maintained its lead, and his replacement at that later moment would be more critical in a close game than Roenicke's replacement now; third, Lowenstein, the obvious man to step in for Roenicke, was too valuable a pinch hitter to use in anything but a must-hit situation; and fourth, Weaver's index cards told him Roenicke was a .371 lifetime hitter against Milwaukee pitching.

Slaton eyed Bumbry on first, but made no pickoff throw. He had an admittedly weak move, unlike McClure, who reveled in his pickoff motion and practiced by the hour in front of a mirror. Slaton also saw little likelihood that Bumbry, who had slowed appreciably in recent years, would be running. And although a good move to first *was* important, and lip service was paid to developing one and making good use of it, the Brewers simply didn't stress holding runners terribly much. Randy Lerch, a tall left-hander who had started the night before for Milwaukee, could no more readily hold a runner on first than he could speak Urdu. And though Bob Rodgers had, in his first spring camp in '81, made much of what was called "the Willie Wilson pickoff play" — the first baseman lining up *behind* the runner rather than right on first, and the pitcher throwing straight at the runner's head — it was the sort of thing that demanded attention in the spring, and generally slipped from front-of-mind consciousness as the season wore on.

Slaton's first pitch to Roenicke went wide of the plate, and Bumbry held. The next pitch, a slider, just caught the outside corner, and Roenicke got only enough of the ball to send it on a looping arc into short left field. Oglivie closed in on it, but at the last moment the wind pushed it toward center field, where Yount, 60 feet beyond his normal position, caught it falling over backward for the third out.

Jim Slaton had thrown three fastballs and one slider. Only one pitch was out of the strike zone, and the two balls Bumbry and

Roenicke actually hit didn't together generate enough force to reach the deep outfield.

	1	2	3	4	5	6	7	8	9	R	H	E
Baltimore	1	2	0							3	6	1
Milwaukee	2	0								2	3	0

As the Brewers ran in to their dugout, the Orioles deserted theirs for the field. With the Brewers at bat, the Milwaukee dugout contained those players not in the bullpen, the batter's box, the on-deck circle, and the clubhouse (Cecil Cooper and his pulled hamstring were in the whirlpool, attended by trainer Freddie Frederico). Pat Dobson sat next to Harvey Kuenn, equipment manager Bob Sullivan watched the game from the far end of the dugout, and assistant trainer John Adam stood near the runway to the clubhouse. (Adam was yet another, if peripheral, member of the Dalton Gang. He had originally been a pitcher in the Baltimore organization, and when his arm went bad he learned the trainer's trade; Dalton eventually hired him as trainer with the Milwaukee Class AA farm club in Holyoke, Massachusetts, and he reached the major leagues, in his white ducks and blue Milwaukee golf shirt, in 1980.)

League rules allow only uniformed personnel, the trainers, and the equipment manager on the bench during a game. A telephone connected Kuenn to the bullpen, to Tom Skibosh in the press box (it enabled players angry about the scorer's calls to send their rage *somewhere*), and to Harry Dalton in his private box on the first base side of the press level. Dalton called only when an injury occurred. During a game, his phone was more likely to be connected to a scout on the West Coast than to the dugout.

Bob Sullivan worked for Tommy Ferguson, the traveling secretary and vice president, administration. (It was Ferguson's primary — and thankless — task to serve as travel agent, concierge, and peripatetic den mother to a traveling party of one manager, four coaches, twenty-five players, two trainers, two reporters, four broadcasters, two broadcast technicians, and Mrs. Paul Molitor, who traveled with the team so frequently that the players began to call her "the twenty-sixth man.") Like Ferguson, Sullivan had begun his baseball career as a batboy in Boston, and had moved slowly up the nonplaying ladder until he took charge of the Milwaukee clubhouse. He was, in many ways, a bona fide member of the team. A fit, youngish man with a pronounced Boston twang, he was guardian of the hoary clubhouse dictum "What you see here stays here." He probably knew more about the players than anyone in the organization. His specific responsibilities made him sort of their majordomo. He was responsible at home for the postgame meals, the constant availability of candy bars and cigarettes, the maintenance of the clubhouse, the guardianship of the safe in which the players placed their valuables during the game, the shine on the players' shoes and the cleanliness of their uniforms. He also made sure that the boxes of giveaway balls got autographed, and had to put up with the gibes attendant to this most ritualistic of clubhouse tasks. (One afternoon, attempting to discern what the ball in question would be used for, Charlie Moore asked, "Is that a bartender ball or a pussy ball?")

On the road, Sully stayed always with the bags of equipment and luggage that traveled with the team, riding from airport to ball park and back with the truck that ferried the bats, gloves, uniforms, the two trunks of trainers' supplies, and the luggage of the players, coaches, trainers, manager, and writers. Sullivan received a salary from the club, and sizable tips from the players at season's end. (The manager of the visiting clubhouse receives tips from the visiting players at the end of each series. In Seattle, clubhouse manager Freddie Genzale kept a list of visiting players, and as he got tipped he'd check off the player's name, putting a star next to the names of those who were particularly generous. Don Baylor, then with the California Angels, foiled the practice by collecting his teammates' tips himself and giving Genzale a fistful of bills, undifferentiated by donor.)

Near Bob Sullivan in the dugout sat Mike Caldwell, the left-handed pitcher, who was keeping the chart on June 10. The chart is an 8½-by-14-inch document that records the progress of the Milwaukee pitchers throughout the game. As each pitch was thrown, it was Caldwell's job to record whether it was a fastball, slider, curve, or whatever, whether it was a ball or a strike, and whether or not it was hit. Those hit in fair territory were mapped out on a miniature schematic map of the playing field; in the off-season, Kuenn had, when he was a coach, collated the records of the flight of every ball hit by every player on every team against every Milwaukee pitcher. In his Arizona winter home, Kuenn would graph the information for each opposing hitter on a large chart of the playing field, all balls hit into play represented by a different-color pencil for each Milwaukee pitcher. These elaborate and rather handsome abstracts were taped to the wall of the Milwaukee dugout for every game; the idea was that the players would consult them before they went out in the field each inning, the better to position themselves for the opposing batters. A few of them actually did.

Caldwell took charting relatively seriously, and with uncharacteristic moderation. When Pete Vuckovich kept the chart, it would be filled with various written ejaculations of doubtful temperance, mostly concerning the home plate umpire's calls. Caldwell's chart on June 10 was free of editorializing, save for the heading: Caldwell titled today's effort BALTIMORE AT 'DRAB CITY.'

It was an exceedingly mild description from Caldwell. Though he was one of the few Brewers to hold a college degree in an academic subject (he received his degree in sociology at North Carolina State University), he seemed — in contrast, say, to Simmons, who wished very much to be perceived as a cultivated man — at times to want the baseball world, at least, to perceive him as an ape. He was foul-mouthed and foul-tempered, a vicious and constant bench jockey whose most common dugout word was "cocksucker," usually directed, with considerable volume, at the umpires. Gorman Thomas was once thrown out on a close play at first and, returning to the dugout, found himself standing in front of an inflamed Caldwell, who was showering vituperation on the umpire who made the call. The umpire turned in the direction of the screaming, saw Thomas, and ejected him from the game. Five other players had to restrain the irate Thomas from charging the umpire.

Caldwell was often unshaven, and the utter absence of even a momentary smile on his visage earned him the nickname "Mr. Warmth" (he even wore a T-shirt emblazoned: MR. FUCKING WARMTH). His upper lip covered by a muddy-brown mustache, his pugnaciousness visible in the way he held his head, hanging forward from his slouched shoulders, Caldwell appeared at times to resemble something apelike. He was also the Wisconsin sports chairman of the Cystic Fibrosis Foundation, and had intended to pursue a career in criminal justice if he hadn't found success in baseball.

Caldwell had hated Bob Rodgers and Bob Rodgers had hated him, and there was no one else on the team as happy to see Rodgers gone. Caldwell had flourished under George Bamberger, who worshiped Caldwell's competitiveness and who had helped Caldwell perfect a spitball that had earned the pitcher a spot on American League president Lee MacPhail's "scrutiny list" of pitchers suspected of doctoring the ball. (The list was prepared for the umpires, who largely ignored it, feeling the league lacked the will to enforce the stricture against altered balls. Umpire Larry Barnett said, "Until I see a big blob of shit on the ball, I'm not going to do anything.")

But even Rodgers liked giving Caldwell the ball. At the 1981 winter meetings, Harry Dalton had rejected Philadelphia's offer of several promising young players, including an infielder named Ryne Sandberg, for the combative pitcher. Even though Caldwell could barely hit 80 mph with his fastball, and though he kicked and strode on a pair of ankles that were a textbook case of catastrophic pathology, he was able to win by keeping his pitches down and by varying the pitches' speed. The basic trick to the latter lay in how snugly the ball was held against the pitcher's hand: a ball gripped at the tips of the fingers increases the radius of its sweep through the air before delivery; as more hand makes contact with the ball, this radius is decreased, friction is increased, and a ball pitched with an otherwise identical motion slows perceptibly and, to a hitter, disruptively. As with Caldwell, Jim Slaton — a different pitcher in every other regard — changed his speeds often, and it helped him immeasurably.

For the bottom of the third, Gary Roenicke moved to left as Al Bumbry, who had hit for Benny Ayala, went to center. Though Bumbry had lost some of his speed, he had spent his entire career in center, and knew how to play it. Roenicke had played all three outfield positions, and could better adapt to moving around.

Bumbry's experience, though, paid off on the first pitch Stewart threw in the bottom of the third. Robin Yount attacked the pitch viciously, sending a high line drive 390 feet to center field. Bumbry knew not to shade Yount to left; though his power was mostly a pull hitter's power, Yount was able to hit with strength to the right side as well. The ball was hit hard enough, and low enough, to make it catchable only by someone who had positioned himself perfectly: someone like Bumbry, who was seemingly off with the pitch and under Yount's drive when it arrived at the warning track.

Don Money, whose home run had accounted for both Milwaukee runs, took his stance stone still in the rear of the right-handed batter's box, his bat perfectly erect, his hands in front of him, actually positioned over the inside edge of the plate. Stewart began with a fastball low and outside that Morrison called a strike. Money, a patient hitter, rarely swung at the first pitch, and was consequently often behind in the count. It is an article of faith to most managers and pitching coaches that the character of an at-bat is determined by the first pitch. George Bamberger so swore by the one-pitch, one-strike rule that he insisted that hitters who began at 1 and 0 batted .400 and that hitters who started off 0 and 1 batted under .200. (The difference is real, but not nearly so great as Bamberger perceived it to be. Still, statistician Pete Palmer found that more than 80 percent of all walks occurred when the first pitch was a ball, and batters starting at 1 and 0 produced twice as many runs as those starting at 0 and 1.) Don Money was careful, had a good eye, and seemed always to want the pitcher to prove he had control. Of the Brewers, only Gorman Thomas, who was often pitched around, walked more frequently.

The next pitch, too, was a strike, this time a curve that swept over the outside half of the plate and dipped into Rick Dempsey's glove about a foot off the ground. Stewart was working the area that was, in most cases, the place for a pitcher to be: an area defined by an *L* that stretches down the height of the strike zone from letters to knees on the inside edge of the plate, the bottom stroke of it along knee level to the outside corner. Most pitchers, if they can keep the ball in the *L,* see success.

Logically, Stewart would now come inside and high, and indeed Dempsey signaled for the pitcher's fastball and set up his glove on the inside edge of the plate. Stewart was not a sinker ball pitcher, and his fastball, thrown with the palm of the hand facing the plate, would either stay on one plane or move slightly upward as the backspin imparted by his fingers created an airplane effect as it hurtled through the ambient air.

High and inside, and ideally not even in the strike zone, was the perfect pitch for the 0-2 situation, especially for a batter who crowds the plate. But as Stewart released the ball, he erred mechanically and the pitch crossed the outside half of the plate at Money's chest level. The batter pulled back his bat as Stewart went into his motion and whipped it around on an even plane, never taking his hands from the level at which he had cocked them. Money lashed the ball past Stewart and into center field: a single.

Ben Oglivie batted next. The first pitch was a ball, high and outside. Then Stewart threw idly to Murray at first, and Money retreated to the base as coach Ron Hansen shouted "Backbackback"; it was an urgent, high-pitched shriek, and Hansen used it on every throw to first, no matter how desultory. A slider, which Oglivie watched, crossed the outside corner, a strike. Another ball, inside, and the count was 2-1. Along the left field line, Gary Roenicke in the outfield and Cal Ripken Jr. at third base were playing way over toward the center of the diamond. In Oakland the week before, Oglivie had repeatedly tried to hit against this sort of defense. Today, though, he failed even to take notice of the defensive alignment, and later he said that he was so successfully concentrating on the pitcher that he didn't even notice there *were* other fielders out there.

Though various observers had attributed Oglivie's success as a power hitter to his wrists, comparing them to Henry Aaron's, it wasn't really an apt analogy. Aaron, at the height of his career, outweighed Oglivie by nearly 15 pounds, and the older man's weight was compressed into an even 6-foot frame. Oglivie was two inches taller, his chest less full across, his legs relatively slender. His power was generated from astonishing speed in his wrists, but also from a kinetic force generated throughout his lean body.

On June 10, at the plate in the third inning, he waited for Stewart's next pitch near the rear of the box, his bat waggling furiously, like some sort of unnatural, oversize tuning fork. His hands were pulled back, his upper body muscles stretched tight. It was a slow curve, and Oglivie, his mind focused entirely on the ball's red stitches as it spun toward him, immediately discerned its direction. Unlike the batter who stands near the front of the box and is able to reach the curveball as it begins its dip downward, the batter who waits three feet farther back has to make his adjustment in midswing. This Oglivie did as his right foot stepped forward, opening his body up toward the ball. His rear ankle turned parallel with the front ankle, and the movement sent his legs in a similar pattern, his hips opening up as the pitch approached the plate. The hips, in turn, set the arms in motion, in Oglivie's case working against a little backward jerk that classicists call a "hitch" in the swing and that Kuenn called evidence of "rhythm." Now the shoulders came around, then the arms, then the bat at the far end of a blurry crack-the-whip. Oglivie's bat intercepted the ball with his hands in front of the center of his body's weight, in front of his tensed upper arm muscles. As bat and ball made contact, his wrists added the last movement in a perfectly coordinated swing. But by then the ball had already met the bat; the wrists merely completed the accelerating series of arcs and brought his bat around his body for the follow-through, as the ball rocketed between first and second base and on into right field. Money, whose progress was slowed as he pulled up to let the ball pass him, advanced to second base, and Oglivie perched at first.

Gorman Thomas was next. Twice Stewart had let a curve stay too high up in the strike zone, and twice he had been fortunate that the hitters had made contact with the ball perhaps a thirty-second of an inch too high, and had sent the balls through the infield on the ground. Thomas, with his uppercut swing, was less likely to hit a Stewart mistake for a ground ball, and Ray Miller, the pitching coach, came out to talk with Stewart and Dempsey. Thomas was murder on the low inside pitch.

Thomas had, basically, two swings. One was for the "bump," which is what he called a home run, and one was for a single. He used the latter when there were two strikes on him, and men on base. He'd bring his feet closer together, shorten his swing, and attempt to send the ball, especially an outside pitch, over the infield for a single.

After watching the first pitch from Stewart sail outside, he got his meat pitch, a slider down and in, but Thomas, whose team had not won for four days, and who saw two men in Milwaukee uniforms on base, went with Swing Number Two and dumped it in front of Al Bumbry, who was playing Thomas deep in left center field. It appeared at first that Bumbry might reach it, so Money proceeded cautiously, and when the ball dropped and Dan Ford came over from right to cut it off in front of the center fielder, Money had to stop at third. The bases were loaded.

In the stands, there were few people who felt that of all the Milwaukee hitters, Roy Howell, the DH, was the one they wanted at bat with the bases loaded in a game in which the Brewers were trailing. Howell had come to Milwaukee before the 1981 season, signed as a free agent off the roster of the Toronto Blue Jays. In 1972, Howell, from Lompoc, California, had been one of the most avidly scouted amateur players in the country. He had played American Legion ball in the eighth grade. He met his first scout when he was 13. In high school he was, said Brewer scout Harry Smith, "like a 25-year-old playing with a bunch of kids." He was strong, he had good instincts, and he could hit. Dee Fondy, Dalton's special assistant and a sort of "superscout," remembered Howell, too, as "soft-handed," an adept third baseman who was also blessed with a strong arm. The Texas Rangers drafted him as the fourth player picked in the entire country, and he reached the major leagues to stay barely two years later. In the ensuing six seasons, he hit ably, if unspectacularly, for Texas and then for Toronto.

By the time Howell approached free agency at the end of the 1980 season, he knew he didn't want to stay with the Blue Jays. He was a quiet, intense man, and he had spent his entire professional career amid the frustration of playing for losing teams. As his agent, George Kalifatis, began discussions with various ball clubs in the winter of 1980, Howell determined that, more than anything, he wanted to play with a contending team; when Harry Dalton made Kalifatis a competitive offer, the agent and the player accepted, even though there were two third basemen ahead of him on the Milwaukee roster and Howell's playing time could not be guaranteed.

One of the third basemen was Sal Bando, though, and even though Bando had a year left on his contract entering 1981, it was fairly well understood that he'd be retiring, especially if Dalton found another man to play third. Don Money was the other, and though he was the model of a professional — "the crafty veteran," bullpen coach Larry Haney called him, relishing the cliché — he was plagued by all manner of ailments. Too, Howell was a left-handed hitter, and Dalton and Rodgers liked the idea of the flexibility that Howell would give them: a left-handed bat to spell or alternate with Money at third, a substitute first baseman when Cecil Cooper was given a day off, another DH candidate if Larry Hisle, recuperating from shoulder surgery, failed to return to his 1978 form, and a strong left-handed bat off the bench when Howell wasn't in the regular lineup.

Howell, for his part, decided he was willing to forgo his accustomed position as a regular (he had played at least 125 games in five of his six major league seasons). Not only did he want to play with, as he called them, "people who want to win"; he also saw that the end of Bando's professional career had likely arrived, and Money's could not be too far off.

But, in spring training in Sun City in 1981, Bob Rodgers and his coaches saw that Roy Howell, at third base, was an adventure they didn't particularly enjoy. When players are acquired from other teams, a certain wishfulness is operative: even the most hardened scout will find a way to rationalize one part of a player's makeup (in Howell's case, his glove) because he relishes another (his left-handed bat). Howell was definitely no longer the soft-handed youth Dee Fondy had admired, and in Sun City he fielded the position atrociously. Bando was dissuaded from retiring, and Howell played third in fewer than half of Milwaukee's games, despite Money's being immobilized by injury most of the second half of the season.

Howell took it well enough, preparing to pick up yet more playing time in '82; Bando made it clear long before the 1981 season ended that it would, for sure, be his last. But the specter of ground balls clanging off Howell's chest horrified Rodgers and Dalton, and they decided late in 1981 to give the third base job, uncontested, to Paul Molitor.

Howell came to regret his decision to sign with Milwaukee when he learned that Molitor, whom he acknowledged was a superior athlete, would immovably block his path at third. He felt he was a better third baseman than the Milwaukee decision makers thought he was, and that he hit well enough to justify greater faith than Rodgers and Dalton had granted him. Angry, he told the *Milwaukee Journal,* "No words are going to change it. What am I going to do, *tell* him [Rodgers] I can play? I guess I have as much respect for him as a manager as he has for me as a player." Howell went to Dalton's office in Sun City early in March, aired his frustrations, and asked to be traded.

Dalton rarely liked to accommodate a player's trade wishes without question; in 1982, in fact, he offered to make such an effort only on behalf of Charlie Moore, who saw Simmons eternally behind the plate (despite his weak 1981 hitting) and knew how much Rodgers liked Ned Yost, the young third-string catcher whom the manager thought was the best defensive catcher, and the best handler of pitchers, he had. Dalton had promised Moore, when he signed a long-term contract the year Simmons joined the team, that he would honor Moore's request for a trade if it turned out that he did not get sufficient playing time. (Moore actually made the request in March of 1982 but withdrew it before Dalton had had time to act on it.)

Still, despite his displeasure with Howell's reaction to Molitor's insertion at third, Dalton began to look for a deal — but only a deal that would otherwise enhance his club's prospects. Which is to say, he looked halfheartedly, and with the aces in *his* hand, not Howell's. Even this strategy was complicated by Howell's very visible displeasure during the exhibition season in Arizona. Quiet and remote to begin with, Howell fell into a sulk. He told those who offered their good wishes, "In the dictionary, sympathy comes between shit and syphilis." During pregame practices, he visibly loafed, and Dalton felt impelled to tell Howell that the more he made it clear that his heart was not in playing for Milwaukee, the less interested would be the scouts who came to appraise him. When the team went north, Howell was still a Brewer, and an unhappy one.

Nonetheless, he realized that his future was out of his hands, at least so long as he was under contract to Milwaukee (another two years). "That's baseball," he said. "Nine positions and 25 guys. Why should I kick my dog, yell at my wife? I can't say I like it; I don't. But life's too short." Soon enough, Howell adjusted to his role as a half-time DH — Hisle, for the third time, had failed to make a sustained comeback from his injury — and learned to make his contribution in what ways he could. He was an active dugout cheerleader, and an able sign stealer, training his eyes on opposing third base coaches for the telltale sequences that would enable him to break the encryption. He was also, though not blessed with extraordinary speed, a good baserunner and an especially creative slider. Against Cleveland in 1981, he avoided a sure tag-out when he executed a perfect half-gainer over second baseman Dave Rosello, vaulting over defender and base; only after landing on the outfield side of second did he reach back to touch safely.

Still, these were values appreciated more by his teammates than by Milwaukee fans, to whom Howell was stone-handed, remote, and simply not the stuff of hero worship. They loved Gorman Thomas, who played to the crowd and embodied all the Milwaukee virtues: blue-collar, beer-drinking, unfancy, and, despite his South Carolina Tidewater origins, somehow ethnic. They also swooned for the good-looking, boyish Molitor; for Robin Yount, whom they had seen grow up on the County Stadium field; for the elegant Cecil Cooper. Howell? He was a body.

There was one out, the bases were loaded, and Milwaukee still trailed 3–2 when Howell reached the plate. A sacrifice fly would tie the game, and Howell could mentally tick off the two critical things to avoid when attempting the sac fly: not to sucker for a low pitch that would be difficult to lift into the air and not to try to pull the ball. (This last act sometimes causes the hitter to turn his bat over, which in turn can cause him to drive the ball into the ground.)

Howell swung at Stewart's first pitch and popped it up beyond the Baltimore dugout, where Ripken got to it in time to make, apparently, the second out. But the third baseman fell as he caught it, and the ball dropped out of his glove. The pitch, a slider down and in, was the "book" pitch on Howell: every right-handed pitcher in the league tried to get him out with it, tying him up as he strode into the plate on his swing.

But Stewart's next pitch was a curveball that swooped just into the outer part of the strike zone as it passed the plate, a pitch Stewart meant — but failed — to throw for a ball. Howell reached it readily and pushed the pitch into left field for a double. Money and Oglivie scored, and Thomas moved to third. Milwaukee took the lead, 4–3, and Earl Weaver went out to the mound to take the ball from Sammy Stewart.

Milwaukee's players knew Sammy Stewart well. Over his three years in the major leagues, they had seen 40 innings of his pitching, knew his ability to change speeds, and particularly his usual deftness with his breaking pitches. Knowing what he threw didn't mean they could necessarily hit it, but at least they could approach the plate without having to worry about surprises. But Storm Davis, his successor, was a cipher: he had come up from the minor leagues a bare few weeks earlier, and no one on the team had ever faced him before. The call went up on the bench, in an effort to find someone who had played against Davis in the minors or in winter ball, but it was unavailing. Kuenn surmised Davis had good control; he hadn't given up a single walk in the 14-plus innings he had pitched since joining the Orioles. He presumed, too, that Davis, who had struck out 9 men in those same 14-plus innings, had a decent fastball.

Kuenn was right. On June 10 Davis was the youngest player in the major leagues, having reached his twentieth birthday the previous winter. He threw hard, and he was also able to get his curve and his slider over the plate for strikes. But beyond that knowledge, Kuenn's batters would have to proceed on automatic pilot, on their own confidence that they could hit. They would correctly presume that Davis would employ his fastball, curve, and perhaps an occasional change-up; he'd pitch high and tight, then low and away; he'd change speeds. He would, in a word, do what pitchers do. Coming out of the Baltimore organization, he likely wouldn't proceed on the basis of the creaky (and fairly preposterous) truisms that fluttered perpetually in big league clubhouses and hotel bars. Bob Rodgers reported that he had, in his career, heard the following: "Throw the curve to guys under 30, the fastball to guys over 30; throw the fastball at night, the curve in the day; throw the curve in April and May, because the hitters aren't ready for it, and the fastball in August, when they're tired. I've even heard people say jam the black guys." Gates Brown, the Detroit batting coach, added another saw when he told *Sports Illustrated,* in all earnestness, "If a man's wearing glasses, pitch him low and away."

Charlie Moore came to the plate. Gorman Thomas, standing in foul territory as he took his lead at third, plucked at the shoulders of his jersey in an abbreviated version of his at-bat ritual. Roy Howell walked off second as Davis brought his hands into the pitcher's set position. Though not nearly so adept at it as Money, Howell had a good eye for stealing a catcher's signs from second. If he could break the code Rick Dempsey was using with Davis, Howell would flash a discreet signal to Moore, almost imperceptibly lifting his fingers from a knee as he crouched in his lead off second: breaking pitch.

On a 2-2 pitch that rode up and in, the right-handed Moore threw his bat off his shoulder in a motion reminiscent of a left-handed tennis player's slicing a backhand, his top hand coming off the bat as it made contact. The ball skipped along the ground toward Rich Dauer at second base, and Thomas scored as Dauer looked toward home before throwing to first. Had Moore taken his normal position at bat, closer to the plate, he would have had his hands tied by Davis's pitch, and would not likely have managed to dump the ball on the one spot on the infield that ensured Thomas's safe progress to home.

It was now 5–3, two outs, Roy Howell standing on third, and Marshall Edwards, his mouth open in a nervous rictus, his hands dancing up the barrel of his bat, hit a ground ball off Eddie Murray's glove that gave Milwaukee a 6–3 lead. Though Jim Gantner followed with another single, Paul Molitor grounded out to end the inning.

The Milwaukee offense, on their way to hitting more home runs in a season than any team in twenty years, had scored their 4 third-inning runs on 5 singles and a double. Cecil Cooper, the team's best hitter, was in the clubhouse. Robin Yount and Paul Molitor, the other men who, in the dugout cliché, "set the table" for the Milwaukee offense, had made the first and last outs of the inning. Gorman Thomas and Ben Oglivie, home run champions both, had managed hits that were only utterly mortal singles. The weary Don Money, the unappreciated Roy Howell, and the fretful Marshall Edwards built the four-run offense.

	1	2	3	4	5	6	7	8	9	R	H	E
Baltimore	1	2	0							3	6	1
Milwaukee	2	0	4							6	9	0

Up on the terrace beneath the press box, Sal Bando was joined by his business partner, a former professional basketball player named Jon McGlocklin. The two men shared control of a Small Business Investment Corporation, which had assets of $2,500,000 and which, with interests throughout the Milwaukee area, had made them both wealthy. Bando's last playing contract, signed at the end of 1976 when he earned his freedom from Charles O. Finley of the Oakland A's, had in the ensuing years been dwarfed by agreements executed in behalf of far lesser players, but he never complained (not that $281,000 a year should merit complaint). He was a man of his word, and like some others on the team who had either outperformed what had been expected of them when they signed their long-term contracts or had seen the hugger-mugger race to sign free agents escalate the price of mediocre talent beyond the standard that had been used for genuine stars only a few years earlier, Bando never asked to renegotiate. (The same held for Pete Vuckovich, who signed his long-term agreement in 1981 and then went on to be the best pitcher in the league that year, and Rollie Fingers, whose once-fat $215,000 a year had been dwarfed by the time the Brewers signed him to a lush new contract in '81. On the other side, Cecil Cooper had successfully pushed Dalton to the wall for an "extension" of his own contract — that is, a transfusion of new money on top of old money in exchange for the addition of a year or two at the contract's end.)

Although his ethical sense certainly had much to do with Bando's contractual contentment, so did the peak and wane of his career. He had come to Milwaukee on the cusp of his prime; he had given the club credibility and, in 1978 especially, helped mightily to make the team competitive. By 1980, though, Bando's career was clearly in decline, and in 1981 he came close to retiring and forgoing the pay due him that year — until the Brewers' management saw the true state of Don Money's back and Roy Howell's glove in spring training.

Among the other things Bando did in 1981 — such as watching his younger brother, Chris, a catcher, break in with the Cleveland Indians — he played what might have been a critical role in baseball labor relations had not the singularity of the game's ownership class made itself manifest. In what some considered a stall, and others considered a genuine effort to avoid a cataclysmic strike, the Major League Baseball Players Association and the Player Relations Committee, Inc., the two adversaries who represented labor and management in baseball, agreed to establish a four-man study committee in the winter of 1980–1981. Management was represented by New York Mets general manager Frank Cashen and by Harry Dalton; labor's envoys were Philadelphia catcher Bob Boone and Sal Bando.

"I really think we could have solved it," Harry Dalton said, "if we had been left to ourselves to work it out. But every time outsiders were present" — he presumably meant Marvin Miller, the executive director of the Players Association, or Ray Grebey, the chief negotiator for the PRC — "we were back to slogans. It was hopeless." Bando allowed that he agreed that Cashen and Dalton, both of them relative doves on the free agency issue, and Boone and Bando, representative of the more thoughtful players in the game, had a better shot at reaching agreement than Grebey and Miller had.

Whatever, the study committee made no progress at all, and neither did the professional negotiators. The players went on strike after the completion of the games of June 11, 1981, and for seven weeks the nation endured a summer without baseball. Sal Bando thought it suited him just fine.

"For the first time," Bando said, "I found what it was like to be at home with my family for a length of time when the kids weren't in school. I got to bed early; I had breakfast with my wife and kids; I had an office to go to. Of course, I was lucky because my career was just about over, and because I had my business with Jon. But it sure told me that retirement was something to look forward to."

Bando was deeply religious, and his theology had been profoundly affected by the born-again evangelical movement despite the fact he was a Roman Catholic. While retaining devout belief in the doctrines of the church, he nonetheless saw a hopeful ecumenicism in the born-again movement and became the Baseball Chapel leader on the Brewers. On the road, he often passed the boring afternoon hours in his hotel room, studying the Bible; often he invited reporters, executives, and others to come to Chapel meetings. He took Paul Molitor, also a religious Catholic, under his wing, and helped Molitor through a difficult time when the younger man's parents were being divorced and were making strenuous demands on him.

Yet there was nothing sanctimonious in Bando's religion, even in his proselytizing. He never pressed nonbelievers, and never condemned them either. In fact, he was most likely to criticize his fellow brothers in religion who cited "God's will" as the reason for a particular athletic misstep.

To many in baseball, such constant reference to God and His will — especially when the latter had something to do with a swinging strikeout with men on base — reeked of alibi, not to mention a sense of proportion that was somewhat lacking. But few in baseball addressed the problem out loud, fearful of appearing ungodly themselves. They were also reluctant to risk offending the Baseball Chapel itself, a rather strident organization of evangelical mood that sponsored religious sessions on Sunday mornings in every clubhouse in organized baseball and that published a newsletter that trumpeted such notable events as two minor leaguers' burning "$500 worth of rock records because of their satanic implications." The San Francisco Giants organization in particular was plagued by rampant religious excuse-making, and gatherings of scouts often featured a resentful disdain of the Giant players who used their faith to excuse their errors of commission and omission.

Harry Dalton did go on the record about the issue, however. He said that such excuse-making was, indeed, inexcusable, and he took steps to deal with the peer pressure that aggressive Chapel members might bring to bear on nonbelieving or at least nondemonstrative team members. With the Brewers, it all began in the minor leagues when the father of a Jewish Milwaukee farmhand telephoned Ray Poitevint, then the farm director, to express his concern that his son was being ostracized by his born-again teammates for sitting outside the locker room while Christian doctrine was being celebrated within. Poitevint immediately took steps to ensure that any chapel services on a Brewer farm team had to be concluded 90 minutes before the time at which team members were required to come to the park. Dalton instituted the same policy on the big league club.

Bando was dismayed that there was controversy about faith. Yet he reminded himself, always, to keep his perspective: if nothing else, Bando had learned that perspective, above all, was required of a big league ball player, who lived his life in a fishbowl, expected the world to gaze in admiringly, and could find it too easy to succumb to the blandishments of fame. He needed his religion to remind him there was something *other* than baseball; too many others saw the two as concurrent.

"You just try to retain some human values," Bando said. "I remember last year when my son and I were waiting in a long line in a restaurant in Milwaukee and it looked like we'd never get seated. My boy said to me, 'Come on, Dad, tell 'em you're Sal Bando and they'll serve us right away.' I thought I had failed as a father.

"You see," Bando went on, "it's so easy to get caught up in this life: people always want to give you things, hold the door open for you, wait on you. When you travel, someone else makes your reservations, holds your ticket, and carries your bag. Athletes today are 30-year-old kids. When a manager or someone else in the front office says, 'These are adults,' they're copping out. It's as though people were afraid to let athletes *be* adults."

For Bob McClure, perspective was blurred by zealousness. While he was floating through his big league career and performing with relative indistinction, McClure had found Jesus. Then, in 1981, scheduled to be a member of the Milwaukee starting rotation, the pitcher suffered from what appeared to be tendinitis in spring training. Soon thereafter, the condition was diagnosed as a rotator cuff tear, and McClure had to face the reality that his career might be over, that all his professional attention would have to turn to his chain of hairstyling salons. Suddenly, his religion loomed ever larger, and when he found his injury healed, he could perceive the Hand of God.

Although he remained the easygoing practical joker he had been before, talk of God crept ever more insistently into McClure's conversation. Simple questions — "How's the arm?" or "What do you think of your season so far?" — brought convoluted answers. Reporters with Milwaukee, as so many reporters with other teams, suddenly found themselves confronted with developing interviewing techniques that would enable them to slice through words that however worthy and respectable, had little to do with matters at hand.

It could have been worse for Tom Flaherty of the *Journal* and Vic Feuerherd of the *Sentinel*, the two writers who traveled with the Brewers. McClure may have retreated to what the cynic might consider vacuities, but he remained accessible. He could have been like some of his teammates who had chosen to make the game of ring-around-the-reporter as difficult as possible.

There were 25 men on the team, and 25 ways of dealing with the press, but some techniques were particularly notable. These ranged from the direct, almost eager cooperation of the veteran Rollie Fingers, who was always available but seemed careful never to say anything too interesting — save for his stinging condemnations of Bob Rodgers in the days before the manager was fired — to the abrupt close-mouthedness of Ted Simmons. This was, for the reporters, a doubly vexing situation because Simmons was, when he spoke, thoughtful and articulate; furthermore, a catcher so often has crucial insights on the progress of a given game.

Simmons had only recently stopped talking, and no one knew for sure why. The season before, as the Milwaukee representative on the governing body of the Players Association, the catcher had maintained constant and good relations with both Feuerherd and Flaherty, and had become a valuable source of information on both strike-related and other matters. Yet through the '81 season, and into the first two months of '82, as Simmons struggled on the field, both Feuerherd and Flaherty pointed fingers in print at the unproductive catcher. He became testier as May progressed, and finally — when Flaherty wrote that the recently deposed Rodgers had felt that Simmons, along with Mike Caldwell, was a "cancer" on the team who had tried to "stab me in the back" — he stopped talking altogether.

It was a not uncommon response for a modern ball player, and not even uncommon for one so relatively well spoken as Simmons, who before his silence was as likely to discuss the Equal Rights Amendment (he even testified in its behalf before the Missouri legislature) as he was eager to talk about baseball. Admittedly, it was somewhat understandable — if not entirely admirable — for ball players to weary of, and eventually to become enraged by, the constant questioning in person, the direct criticism in print. Some players dealt with the constant questioning by answering all questions in monosyllables; others set rules by which they asked reporters to abide: no questions before the game, or away from the park, or on days when they went hitless. Others established distance by intimidation. Alex Johnson, a gifted hitter for several teams in the '60s and '70s, was one such aggressive antagonist. One year, Johnson had hit 7 home runs by midseason, compared to 3 the year before. A Philadelphia writer asked him, "Alex, what's the difference between your homers last year and your homers this year?" Johnson glared at the reporter and said, "Four, you motherfucker, four!"

The most famous clubhouse mute of the '80s was Philadelphia's Steve Carlton, a man of substantial intellect whose self-imposed silence of nearly six years was especially frustrating to writers who not only sought insights from the men they covered but desperately hunted for players who had wit enough to offer something other than the usual clichés and homilies — players, in fact, like Ted Simmons. But what was especially rare about Simmons' silence was that it occurred in Milwaukee. The Brewers were generally cooperative, if peevish, toward the press, and Simmons himself, in spring 1982, asserted, "It makes sense here: you've only got two guys covering the team, and if you can't get along with them, you can't get along with anyone."

Feuerherd and Flaherty alone constituted the Brewers' traveling press corps. Also along were radio broadcasters Uecker and Mosley and the television voices, Steve Shannon and Mike Hegan, but the latter four, though not employees of the club, served with the club's approval and through direct contractual relations with the club's two most important business associates, radio WISN and television WVTV. The newspapermen, though, were nominally independent. This placed them in a position of considerable paradox.

It is the habit of the nation's newspapers to take a conflicting attitude toward the professional teams in their circulation areas.

On the one hand, they presume journalistic remove. They cover baseball as news, their reporters and editors turning to the game as cityside staff members cover, say, local politics. When a club bars a writer from its premises, as the Green Bay Packers football team did with the *Journal*'s Dave Begel in 1978 and 1980, formal complaints are filed and First Amendment justifications cited. At the same time, the reporters who covered the Brewers (and scores of other professional teams all over the country) traveled on the team plane, had their hotel reservations made and baggage handled by the team's traveling secretary, and drank night after night in the hotel bars with the team's personnel.

The Milwaukee papers, both owned by a muscular journalistic holding company called Newspapers, Inc. (which also controlled the Milwaukee radio and television stations that operated under the call letters WTMJ), had participated in recent years in the trend on the part of newspapers to set up conflict-of-interest safeguards that put their employees at some distance from the organizations they covered. Most clubs had long ago dropped the special privileges that Walter O'Malley extended with the old Dodgers (the club picked up the newsmen's hotel bills and air fares), but the press dining room remained a fixture everywhere, as did the constant grilling of franks and pouring of beers in the press box itself. Though Flaherty, for one, would eat in the dining room, his paper sent Bud Selig a check at the close of each season for hot dogs consumed in the line of duty. Both Milwaukee papers wisely forbade their writers from serving as official scorers, thus removing them from the line of nonjournalistic conflict with the players they wrote about.

Still, Flaherty and Feuerherd were in a difficult position. Flaherty, a Montanan in his early forties, had covered the Brewers on and off since their arrival in Milwaukee in 1970. He had known Gorman Thomas when the outfielder was a 19-year-old shortstop in Clinton, Iowa, and he had helped other Brewers, such as pitcher Moose Haas, find their way around big league cities when they first emerged from the minors. Most of the players on the team were Flaherty's friends, partly because he was an easygoing, likable, and eminently fair man but also because of the undeniable fact of proximity, of years of flying in the same airplanes, eating breakfast in the same coffeeshops, and engaging in daily encounters in the clubhouse or by the batting cage. Though Flaherty and Feuerherd, a New Yorker in his late twenties who began covering the club in 1981, were constant seatmates on buses and in press boxes, and though they worked for the same corporation, theirs was a competitive situation, and Flaherty was well able to call on his long associations to get stories sooner than Feuerherd, or to get access to certain of the players who might be tougher interviews for Feuerherd. It was hard, after all, to evade a man who knew you when you were 18 and who seemed to be the epitome of worldliness at the time — even if, today, the same man criticized you in print and earned annually perhaps a tenth (or less) of what you were bringing down.

By and large, the players didn't know quite what to make of the reporters. "They should be positive," said Mike Caldwell. "They should want the team to win, and do what they can to help." Even Caldwell, the sociology major, was unable to distinguish the interests of the newspaper from the interests of the quite separate corporation that owned the ball club: Flaherty and Feuerherd were around so much, it appeared they were, indeed, part of the club themselves.

Yet if such apparently peculiar ideas of a free press pervaded the clubhouse — and Caldwell probably spoke for a majority of the team — neither were the papers themselves free of contradictory poses. In a town like Milwaukee, intimidated by the proximity of the far larger, far wealthier Chicago, an intense civic activism was a communal habit. Just as Bud Selig, who had longed to be involved in baseball his entire life, who relished the men's club atmosphere of sport, and who positively worshiped the memory of the Green Bay football coach Vince Lombardi (he had even hired Lombardi's former secretary, Lori Keck, as his own secretary) — just as Bud Selig could say that he and his partners "bought this ball club for the people of Milwaukee," so did the newspapers play their role in the chronic boosterism. The newspapers knew that the presence of a big league team enhanced the city's image; they wanted to see the club succeed, and sought at some perhaps subliminal level to help it along its way. Until very recently, the annual January Diamond Dinner — little more, in reality, than the kickoff of the yearly ticket sales drive — was, in fact, sponsored by the newspapers, through its employees who were members of the nominally responsible Baseball Writers Association.

But the newspapers also knew that they needed baseball fully as much as baseball needed them — more, perhaps, in an electronic age, when scores and stories are available on the air long before the delivery boys begin making their rounds. The *Journal,* by far the more powerful of the two papers, was one of the rare big-city papers in the country that did not have a separate sports section, but it was clear that a newspaper without baseball news during the summer would suffer greatly. The morning *Sentinel* was even more profoundly affected, actually increasing its daily press run for newsstand distribution when there was a ball game to report. His eye on increased daily newsstand sales of 20 to 50 percent, the paper's assistant circulation manager, Charles E. Koeble, told how news deadlines were extended for Feuerherd's stories from the West Coast, at great cost to the paper, because of the sales engendered by those extra copies available on downtown newsstands the following morning. "We'll keep the paper open until two A.M.," Koebel said, "when the Brewers are out west playing the Dodgers or San Francisco." Had Milwaukee been in the same league as either of those teams, one might feel that Koeble actually read Feuerherd's stories.

As the junior man from the junior paper, Vic Feuerherd didn't have the ready cooperation of some of the more distant players, men like Gorman Thomas or Caldwell. He was also somewhat disadvantaged by Flaherty's position as the Milwaukee correspondent of the *Sporting News,* the national newspaper that arrives in stacks each week in every major league clubhouse for free distribution to the players. For a bare $50 weekly, Flaherty and 25 other baseball writers around the country filed stories about the teams they covered, which offered them high visibility in exchange for the minimal compensation. In each city, the man from the *Sporting News* holds an edge in prestige among players who rarely read anything more than the box scores in the daily papers but absorb every word of the page upon page of baseball coverage in the *Sporting News.*

In September of 1981, Flaherty wrote a story that had immense repercussions on the team. The Brewers were engaged in a tight race for the second-half championship of the Eastern Division in the American League, but the "yellow cloud" Peter Gammons had written about in the *Boston Globe* permeated the clubhouse: the players simply disliked their manager, Bob Rodgers. One September Sunday, Flaherty's byline appeared on a banner headline story that revealed the full extent of the unhappiness with Rodgers. Players on the team, quoted anonymously at their insistence, said Rodgers was the problem. When his team played on national television the following week, Rodgers, citing the unattributed nature of the criticisms, said on the air that he had "no respect for the players who said those things, no respect for the paper that printed it, and no respect for the reporter who wrote it." That evening, Flaherty and Rodgers and the other coaches and reporters were back sharing drinks and conviviality at the hotel bar. "Tom knew why I had to say that," Rodgers told another writer.

But the players' reactions were even more remarkable. Gorman Thomas, whose distaste for Rodgers was well known, was widely thought to be one of the unnamed sources for Flaherty's story. When the ensuing controversy erupted, Thomas told a television reporter, "The guy who wrote that story is gutless." But Thomas proceeded, in a later conversation about the role of the press, to refer to Flaherty thus: "Flags? Hell, he's not like a reporter; he's my friend." Pete Vuckovich, who blamed Flaherty's editors and not the writer himself — he had to live with Flaherty — had the most peculiar relationship of all with the reporters. When he pitched poorly, he'd stand patiently by his locker and withstand the barrage of blaming questions and speak eloquently, forthrightly, and quotably about his failures; when he pitched well, he'd quickly tell the writers and radio people waiting by his locker, "I owe it all to my teammates, my manager, and the coaches," relishing the way his intentional vacuity made the reporters squirm with frustration.

Flaherty used his competitive edge judiciously and somewhat cautiously. It was largely a matter of personality; Flaherty was not by nature a competitive man. While other press box occupants engaged in a freewheeling game of insults aimed at the distant players more than at one another, Flaherty amused himself by parodying his profession. In the top of the third, returning late from the coffee urn, he had asked, "How did they retire the premier swatsman this canto?" He enjoyed his job, his relationships with the players and the coaches, and he confessed he had little interest in doing the sort of journalism that had become common, say, around the New York Yankees: the aggressive hugger-mugger after players who would criticize management in print, or the continual search for distress signs in the relationship between owner and manager.

In the ferociously competitive New York market, where more than a score of reporters were accredited to the average game, and nearly a dozen traveled with the club on every road trip, a new form of journalism had evolved over the years since the end of

World War II. As television sets spread to every home, baseball reporters saw their primary job — telling who won, who got the hits, who made the errors, telling the essential story of the game — made obsolete by the immediate availability of the same details on the 11 o'clock news. Kuenn said his biggest surprise upon assuming Rodgers' chair occurred that first day in Seattle. "All those radio guys stuck mikes in my face and nobody said anything." Today the radio and TV reporters wait for the more experienced and knowledgeable newspapermen to ask the questions, then broadcast the answers within minutes, along with the score of the game and the other salient facts. Thus, where once reporters sat in the press box and composed graceful (or, in the worst cases, laughably overwrought) essays on the movement of a game, that technique no longer serves. Led by Dick Young of the *New York Daily News,* baseball writers in the early '50s moved out of the press box and into the clubhouse, in search of less visible stories. Today, men like Joseph Durso of the *New York Times* still write "game stories" of excellent form and revealing substance, but they are dinosaurs of a sort. Thirty years after Young's charge into the clubhouse, baseball writers everywhere are in desperate search of what television and radio reporters cannot provide. Young himself, who has an uncommon sympathy with ownership and almost none at all for players in the era of free agency, characterizes the most aggressive of his modern successors as "chipmunks," little, chattering animals scurrying frenetically to find stories that don't really exist.

But Young had started the revolution, and by 1982 it had reached the remotest outposts. Reporters daily entered the same locker rooms to ask the same questions of self-involved young men who spoke generally in clichés, and to whom introspection and reflection were alien. Tom Flaherty despairingly concluded that, past a certain point, "there are no good questions." The basic thematic demands of the beat writer's job never vary, and the answers he gets from players and managers can in many cases be written in advance. Many ball players, for their part, puzzle over the constant questioning; the agreeable Buddy Bell of the Texas Rangers perhaps summed up the heart of the dilemma when he confessed to a writer, "Frankly, I'm pretty dull." The reporter in search of something new relies on those players and managers who, it sometimes seems, occupy dull moments during the game obligingly thinking up pithy quotes, or else he finds himself engaged in the preposterous. In the late

1970s, *New York Times* writer Tony Kornheiser found himself in the Yankee dugout with several other reporters and the New York manager, Bob Lemon, whose years of bibulousness had left their evidence on his face. "Tell me, Bob," Kornheiser asked in a lull in the conversation, "are you aware of your nose?"

In Milwaukee, though Tom Flaherty always had his ear to the ground, for evidence of any rumbling in the near distance — thus his September 1981 story on Rodgers — Vic Feuerherd was more typical of the new school of baseball journalism. A tall, thin man, a writer with imagination and style in his prose, Feuerherd carried himself with a certain cynicism. His primary antagonist on the team was Caldwell; after one critical piece in which Feuerherd said the Brewers "didn't have enough guts to string a junior-size tennis racket," Caldwell snarled, "Fuck your junior-size tennis racket," and overturned a table in front of Feuerherd. Caldwell scowled whenever Feuerherd approached, and wouldn't so much as nod a hello if they encountered each other in the hotel lobby.

Yet even in his surliest moods, Caldwell, who was an adept manipulator, would on the day he pitched answer any of Feuerherd's questions, never hiding in the off-limits training room, the redoubt of players who hated the press, were ashamed of their own on-field failures, or both. In Boston, during the years Don Zimmer was manager and the Red Sox clubhouse was a minefield for reporters, outfielder Dwight Evans would stand tauntingly in the doorway of the trainer's room, gazing at the reporters two feet away, refusing to answer their questions if they attempted even to whisper a few words across the sacrosanct threshold. Of course, the Red Sox clubhouse was a fiefdom unto itself, with the direct encouragement of club management: a two-part room, one wing was reserved for the regular players, the other for the reserves. The caste system was so rife that when Frank Duffy, a reserve shortstop who had been with the team for a year and a half, was released in June of 1979, he told a reporter that in all of his time with the club, star outfielder Jim Rice had never deigned to say hello to him.

Throughout baseball, there are always the surly and rude players, like Rice, the combative, like Caldwell, and the temporarily indisposed, like Simmons. Their conflicts with reporters take different forms. Only a handful, like Philadelphia's Carlton, had the consistency and ego strength to refuse interviews to anyone — network television personalities as well as local newspaper reporters — and there was, in their cases, a certain integrity, no matter how inconveniencing. George Hendrick, a St. Louis Cardinal outfielder of considerable talent, was another who never gave interviews, in a stand of determined (if obscure) principle, but Hendrick was thought by reporters who covered the Cardinals to be a fundamentally decent, even warm individual. He'd talk with reporters about the weather, or road trip restaurants, or about professional basketball; Hendrick simply did not want to be *interviewed*. Less principled than Hendrick, and less consistent than Carlton, was the itinerant Dave Kingman, who would periodically go into wild anti-press rages, then make a great show of making up, and finally retreat into his shell, designating which reporters could talk to him, on which days, and about which subjects. Writers who covered Kingman when he was with the Chicago Cubs perceived the player as imbalanced, so egregiously sensitive, said one, that he'd bet he'd end his career "in a padded room." More generously, New York Met catcher John Stearns, trying to characterize the enigmatic Kingman, said, "Dave has the personality of a tree trunk. He's not a bad guy, but if you try to talk to him, about all he does is grunt."

There were no Kingmans on the Milwaukee team, and even Simmons in the midst of his uncommunicative 1982 didn't refrain from basic cordiality with Flaherty and Feuerherd. Yet there was still a journalistic disadvantage for the two writers, to the degree they had to compete — for leads, for off-the-record insight, or for true intimacy — with two of the Milwaukee broadcasters, Bob Uecker and Mike Hegan.

Hegan, who shared television play-by-play duties with Steve Shannon, had played for the Brewers, retiring in 1977, and had known many of the players as teammates. Uecker's reputation as a television comic (he was a regular on *The Tonight Show*) was built on the self-deprecation of his own stunningly undistinguished major league career. (One of Uecker's favorite stories concerned signing his original contract with the old Milwaukee Braves. "They said 'three thousand dollars,' " Uecker related, "but my dad didn't have that kind of money.") Hegan and Uecker, having been among the elect who had played in the major leagues, shared with *all* the players a feeling of fraternity. They knew and empathized with the players' goals and frustrations, were accepted golf companions, dinner partners, and confidants. Flaherty, Feuerherd, and all other reporters were — and would ever be — outsiders. Flaherty even went so far as to fib to Vuckovich when the pitcher joined the team that he, Flaherty, had pitched Class D ball in the Northwest League in the late 1950s — and Vuckovich's face lit up in recognition and appreciation.

But for all the access they had, Uecker and Hegan rarely made journalistic use of it. Hegan, who had done a sports show on Milwaukee television, did have a reporter's instincts, and would not refrain from criticism of ball players, but both he and Uecker were required to satisfy Selig and the other members of Milwaukee management, or their employers, the stations, would soon learn they'd have to go. Too, they were both subject to the peculiar position of being shills for advertisers, required to read off product endorsements between innings, during pitching changes, or whenever the action lulled long enough for WISN, or WVTV, to make another dollar and cover their substantial investments in the rights to Brewer broadcasts.

As the Baltimore Orioles prepared to bat in the top of the fourth, and as the Brewers trotted out to their positions on the field, WISN took a minute to broadcast a piece of bluegrass music that framed a Pabst Blue Ribbon commercial. Then Uecker's voice exhorted, in behalf of a bratwurst manufacturer, "Hey, fans, try some Johnsonville brats when you're at County Stadium — or, grill some at home. Johnsonville brats, the best you can get." ABC television had once insisted on 105 seconds of commercial time while the teams changed sides, and that had become the standard, fillable space while the players readied themselves for the resumption of action. On the County Stadium field, Don Money stood at first and tossed grounders at his teammates with the infield practice ball Ron Hansen had flipped to him — as first base coaches have for years been flipping to first basemen as the latter come off the field each inning — in the middle of the third. In the clubhouse, Cecil Cooper's whirlpool treatment had ended, and he was getting into his uniform to join his teammates on the bench, perhaps later to serve as a pinch hitter. Bob McClure sat in the trainer's room with ice packed in an Ace bandage wrapped around his left shoulder by Freddie Frederico. Upstairs, Bud Selig got up in his private enclosure and strolled into the adjacent press box.

After the company of his fellow owners — the only people, family excepted, whose calls Selig's secretary, Lori Keck, would put through to him in his box during a game — and after shoulder-rubbing with his players, Selig most enjoyed the give-and-take with the out-of-town reporters who came into Milwaukee with the visiting teams. From the remove of the press box, many baseball reporters amuse themselves during games by exchanging *mots* with one another about the failings of the players on the field. A popular target for the Baltimore writers, until his trade to California, had been third baseman Doug DeCinces; whenever DeCinces misplayed a ball at third, the press box parodists would begin to lampoon his inevitable postgame excuses: " 'You know, that was a real tough one; it hit a pebble at the last minute,' " one would say. "Yeah," another reporter would counter, "if you call your knee a pebble."

Selig loved to partake, and today the target was Benny Ayala, the rather graceless Baltimore outfielder whose hitting had hurt the Brewers badly in the first game of the series. "Benny A*yall*uh?" Selig said, his voice rising in incredulity. "And you guys call this a baseball team?"

Selig walked along the back row of the two-tier press box, tugging on one of his omnipresent Cherry Tipalet cigars, his eyes gleaming, his toothy grin making him seem a boy in a business suit. "Beaten by Benny Ayala! Not since . . . what was his name? The catcher who looked like a beer can?" "Dave Criscione," someone said, referring to an improbable figure from the Baltimore past whose ninth-inning hit in a 1977 game had beaten the Brewers. "Yeah, Dave Crish-ee-*own*-ee," Selig said, masticating the syllables with sarcastic glee. "And now Ben-nee Eye-*all*-uh. Powers! Immortals!"

Selig returned to his box as Ken Singleton came to the plate. The Milwaukee pitching change, from McClure to Slaton, was advantageous to Singleton. Although he was the rare switch hitter who could hit with power either right-handed or left-handed, his elbow injury had diminished his effectiveness greatly as a righty, and with Slaton now in the game he could move to his more productive side of the plate.

In the Baltimore dugout, Earl Weaver emerged from the bathroom under the stands with his eyes darting about, virtually providing an inch-by-inch chronicle of the mental gymnastics in which he was engaged, the last traces of his between-innings cigarette trailing from his lips. As unusual as it seemed to see a cigarette in the hands of a man in a baseball uniform, Weaver was celebrated for his secretive dugout puffing, and besides, he was long past his athletic days, a 51-year-old man of unprepossessing physique. It was stranger to see — in a clubhouse, or a hotel lobby, or in the dugout during batting practice — chain-smoking players like Boston's aging monument, Carl Yastrzemski, or the former Baltimore shortstop Mark Belanger, engaging in such a decidedly anti-athletic habit. Ted Simmons, in fact, when shagging flies in spring training, would bum cigarettes from loitering writers, tucking the filter end into a gap between his glove's lacing and webbing as he ran back to the outfield. From a distance, one could see Simmons periodically raising his glove to his face and, incongruously, seeming to kiss his mitt as he sucked another puff between the batter's swings.

In the Milwaukee dugout, Harvey Kuenn stood at the end closest to home plate, with Pat Dobson and Harry Warner next to him. Kuenn's cheek was distended with his omnipresent plug of chewing tobacco, and he leaned forward every ten seconds or so to spit out the juice. Slightly slouched, his pale gray eyes impassive, his pink face expressionless, his puffy features sagging, Kuenn resembled nothing so much as a turtle without his shell. And so did he proceed, turtlelike, at his job: steady, unexciting, unexcitable. It was fairly easy to be calm with a three-run lead, but this calm was also dictated by the nature of his lineup. When he took over the team from Rodgers, Kuenn had encouraged his players to just "go out there and swing at the ball," and he generally allowed the same nine men to do it, day in and day out. Money was playing today because of Cooper's incapacitation, but otherwise only Simmons' absence from the lineup gave Kuenn any need to make offensive moves. He had only to wait out Slaton, to see if the pitcher had enough today to protect the lead and keep Baltimore at bay.

With the count 1 and 1 on Singleton, Gorman Thomas stood in center field in his characteristic position, his weight on one leg, the other leg languidly bent. Thomas — like all center fielders — never played precisely straight-away; he was always shaded one way or another, no matter how slightly, to be able to pick up the flight of the pitch as it approached the batter. Dead straight-away, his view would be blocked by the pitcher. As Slaton unleashed a fastball toward the inside corner of the plate, Thomas began to step toward right field, and as Singleton's bat came around in a well-timed sweep, the center fielder broke into a run just as ball hit bat.

But Singleton's timing was a fraction too quick, or Slaton's pitch a fraction too slow, for Thomas to figure in the play; getting in front of the ball, the hitter sent it on a low but lengthy parabola to right field. Marshall Edwards, playing nearer to the foul line than to center, raced over with his small, staccato strides and slowed a bit as the ball began to curve toward him. As he was about to intersect its path, Edwards reached out and grabbed the ball at hip level for the first out of the inning.

Charlie Moore signaled for a slider from Jim Slaton when Rick Dempsey stepped in. Moore was not quite as aggressive a catcher as Simmons; too, he was raised in the American League, where the fastball was not the article of faith that it was in the National. But Dempsey was something of a first-ball hitter, and first-ball hitters were usually fastball hitters, for good reason: most pitchers (and catchers, and managers) wanted to get the first ball in for a strike, and the fastball was the easiest pitch to *throw* for a strike.

But Moore had confidence in Slaton's control with the slider, and the ball just nicked the outside corner of the plate; by the time it reached Moore, it was a good six inches outside, but when it first reached the slab of "hard, whitened rubber" that the rule book mandated to constitute home plate, it passed over its beveled edge, the area the players called "the black." Dempsey leaned, but let the pitch go by.

Now Moore offered Slaton the next sign. From the time in the nineteenth century when hitters no longer were given the option of requesting a specific pitch and waiting until the pitcher provided it (in those days, catchers were, until runners were ready to score, little more than human backstops, and would take their position a full 50 feet behind the batter) — from that time forward, one finger denoted a fastball, two a curve (a catcher who called a lot of curves was said to have "an olive stuck between his fingers"). The spread of the slider, developed by George Uhle of the Cleveland Indians in the 1920s, named a decade later by George Blaeholder of the St. Louis Browns, perfected by Red Ruffing of the Yankees, and popularized in the years after World War II, earned it the three-finger signal. Four fingers were reserved for whatever a particular pitcher specialized in for a fourth pitch — for Rollie Fingers, say, his forkball; for most pitchers, the change-of-pace.

Earl Weaver liked to have some of his pitchers, especially Jim Palmer, call their own game, nodding in assent or disagreement as the catcher went through the signals. Until he arrived in Baltimore, Steve Stone, who won the Cy Young Award with the Orioles in 1980, called his pitches by holding his bare hand at his side to indicate a fastball, placing it on the front of his thigh for a slider, and so on. Several teams picked it up over time, much to Stone's disadvantage, and Weaver eventually cured him of it, while still pretty much allowing him to call his game. Kuenn, on the other hand, was largely content with his catchers' dictating the mix of pitches.

Moore flashed his hand once, this time with one finger extended down: fastball. Had there been a man on second, able to pick up the sign and relay it to the hitter with a slight gesture, Moore would've used a more elaborate sequence of several signals. One such, favored by Bob Rodgers, was called "scoreboard signing." If the count was even, the third sign flashed by the catcher was the real sign; if the batter was ahead in the count, the second sign was operative; if the pitcher was ahead, the first.

Moore waited for Dempsey to plant his rear foot in the back of the box, away from the plate, his front foot closer to and even with the plate, waited for him to begin the slow cranking up of muscle and nerve that each batter engages in as the pitcher is about to begin his delivery. Now Moore shifted his weight slightly and placed his glove near his right knee, on the edge of the plate away from Dempsey. Caught flat-footed by the previous pitch, Dempsey might be tempted to swing defensively at one that was yet farther away and that would approach with greater speed. But Slaton was a shade too wide, and the count went to 1 and 1.

Then Moore asked for another fastball, inside, and it was ball two. By missing with that pitch, Slaton had tilted the odds against him: he could come straight over the plate to prevent the count from going to 3 and 1, but that would risk a fat, easy-to-hit pitch. He chose to shoot for the edge again, but his slider came in just a hair low; had the third pitch been in the zone, and the count thus 1 and 2, Dempsey would have had to swing, and would surely have driven the ball into the ground. But Slaton had missed on the third pitch, and Dempsey had world enough and time to wait on the fourth one.

At 3 and 1, Dempsey looked down at the elder Cal Ripken at third, who relayed the hit-away sign that Weaver had given him from the dugout. With Weaver, though, it was a hit-away with a yellow light: his players knew not to swing in that situation if the pitch were not precisely right for them. Moore asked for a fastball, Dempsey moved imperceptibly, and it was a called strike two, belt high on the outside corner. An inch farther away from Dempsey and the batter would have walked; two inches farther toward the heart of the plate and he likely could have hit a hard line drive.

Dempsey was disgusted with the call, and a slow-motion view of the pitch, from the center field camera operated by local Milwaukee cameramen in behalf of Baltimore station WMAR, revealed he was right to be disgusted: it appeared clearly outside. But the baseball rules had in recent years forbidden batters from arguing with umpires over ball-and-strike calls, with a penalty of eviction from the game for violating the stricture, and Dempsey contented himself with muttering as he took a stroll away from the plate and back again. It was a full count, and umpire Morrison had made it clear that he was giving Slaton the outside corner. Moore requested the same pitch from Slaton, and Slaton placed it in precisely the same spot. Warned, Dempsey reached awkwardly for the pitch, made contact, and sent an easy fly ball to Edwards in right. Two out.

Comfortable with the leeway he had apparently been allowed on the outside corner, Slaton started off Rich Dauer, Baltimore's number nine batter, with another fastball, and Morrison sent up his right hand, signaling a strike. He stayed with the fastball for the next four pitches, alternately hitting the zone and tantalizing the batter with "waste" pitches. When Slaton came in with the last one low and inside with the count 2 and 2, Dauer fought it off and sent it to right field, a single.

Two sliders and two fastballs, scattered about the plate, Slaton mixing his speeds as well as his location, and Lenn Sakata, the next batter, lofted a soft liner to Thomas in center, ending Baltimore's fourth as it had begun: Milwaukee, 6–3.

	1	2	3	4	5	6	7	8	9	R	H	E
Baltimore	1	2	0	0						3	7	1
Milwaukee	2	0	4							6	9	0

Robin Yount, who led off the Milwaukee half of the inning, was born in Illinois but soon moved with his family to California. To the young athlete, California was heaven on earth, a paradise that afforded year-round competition beneath a benevolent sun.

The state had always sent athletes to the major leagues; in 1954, when California contained 7 percent of the nation's population, it was producing 9½ percent of major league ball players. But the next quarter century saw such a flowering of California talent that by 1982, fully 25 percent of the major leaguers born in the U.S. were born in California, even though the state accounted for just over 10 percent of the nation's population. And this did not include players, like Yount, who were born elsewhere but who moved to California as children.

There were two reasons for the increase in big league talent from California, and neither was a magical improvement in the quality of the Californian gene pool. First, there was expansion: in 1957 there was no major league baseball in California, whereas by 1969 five teams played their home games in the state. Although the Pacific Coast League had long developed local talent and forwarded it east — the Yankees, dating back to the days of DiMaggio and Crosetti and Lazzeri, seemed to have had a direct pipeline to the streets of San Francisco via the PCL — the absence of major league baseball as a daily factor in California life surely had not stifled major league ambitions among the state's youth. When Walter O'Malley led baseball westward, he found not only an audience but in that audience a pool of talent.

But, more, once other clubs began to see larger numbers of California players reach the majors, they recognized, however belatedly, the opportunities that existed on the state's sun-drenched playgrounds and sandlots. In 1982, 13 of Milwaukee's 33 scouts, including scouting director Poitevint, lived in California, each of them covering in his own neighborhood as many potential prospects as Missouri-based scout Paul Tretiak, say, would encounter in a drive across five midwestern states. The vision of major leaguers Eddie Murray, Ozzie Smith, and Darrell Jackson playing on the same high school nine — or, over in El Segundo, Scott McGregor and George Brett — was incentive to look for more high schools as well stocked with baseball talent; and incentive provided, inevitably, reward. From 1966 to 1974, 34.4 percent of all players selected in the amateur draft were from California; in 1974, the figure was an astonishing 43 percent.

As readily as such talent could be found in the Los Angeles ghetto, where Murray, Smith, and Jackson first played ball, or in the relatively grimy suburb of El Segundo, beneath the flight paths into Los Angeles International Airport, so could it be uncovered by a scout prowling more affluent communities, like Woodland Hills in the San Fernando Valley. There, Yount began at nine as a Little League pitcher, catcher, and shortstop. When he was a high school junior, and primarily a pitcher, he first encountered the scouts who worked the Valley leagues, and they told him he had ability. The season before, his older brother Larry, who had pitched in the minor leagues for five years, appeared in his first — and only — major league game, as a pinch runner for the Houston Astros.

There were two pitchers ahead of Yount on the Taft High School team, so in his senior year he focused his attention on shortstop. The scouts gathered more and more frequently, and in June of 1973 he was the third player in the entire nation selected in the free agent draft. (The two young men ahead of him were John Stearns, drafted by the Phillies and later a capable catcher for the New York Mets, and — the number one pick — the ill-starred David Clyde. Clyde won his first major league start less than a month after he pitched his last high school game, but his career disintegrated in the unreasonable expectations of the Texas organization, a headstrong overvaluation of his own talent, and eventually a career-ending alcoholism problem.)

Yount reported shortly after the draft to Milwaukee's Newark, N.Y., farm club in the Class A New York–Penn League. He played for a team that managed to win only 15 games in 70 tries. He hit a respectable .285, but with scant power (3 home runs, 25 runs batted in). Afield, his .877 fielding percentage — 18 errors in only 64 games — was the worst for any regular in the league. Still, the following April, Yount, age 18, became the starting shortstop for the Milwaukee Brewers.

Even though the Milwaukee incumbent at short was the woeful Tim Johnson, who had batted .213 as a rookie in '73, the elevation of Yount from the second lowest level of the minors was radical action, especially in the face of statistics that would hardly indicate he would thrive against major league pitchers. Yet the Milwaukee front office, then headed by Jim Baumer, saw no reason to retard Yount's progress. Baumer, who replaced general manager Jim Wilson in 1974 and would himself be replaced by Dalton in 1977, might have looked to his own experience: a bonus-baby infielder signed by the Chicago White Sox in 1949, he appeared in 8 games that year, disappeared into the minors, and did not reemerge until 1961, when he played in 12 games for Cincinnati and sank to the minors again, this time for good. But Baumer did not fear that Yount was being rushed. Those first few years, Yount batted between .250 and .270, stole some bases, and hit a very occasional home run. In the field, he displayed considerable range but an erratic arm. In his fourth season, 1977, he finally dragged his average up to .288, and hit a respectable 34 doubles. Until early September, his average stayed above .300. Perhaps his slump was precipitated by the stark reality Yount encountered on September 16 in his fourth big league year: he turned 22.

Throughout these first four years, it was clear that Baumer's judgment on Yount had been sound. He demonstrated a real, if erratic, talent in the field as well as at the plate. On one play he might casually pick up an easy ground ball and then throw it ten feet over the head of his first baseman, but on the next he'd go far in the hole to his right, spin, and his throw would beat the runner by a foot. (Though County Stadium featured natural dirt and grass, Yount was an especially good practitioner of the "turf hop" throw perfected on artificial surfaces by Cincinnati's Dave Concepcion: the throw would reach the first baseman on one clean, direct bounce off the pool-table-smooth playing surface.) Yount also developed a trait shared with Boston (and later California) shortstop Rick Burleson: too often caught flat-footed when the ball was hit, Yount began after his second year to take his fielding stance with one foot a stride ahead of the other, stepping forward as bat met ball. In time he would become as consistent as he was flashy, eventually providing the anchor to the Milwaukee defense.

Along the way, though, Yount took the walkabout that led to the hurried elevation of Paul Molitor to shortstop (after, coincidentally, 64 minor league games — the same number Yount had played) in 1978. Yount's talk of joining the professional golf tour would mean his retirement from baseball before his twenty-third birthday. Hypersensitive as a young man, and depressed by the continuing futility of the woeful Brewer teams, Yount's alienation was deepened when in 1977 there began to be talk of moving him and his still erratic throwing arm to center field. Yount didn't merely reject the suggestion; he brooded about it, resented it, and lost himself in self-doubt. Members of the front office — this was just before Selig swept out the Baumer administration and brought in Dalton — saw Yount's reaction as immature sulking.

But Dalton and Selig remained patient, Yount found his way back, Molitor moved over to second, and in 1978 the Brewers played competitively — for them — through the end of May, and then went on a spree that placed them into the first facsimile of a pennant race they had known. Under the calm, avuncular reign of the newly hired George Bamberger, the team blossomed, and Yount slowly emerged from his shell. He hit .293; more, he batted in 71 runs while playing in only 127 games.

The following season, the Brewers were competitive again, and Yount was about to take a step that would change him from a shortstop who hit respectably to a hitter who would soon become one of the best in baseball. Six feet tall, lean and already muscular, he followed the lead of his then teammate Lenn Sakata and began to work out on a Nautilus machine. When he reported to Sun City, his muscles had become rock-hard cords; on his shoulders and back especially, muscles appeared to sprout other muscles. Even his long, graceful fingers appeared to be made of taut cables.

The next spring, reflecting on the 23 home runs and 49 doubles he hit in 1980 — 9 and 34 had been his previous best — Yount wasn't quite sure the Nautilus machine, and his enhanced musculature, were responsible. He had opened his stance somewhat, his feet more in a straight line, more nearly parallel to the flight of the ball, than they had been. Flies he had previously hit to the warning track, he said, had carried over more regularly; indeed, he seemed in '80 to hit an extraordinary number of balls into the first row seats in left field.

By the time Buck Rodgers took over the team for good at the end of 1980, Yount had also moved into the second spot in the batting order, following Molitor. Rodgers seemed to discount Yount's home run potential, and spoke to him about taking more pitches, drawing more walks (only once had he had more than 40 in a season), hitting to the opposite field — doing the things expected of number two hitters who followed speedy men like Molitor at the plate. In 1981 (the year of the strike), playing two thirds the number of games he played in '80, Yount hit 10 home runs. But he also walked only 22 times, and his average dropped to .273.

He had given Rodgers' theories the benefit of the doubt, or at least lip service, but it seemed not to help. He was, in the emergency, players-only team meeting called by Bando and Simmons in Kansas City in 1981, one of the most vocal complainers. Rodgers had begun to fiddle with the batting order; he was overly reliant on strategic moves on a team that flourished on swinging away; he asked hitters to take too many pitches. Batting order manipulations irritated many ball players; in Toronto, Roy Howell had been deeply frustrated by managers who sometimes batted him third, sometimes sixth, sometimes second, sometimes fifth. "Hitting after Alfredo Griffin, I had to take pitches and hit the ball on the ground," Howell said. "Hitting after John Mayberry, who was so slow, I didn't *dare* hit a ground ball if he was on first. It was inconsistent, and it was tough for me to adjust."

Rodgers maintained the club didn't need home runs from Yount, not with so many powerful hitters scattered through the rest of the lineup. Away from Rodgers, Yount maintained that the very same batting order dictated that he would see more fastballs near the plate than most number two hitters, that opposing teams couldn't *risk* walking him, or anyone else. Rodgers, in the managerial tradition he had become accustomed to while playing for Bill Rigney, thought that the competitive edge lay in guile, cunning, and the courage to make the right moves at the right time. Yount thought that classical baseball "moves" weren't called for, that the Brewers were a team, and he was a player, who should be allowed to hit away. Don Money maintained that on *this* team, the spot where one hit in the order really didn't matter — except hitting second, behind Molitor, which called for taking more pitches than one otherwise would. Kuenn had addressed that by not even asking Yount to take, not even having him know whether Molitor was stealing. The "little things" — hitting behind the runner and the like — were important, but on this Milwaukee team they were a bit less important than elsewhere.

Yount also had begun to learn to control his primary weakness at the plate — suckering for the high inside pitch. There was no mystery to it; he knew it was the chink in his armor, and he knew most American League pitchers worked to exploit it.

Yount's great strength was his ability to extend his arms fully over the plate on his swing, thus getting maximum leverage — and power — on the ball. The high inside corner of the strike zone was the one spot that left him unable to offer his best swing. He didn't need to be reminded that pitchers worked the spot incessantly. "Hitters are smart enough to know how the pitcher's trying to get him out," Kuenn said. "Hell, I can remember how guys pitched me thirty years ago; these guys ought to be able to remember what a guy did last year."

In the first inning, Sammy Stewart had started Yount with a high fastball, just on the inside corner, which the batter had let pass for a strike. The next pitch, a low slider, he had looped into the outfield. In the third, Stewart came in high, but too far over the plate, and Yount's drive had sent Bumbry nearly to the center field wall.

Now, in the fourth, with Yount leading off, Storm Davis was pitching. Though Davis had watched Yount hit twice today, and several times on Monday and Tuesday (Yount was rested on Wednesday, to protect a sore shoulder), he had not yet pitched to him. He would throw pitches specified by Rick Dempsey. It made sense to Yount, and to Dempsey, that the high-inside pitch, that pitching by the book, was called for. Yount stood in his crouch, elbows and knees the most visible parts of him, his bat held at a 45-degree angle away from his back shoulder. Davis came in high and inside, and Yount swung. And missed.

It wasn't a pitch that Yount wanted, but he had had a pretty good idea where it was going to be, and the foreknowledge, he thought, would leave him forearmed. Still, it was not his pitch, and he could not hit it.

With the next pitch, the guessing game began. Dempsey called for another fastball, this one low and away. Yount watched it pass: strike two. Orthodoxy next demanded a waste pitch — not a strike, and not terrifically hittable — and Davis obliged, but missed too far outside to tempt Yount, even with a two-strike count. At 1 and 2, the following pitch would be the one that counted, that would determine the shape of this particular at-bat. Dempsey called for another fastball, up and in, where Yount would have to go after it and would be least likely to make damaging contact. But Storm Davis's flesh did not perform as his mind willed, and Yount hit a belt-high fastball into left field, for a single.

When Don Money came to the plate, with no one out and Yount on first, Harry Warner engaged in the dance of the third base coach: touching the tip of his cap, running his hand across the letters on his jersey, clapping his hands, tapping his shoulder. Yount was a fast runner who had stolen as many as 20 bases in a season. Money, when not cranking his home run swing, was an artful man with a bat, and the sort of player who was capable of executing all those important, very noticeable things — bunting, hitting behind the runner, making contact in a hit-and-run situation — that broadcasters persist in calling the small, unnoticed things. With a 6–3 lead, the Brewers did not have the limiting reality of being behind to contend with (and thus were not needful of the big inning that resuscitates trailing teams and mitigates against the possible sacrifice of an out), nor did they have so lopsided a lead that a stolen base, or a hit-and-run, would violate the chivalric code of fair play that had somehow lingered in the highly competitive world of professional baseball.

On the Baltimore bench — while Money twisted his hands on the slim end of his bat, back and forth, watching the third base coach as he went through his somewhat comic routine — coaches and players who were good at this sort of thing tried to break Warner's code. They had tried in the earliest innings to discern the "indicator," the sign that means that all that follows actually is designed to mean something. Then they tried to identify a corresponding sign, the "take-off," which fundamentally tells the hitter or runner, "Please ignore the following message." These two elements are like the vowels in a cipher, and proper identification of them enables the student to crack the remainder of the code. Once indicator and take-off are defined, then one simply has to have the opposition attempt, say, a hit-and-run: the sequence that followed the indicator will be the sequence worth stealing the next time it is used.

Only a master sign man, like California third base coach Preston Gomez, was truly unreadable: Gomez maintained a different set of signs for every hitter and every runner, and what might mean "bunt" to Tim Foli could mean "steal" to Bob Boone. It was difficult enough for the Angels' players to learn and retain, and impossible for their opponents to crack consistently. Since Harvey Kuenn had taken over the Brewers from Bob Rodgers, he had radically simplified the nature of communication he would use with his players, choosing largely to trust in their skills and their judgments. He never asked Ted Simmons to bunt, because Simmons had never truly bothered to learn how to bunt well. He never told Paul Molitor when to steal, and gave him a "green light" to exercise his own judgment. And he almost never ordered Yount to steal; with Cecil Cooper usually following Yount in the batting order, the possible advantage of a stolen base was heavily outweighed by the risk of the runner's being caught.

Mostly, though, Kuenn trusted in Yount's skills, and in his innate baseball sense. Yount was fairly typical of a certain type of ball player who brings great intelligence to bear on his game, yet one who would in any other context strike someone meeting him as hardly intelligent at all. He had a great capacity to sit on a four-hour plane ride, staring blankly into space, never examining so much as an in-flight magazine. His clubhouse repartee was weak, almost juvenile. In an interview, he was cooperative and patient but also singularly unexpressive, inarticulate, even dense. One *Boston Globe* reporter said, "Robin tries hard, but it's useless. He's just plain dumb."

Certainly environmental or genetic factors hadn't conspired against Yount. His father, Phil Yount, was an aerospace engineer; his brother Jim was an oceanographic geologist, and Larry (he of the one-day career with the Astros) was a real estate developer. Robin had grown up in affluence. But from the time he was nine, he had thrown himself so thoroughly into baseball that it became part of him, and he part of it. Like Joe DiMaggio, so hopelessly inarticulate when he arrived in the big leagues (and never growing too much more loquacious during and after his career) that he admitted he thought a "quote" was a soft drink, Yount had allowed baseball to take over his life, and the life of his mind. Like DiMaggio, he never made a baserunning mistake, or pursued the wrong play afield, or allowed his on-field concentration to wander. He had, not entirely by volition, channeled his thoughts so thoroughly into baseball that there was room for little else. Unlike Ted Simmons, he had not experienced college life in a time of great excitement and ferment (Simmons attended the University of Michigan for three years in the off-season, and though he often carried his catcher's mitt to classes with him, he had had his eyes, and his mind, opened by the events of the late '60s in Ann Arbor). Unlike Ben Oglivie, who had an immigrant's wish to better himself and had attended classes at colleges all over the country as he made his slow progress to major league stardom, Yount had come to the big leagues easily, quickly, and not needful of the "fall-back" of an education. Unlike Cecil Cooper, who had never imagined he would be drafted into professional baseball, let alone enjoy a major league career, Yount had not had to think terribly consciously about his trade and thus develop, as Cooper had, great self-analytical abilities.

Yount just went out on the field and did what he did, and when he did it wrong, he filed it away in his muscle memory, and thereby learned not to do it wrong again. His teammate Larry Hisle approached practice as the opportunity "to do things so many times that the mental and physical adjustments become automatic." So it was with Yount, whose every miscue as a young player made him better as he matured, absorbing the whole fabric of baseball playing. In a way, his was a prodigiously absorptive intelligence, if a narrow one.

Moreover, Harvey Kuenn was concerned with the depth of his players' minds, not the breadth; he needed to know only whether the players comprehended the best means of achieving the team goals and were, in turn, able to make the proper effort to attain them. Unlike Weaver, whose team was shaped precisely to fit his style of managing, Kuenn had had only a small role in making the personnel decisions that had brought together the 25 men who worked for him. But he was convinced that the most productive way of guiding them was to let them loose, on their own, playing a swing-hard, pitch-hard game. If Yount ran with no one out and his team enjoying a 6–3 lead, fair enough.

Weaver didn't expect Yount to run, and the two men who would have to anticipate the prospect and perhaps abandon their positions before the pitch reached the batter, second baseman Dauer and shortstop Sakata, didn't expect it either. Storm Davis, on the mound, and Rick Dempsey, behind the plate, couldn't allow themselves to anticipate it, for that would needlessly — and, with no one out, dangerously — throw off their attack on the man at the plate, Don Money. Money was a fastball hitter, and a pull hitter. He had genuine home run power on fastballs inside. Conventional wisdom dictates that in a steal situation, breaking pitches are a bad idea. This isn't simply because the fastball gives the runner less time to advance toward second. (In fact, the difference between the time it takes a major league curve traveling 75 miles per hour and a fastball traveling 85 miles per hour to reach home plate is less than seven hundredths of a second.) Rather, curveballs, and to a lesser degree sliders, frequently end up on or near the ground by the time they reach the catcher, and the likelihood of a smooth, one-motion throw to second is greatly diminished by the extra handling such a pitch requires.

Davis showed his move to Yount before his first pitch to Money; the baserunner retreated to the base standing up, not really imperiled by the implied threat of Davis's pickoff throw, which was utterly routine. But the gesture had been made, and Davis and Dempsey got down to the business of getting Don Money.

On the first pitch, Money did not get the over-the-plate fastball he wanted and, given Yount's no-outs presence on first, could perhaps expect. Dempsey called for four pitches — two sliders and a curve, all of them away, and a fastball even farther out. But the fastball came at 2 and 0, and the overeager Money lashed it into the seats along the third base line. When Money reacted to the fourth pitch in the sequence — an outside slider — by attempting to check his swing, his bat made meek contact with the ball and a little hump-backed line drive found its way out to Rich Dauer, the second baseman.

Dauer's reaction to Money's looper was perfect: he could easily have caught it, but Yount, mindful of the ball's course, was frozen near first, lest he be doubled off. So Dauer allowed the ball to drop wanly in front of him, whereupon he cocked his arm to throw to first, intending to get the force out on Money and then to watch his teammates impale Yount in a rundown between first and second. However, Eddie Murray, who had come off first as Money's hit arced slowly over to the right side of the diamond, had not yet got back to the base, and would have been unable to make the force-out and begin the rundown. Neither had Storm Davis reached first in his dash from the pitcher's mound, getting a late start on his necessary run in that direction. So Dauer, flummoxed, threw to Sakata at second, and Yount was forced out.

In the course of this one play, Rich Dauer considered four different options, made two decisions, and executed the best play available to him. Yount, in an entirely futile circumstance, moved toward second on the meeting of bat and ball, halted as he saw it might be caught, then accelerated again the second it dropped, passing in front of Dauer as the second baseman made his throw: it was all he could do. Don Money knew it was not, because of the circumstances, a routine infield out, and ran as hard as he could, thus avoiding the double play. Lenn Sakata had moved immediately to second base, there either to receive a direct throw from Dauer or to move slowly toward first if either Murray or Davis began to chase Yount toward second in a rundown. Eddie Murray had stood on the base, holding Yount, as the play started, and had jumped off as soon as Davis released his pitch, moving toward the hole into which, indeed, Money hit the ball. When he determined its precise direction, and noted that Dauer could handle it, Murray reversed course and raced back to first, vainly. Rick Dempsey, clad in his cumbersome and unwieldy catcher's equipment, followed Money down the first base line — he did this perhaps fifteen times a game — to protect against a possible overthrow at the completion of a double-play attempt. Storm Davis, completing his follow-through, had left himself out of fielding position, and was the one man out of the seven involved in the play who had failed to perform as well as he could have. The whole adventure took perhaps five seconds.

Withal, Baltimore was better off than they had been: not only was there one out, but Yount, a good runner, had been replaced on first by Money, a terribly slow one.

Ben Oglivie, who had been slumping, had today walked in the first inning and singled in the third. Again the Baltimore defense shifted heavily toward right field, but again they pitched him outside. He crowded the plate, took three half swings as Davis peered in for his sign, then yanked the bat back over his shoulder, as ever waggling it ferociously, its fat end waving back and forth rapidly, oscillating in ever smaller arcs yet never coming to a stop. Oglivie's hands reached back on each pitch, the bat flexing with them, yet he let five straight pitches pass. In the dugout Kuenn was surprised by Oglivie's uncharacteristic patience. He was an aggressive hitter whose violent, rapid *swoosh* of a swing was as malevolent on an 0-2 pitch as on a 3-1. He had looked pathetic in Oakland the week before, trying to break his slump with a weird inside-out swing, trying to poke a ball down the third base line. Baltimore, Kuenn saw, was apparently trying to provoke him again, leaving the left field line unprotected, making in the dugout an ostentatious show of coach Jimmy Williams' waving left fielder Roenicke over toward center. And they were still pitching him outside, fearful of giving him a pitch he could take to right with his whippy power; Dempsey set up so conspicuously outside before each pitch that it appeared he was taking his first stride back to his own dugout. Of the five pitches Oglivie saw here in the fourth inning, one was a tempting inside slider, but too low. The other four were, all of them, outside, and all were at the letters or above. Oglivie was in a zone of induced self-control, and he found it easy to let Davis stay away from him, and in the process put him on base.

Gorman Thomas was next, with two men on base and only one out. Ever since Thomas had ascended to the major leagues for good, he had regarded Harvey Kuenn as a kindly uncle, a man with his interests at heart, yet not so much that Kuenn would hector him or even offer any advice at all without Thomas's first soliciting it. Where Yount operated on an instinctive plane, and Oglivie on a level he could attain through his introspection and his passion for self-improvement, Thomas was frankly Olympian: "If I say I am, I am," he seemed to shout, brimming with self-confidence, no shyness about his ego, no doubt about his abilities. He thought he was a great center fielder. He thought he was a great hitter. He knew the fans loved him. He knew the clubhouse, in some way, revolved around him. He might despise a particular writer, but he knew he was capable, always, of being good copy, even when he wasn't talking. He played with guts and with great energy, stirring his body to attempt the impossible — to hit the home run that would never come down, to pulverize the outfield wall that stood in his way, to outrun the best shortstop's throw to first. (Watching Thomas try to beat out a slow roller in a 1981 game in Boston, Tom Flaherty said, "He *always* hustles. He'll still never beat one out, but he'll always hustle.") Thomas was rarely clean-shaven; his shirttails were forever hanging out; he drank his beer and smoked his Marlboros and walked and talked and behaved the tough guy. He loved talking about how he went to college to avoid the draft, and how he "majored in shooting pool," and about how he, a blue-collar player, couldn't be happier than he was playing in Milwaukee, a blue-collar town. Mostly, though, he loved talking about "dialing 8" — long distance in every road hotel — when he came to the plate. He lived for the home run, and though he was grateful that Kuenn had taught him to shorten his stride and his swing with two strikes on him, he only rarely resorted to this cautious policy *before* there were two strikes on him. "I might be able to hit .280 or .290," he said, a lifetime .232 hitter when the 1982 season began, "but not with 35 bumps. I'm here for the bumps."

He had delivered his "bumps," in fact, with as much frequency as anyone else in baseball. During 1978–80, he hit more home runs than any other player in the game; only an exceptional performance by Philadelphia's Mike Schmidt in the strike-plagued season of 1981 dropped Thomas from the number one spot in the years since he had become a full-time player. And, today, with two men on and the Brewers in the lead? The prospect was delicious.

Before assuming his stance in the box, Thomas tugged at the shoulders of his jersey, flexed his neck by swooping his head back and forth in an open-topped semicircle, wiggled his fingers, fidgeted with his cap. The routine, which he engaged in whenever he was at bat, seemed to settle his energy, and he took his position beside the plate with his legs spread wide, his rear foot at the back edge of the box, his potbelly sucked tight. (Thomas was in terrible condition for a professional athlete; Paul Jacobs, the team physician, often worried about how he failed to take care of his body.)

Thomas let the first pitch go by, and then his bat swept across the plate with enormous energy and he hit a huge, soaring, sinewy rocket into the air, where it hovered and floated for an eternity before it settled into Lenn Sakata's glove, just at the edge of the infield.

The unprepossessing Roy Howell, who followed Thomas to the plate, produced a dwarfed version of the same spectacle, an inning-ending pop-up in front of the plate that might have been a commentary on Thomas's somewhat buffoonish effort. But, actually, the first pop-up in some way defined the second one. Those who, like Thomas, fill the screen of vision and play the buffoon are ballast for the introverts, for the philosophers, for the graceful and lean. Gorman Thomas had a role to play, sure, but it was a role that enabled many of his teammates to go about their business without the pressure that Thomas shouldered for all of them.

5

	1	2	3	4	5	6	7	8	9	R	H	E
Baltimore	1	2	0	0						3	7	1
Milwaukee	2	0	4	0						6	10	0

On the night before June 10, Sammy Stewart and Bob McClure had gone to the bullpens to prepare for today's game. The Brewers had suffered their third loss in three days to the Orioles; like each of the two earlier games in the series, the score hadn't even been close enough to tempt Earl Weaver to use a relief pitcher. Milwaukee's fearsome batters had looked pale and miserable, and after the Wednesday game, Kuenn announced that the team would forgo batting practice Thursday. For the laconic manager, it was about as radical, or noteworthy, a move as he would make.

Also on Wednesday evening, Bud Selig was less than cheery. He sucked his Cherry Tipalets alone in the privacy of his enclosed box, not once venturing forth into the press rows to play his teasing games with the writers. The following morning, he arrived at his office beneath the stands an hour late, dark glasses covering his eyes, a scowl on his face, cool abruptness and a little discourtesy in his voice. He had missed two appointments, one with a staff member and another with one of the writers; Lori Keck, his secretary, had had no idea when he'd be in.

On the photographers' terrace in front of the press box Wednesday night, one of Selig's fellow shareholders in the club, Milwaukee public relations man Ben Barkin, was seated with someone even less happy than Selig. Barkin, an elegant man in his late sixties, was by nature and by profession an optimist. For decades he had charted the public posture of the Joseph Schlitz Brewing Company, leading the firm into the sponsorship of various events and programs that enhanced its image. He had also, by virtue of his acquaintance with the men who ran Milwaukee's business community, played a large role in helping Selig put together the investors who had purchased the old Seattle Pilots and dragged them to Milwaukee in 1970. One of the biggest of the shareholders in 1982 was Laurie Uihlein, the widow of Robert Uihlein, who had run Schlitz for years and had been its biggest shareholder. Laurie Uihlein, a gracious woman who was part pixie and part dowager, perpetually and vocally gave her support to Selig whenever he wanted to spend more money to get better players. She would arise in shareholders' meetings and say, in effect, that if player X would help the ball club, she was all for paying what was necessary.

The unhappy man with Ben Barkin Wednesday night was Jack McKeithen, who had succeeded Robert Uihlein as the chief executive officer of Schlitz. On Thursday morning, McKeithen would preside over his last stockholders' meeting of Joseph Schlitz; burdened by a radical downturn in the firm's business, McKeithen and the other directors had been unable to stave off the effort of Stroh's Brewing of Detroit to take over the firm. Barkin was McKeithen's companion at a sort of wake. The company one of them ran, and the other of them had advised, would be in other hands by noon the following day.

The demise of Schlitz, once the largest of Milwaukee's three major breweries, reverberated within Milwaukee's baseball team; the brewery had much to do with the club's very existence. Bob Uihlein, as much as anyone but Selig himself, had made it possible for the Brewers to come to Milwaukee; his presence in any civic or business effort gave it the stamp of legitimacy, and he was one of the first men Selig had approached to help keep baseball in Milwaukee after the first rumors of the Braves' impending departure circulated in 1964. When Selig met Uihlein for lunch at the Milwaukee Athletic Club in 1964, and said he was the first member of a group forming to keep the Braves in Milwaukee, Uihlein thrust out his hand and said, "The group is now you *and* me." Buddy (it was the name by which his family and his closest friends knew him) Selig was 30 at the time, the brush-cut, toothy son of a wealthy Ford dealer — hardly the model of a community leader. It was long before the time when, as president of the ball club, he was elevated into the inner circle of the city's establishment, well before the time when his visibility in one sector of civic endeavor caused a certain griping in another as members of the Milwaukee Jewish community complained Selig had abandoned his own background to play in palmier social and charitable circles.

Yet in 1965 Selig was able to do a number of things that would change the course of his slightly undirected life. He insisted, a decade and a half later, that his work for a venture called Teams, Inc. — the group that tried first to keep the Chicago-owned Braves from leaving, then immediately went to work to get a new team in town — was done for the benefit of the community, that a city like Milwaukee, so overshadowed by its neighbor 90 miles south, *needed* a big league baseball team. His detractors said he did it because he wanted to be a bigshot, and while the Bob Uihleins and Ralph Evinrudes (of the outboard motor company) and Oscar Mayers (of the meatpacking family) could throw their money and their names into the effort, Buddy Selig could do the necessary trench-digging work, and thereby elevate himself into the city's elite. And, whether toiling out of civic duty or lesser motives, Selig would — if his energy and resourcefulness paid off — end up with what he had dreamed of since his boyhood afternoons at Borchert Field, where the old minor league Brewers played. He would end up with a major league ball club.

The first assault that Selig and his supporters carried off was on the National League itself. There appeared to be irregularities in the transfer of the Braves franchise to Atlanta; Teams, Inc., and Milwaukee County, the owner of the stadium, brought suit against the owners of the Braves and against the National League. In addition to the legal merits of the case, the Milwaukeeans argued that there was an alternative buyer for the Braves — Teams, Inc. — and that its willingness to purchase the club should take precedence over the wishes of the current owners to move to Atlanta. Yet an attorney from the New York firm of Willkie Farr & Gallagher — a young man named Bowie Kuhn, who made his impact on the men who ran baseball with his performance in the Milwaukee case — prevailed in court, and Milwaukee was without a ball club.

Selig and company redoubled their efforts. Every time baseball's government gathered — at the winter meetings, at league meetings, at the All-Star Game and the World Series — the Milwaukee contingent was there, lobbying for a ball club. Defeated in court, they made a midcourse correction and came to baseball, and especially the National League, hat in hand, positioning themselves to be granted an NL franchise should a club come up for sale, or should the league undertake further expansion. At the same time, they lobbied the American League for a crack at the foundering Chicago White Sox. In 1968 they cut a deal with the White Sox owners to play a portion of their schedule in Milwaukee, demonstrating that baseball could still draw well in the Wisconsin city; Teams, Inc., took over the local promotion and ticket sales for each of the 10 White Sox games to be played in Milwaukee.

At the end of '68, each league determined, indeed, to add two new franchises to its rosters. The American League had a concrete debt to Kansas City, which Charles O. Finley had abandoned in 1967 for Oakland, and a long-term, aggressive effort by Seattle promoters had placed that city on the short list. The National League had its eyes on San Diego, with a spanking new stadium ready for occupancy, and, Selig thought, on Milwaukee.

"I'll never forget that meeting in 1968," Selig recalled in 1981. "[Los Angeles Dodger owner] Walter O'Malley came out of the meeting room to announce the names of the two cities who were being given franchises, and we were standing there cocky and confident. He said, 'San Diego,' and then his lips formed an *M* for Milwaukee. Except he said 'Montreal.' " Judge Robert Cannon, part of the Milwaukee contingent, intoned, "It's unthinkable that baseball would do this to cities in the United States, which made baseball what it is." Selig later learned that Milwaukee had got but one vote. "And about eight of them told us they were the one."

Stunned, Selig and his associates watched with despair as the 1969 season progressed. Seattle's perpetual rain kept the grossly inadequate (and aptly named) Sicks Stadium empty, and Montrealers squeezed themselves into the limited capacity of that city's Jarry Park — all while County Stadium's 47,611 seats sat ample and empty.

But the Seattle situation was so monstrously bad that the club's owners simply could not make a go of it, proceeding through the 1969 season underfinanced and unattended; their draw of 677,000 was the lowest of any new franchise in modern history. The clouds of receivership gathered over the heads of the Seattle entrepreneurs, and the American League itself was on the brink of taking over the franchise when, patiently waiting, the Milwaukeeans made it clear they were ready. As the 1970 Seattle Pilots broke camp in

Arizona that spring, their destination was still so unsure that manager Dave Bristol reported telling the airplane's pilot, "When we get to Salt Lake City, ask me whether to turn right or left." They turned right on March 31 — barely a week before the season began — and became the Milwaukee Brewers, the Milwaukee name and insignia hastily sewn onto uniforms designed for the Seattle Pilots.

Selig and his partners paid $10.8 million for a decrepit expansion team, and had to open the season with it barely a week after the deal was closed. Years later, Selig grimaced with the memory of his purchase: "Ten eight!" he exclaimed. "For Steve Hovley and Jerry McNertney!"

Hovley and McNertney were notably undistinguished ball players who typified the Seattle talent; the "ten eight" especially galled Selig when he learned, in 1981, that the New York Mets had been sold for more than $21 million. A baseball club in the most populous market in the country, with vast potential from both gate attendance and broadcast revenue, had sold for fundamentally the same price — once inflation had been figured in — that the Milwaukeeans had paid for the Seattle Pilots in 1970.

There was, early on, some shuffling in and out of the Milwaukee ownership group, as various members found the accumulating deficits too intimidating, or the pleasures of owning a perpetual loser rather limited. By and large, though, they all stuck it out: Ralph Evinrude, who was originally the largest shareholder; Oscar Mayer; the Uihleins; Ben Barkin; and, of course, Selig. Occasionally, the dispensation of an estate, or the exhaustion of a shareholder, would make a piece of the partnership available, and the remaining partners would buy it up. Eventually, Selig himself — the auto dealer's son — held the largest share of the club.

In the early years, the original $10.8 million investment looked dreadful. The team played abysmally and drew poorly. Even the major league rule that a physician must be in attendance at every game was difficult to uphold; the team was so bad that when the regular orthopedist couldn't make it, he had to beg other doctors — gynecologists, pediatricians, *anyone* — to take the free seats next to the dugout. Mark Paget, who later graduated to the club's group sales office, recalled his days as "Bernie Brewer." For $5 a game he'd sit high above the bleachers and slide down into an enormous ersatz beer mug whenever a Brewer hit a home run. "It was an easy job in those days," Paget said. "I would go two weeks without a dunking."

As late as 1976, Selig said he couldn't see how other clubs could afford to invest so much in player development. He had only four clubs in his farm system and a full-time scouting staff of only four men. (Milwaukee in those years drew most of their scouting information from the Major League Scouting Bureau, a cooperative organization whose researches any club can draw upon.) In its civic generosity, the local ownership was providing Milwaukee with professional baseball, but usually only in the form of the various American League teams who wore visitors' uniforms at County Stadium. Finally, in 1977, Selig's frustration peaked (the Brewers had finished last or next to last every season of their existence), and he plunged into the free-agent market to sign Sal Bando. After yet another sixth-place finish (only the brand-new Toronto Blue Jays saved them from last), Selig discharged GM Jim Baumer, manager Alex Grammas, and various others among his top baseball people in one swift move, and brought in Dalton.

Dalton, of course, built on what his predecessors had done, but his hiring of George Bamberger alone pushed the Brewers forward. In 1978 they became a truly competitive team, and this maturation was reflected at the turnstiles: 1.6 million people paid their way into County Stadium, and the Brewers showed a profit. In 1979, following the season-long advertisement that was the 1978 season, attendance mushroomed to 1.9 million, and the Brewer partnership paid a dividend of roughly $750,000 to the investors, retaining an equal amount of profit for reinvestment. The dividend, which at least enabled the owners to pay the taxes on the total profit, represented a 5 percent return on the $13 million (including investor overcalls) they had put into the club to date. It came, however, after an eight-year period in which the total return was negligible.

At the same time that attendance increased, so did broadcast revenue. The days were long past when Selig would sell the radio rights to Schlitz for $400,000 and then allow the brewery to make whatever arrangements it chose with broadcasters and advertisers.

By 1982 the club's break-even attendance figure, which Selig had estimated at 800,000 in the days of Teams, Inc., had ballooned to 1.9 million. There were some people in the Milwaukee office, and with other clubs, who grumbled that Selig, under the spell of the persuasive (and persuasively successful) Harry Dalton, was giving away the store. Baseball's formal salary arbitration procedure, which entitled any player with two full years of major league service to submit his request for a raise to an independent arbitrator, had not yet seen, alone among all big league clubs, a single Milwaukee player. Neither had a player of any real value departed the club for free agency. Dalton's supporters said he was simply a good negotiator who made few mistakes, and hard-liners argued he was a soft touch who had been lucky and had not yet awarded an immense contract to an undeserving player, as so many other teams had. But neither could they say he had pandered egregiously to players' desires, as the New York Yankees had done when they contractually guaranteed first baseman Jim Spencer that he'd start against all right-handed pitchers. What was especially extraordinary was that the stipulation wasn't suggested by Spencer's agent but by New York owner George Steinbrenner himself.

Until 1982, Dalton had in four seasons in Milwaukee made only two contractual commitments that had proved to be real mistakes. In one, he had signed left-handed pitcher Jerry Augustine to a five-year deal averaging $180,000 annually after the pitcher had won 13 games in 1978; only the guaranteed contract enabled Augustine, in 1981 and again in 1982, to fulfill his basically superfluous role, which could as readily have been achieved with a rookie pitcher earning the major league minimum, barely one sixth Augustine's fee. He had also committed the Brewers, at the end of 1980, to a three-year deal worth $1,035,000 to Moose Haas, and though Haas continued to show occasional brilliance, he had by the end of 1982 dropped out of the Milwaukee starting rotation. (Haas was to earn his keep only in 1983, the last year of his contract.)

Otherwise, Dalton (who had struggled in 1967 to keep the entire payroll of his world champion Orioles under $850,000) threw checks of satisfactory size to Rollie Fingers and Pete Vuckovich after they joined the club at the close of 1980, tying both men up for three seasons, the former at a total $2.4 million, the latter at $1.63 million. Around the same time, he got Gorman Thomas, for five years at $3,450,000. He had obtained Jim Slaton, after a one-year exile in Detroit, from the free-agent list for $1,460,000 spread over six years. He allowed Cecil Cooper an "extension" — in actuality, a renegotiation — and he kept Yount, Molitor, and everyone else contractually happy.

In June of 1982, apart from Augustine's the only contract that had become truly problematic for Milwaukee was Larry Hisle's, but for circumstances beyond anyone's control. Hisle had signed with the Brewers for five years in November 1977, just days before Selig appointed Dalton to the general managership. His six-year guarantee, at the time, was the largest single contract in baseball, totaling $3.155 million (plus "moving expenses"). Though it included a variety of bonuses and deferments, it nonetheless amortized at $525,000 a year — which is to say more than ten times the amount the average Brewer was being paid in the season before Hisle signed (indeed, Hisle himself had earned only $47,200 in 1977).

In the first year of his contract, the powerful Hisle earned his keep, batting .290 with 34 home runs and 119 runs batted in. But on April 20, 1979, against Baltimore, Hisle ripped the rotator cuff of his right arm while making a throw from the outfield. Mindful of the depressing odds against returning to full capability after surgery, Hisle rested his shoulder most of that year, eventually appearing in only 26 games. In 1980, he injured the arm again, on May 19, and appeared in only 17 games. Finally, he relented, submitting to surgery on July 23 of that year.

In spring training of 1981, Buck Rodgers and Harry Dalton were counting on a renewed Hisle to be a full-time designated hitter. Gorman Thomas had moved to right field, Paul Molitor had moved to center, Jim Gantner had replaced Molitor at second, and Rodgers and Dalton were counting on Don Money and Roy Howell at third.

Hisle was desperately earnest about his return to the lineup, as he was about almost everything. A native of Portsmouth, Ohio, he had excelled in basketball as well as baseball in high school (Al Oliver, later a National League batting champion with Montreal, was a teammate), and had agreed to go to Ohio State University on a basketball scholarship.

But the major leagues intervened when Hisle was offered a contract by the Philadelphia Phillies. He hadn't thought he had much chance as a baseball player, but when Phillies president Bob Carpenter, his son (and eventual successor) Ruly Carpenter, and Philadelphia personnel director Paul Owens themselves flew to Columbus to sign him, he decided that perhaps he was wrong. "I didn't know whether I had what it took to be a good baseball player," Hisle recalled. "But if the *owner* of a team would come to see me, I figured there must be good reason to." Until that day, Hisle had planned to become a dentist.

He progressed quickly through the Philadelphia system, hitting over .300 (once, over .400) in each of three minor league seasons before joining the Phillies for 7 games at the end of the third year. In 1969, Hisle and another cherished Philadelphia prospect, Don Money, joined the major league club. Hisle played well as a rookie, but his confidence deteriorated over the next few seasons, and 1973 found him, after three trades and two more minor league tours, with the Minnesota Twins, where he finally became a regular.

Hisle was, in many ways, the antithesis of the major league ball player. He was quiet and reserved, his reticent off-field personality the inverse of the powerful, aggressive game he played. He was 6'2", 195 pounds, a dark-skinned Negro who was endlessly teased by his teammates for being world-class ugly; it wasn't so much that he was ugly as that his perpetually furrowed brow, his "excuse me" manner, simply made him an appropriate butt for teasing. He spoke very quietly, almost deferentially, and kept pretty much to himself. He managed, he thought, to turn around his career (he hit with increasing and impressive power throughout his five years in Minnesota and his first in Milwaukee) by building up his confidence. He had seen his boyhood friend, Oliver, rise to stardom on a combination of skill (which Hisle deemed comparable to his own) and an insuperable self-belief (which Hisle utterly lacked). Through constant reading of any self-help book he could find, Hisle worked to build up his ego; he even did his training runs with earphones and a tape recorder, the tapes playing inspirational speeches and exhortations over and over. Don Money, whose baseball skills were instinctive, and whose introspection was largely expended on the endless hours of television shows he watched each morning and afternoon ("I guess you could say I'm a TV nut," he said) — Money thought Hisle turned himself around by listening to himself. "Back in Philly," Money said, "Larry was always listening to everyone else, and getting involved in a lot of that black power stuff because of people like [Philadelphia outfielder] Tony Gonzales. He was reading things he didn't understand, and he got his mind off baseball." But Hisle's natural reticence needed *some* sort of external force to move him, and he found it in his self-help books and tapes. He became suspicious of self-help theology only once, when he attended a particular motivation class in Minneapolis. "I asked the instructor if he could guarantee I'd have a better second half," Hisle remembered. "He said no, but he could guarantee I'd have a better family life and more friends. I said, 'No, thanks, I've got those already.' " Hisle stuck with his tapes and books.

But after his first shoulder injury, the outfielder found that packaged exhortation wasn't enough. He became depressed, and though he never sulked, Hisle did find himself discombobulated. His fine athlete's body had been rendered unusable by a tiny rip in one small piece of tissue. He couldn't, in some ways, accept the fact that the injury just wouldn't heal on its own, and when he aggravated it after his first comeback, in May of 1980, he felt the burdens of Job. Finally, that summer, he agreed to an operation, and both Hisle and his employers were confident that he would be able to return to his prodigious offensive effectiveness.

It was only offensive effectiveness that the Milwaukee front office and coaching staff wanted from Hisle; they saw him, twice knocked out of a season by injuring the shoulder afield, as simply a designated hitter. The designated hitter rule, instituted in the American League in 1973 in an attempt to improve attendance with more offense, had from the first been unpopular with most players. Offensive players who might be used as DHs disliked it because it explicitly indicated that they were athletically deficient, not whole. Pitchers, by and large, disliked it, too (despite its freeing them from the burden of at-plate embarrassment). They saw that the rule, which eliminated the need to pinch-hit for pitchers, meant American League clubs could get by with one fewer pitcher on the roster than could National League teams. Still, by 1982, only the National League, and Japan's Central League, allowed pitchers to hit. In every other baseball league in existence, from Little League and high schools through all of the American minor leagues, the DH rule prevailed. Its spread was all the more noteworthy given the fundamental conservatism of the game; it had, after all, been fully eighty years since there had last been a major change in the playing rules, when the pitching mound was moved back from 50 feet to 60 feet 6 inches.

Larry Hisle was not so much insulted by the prospect of becoming a DH as he was demoralized by a genuine feeling that he would thus not contribute as much to his team as would the other regulars. In Sun City in March 1981 Rodgers spoke continually about how he hoped he'd get 150 games from a healthy Hisle — all of them at DH. His outfield was set with the Molitor-Thomas maneuver, and there wouldn't be room for Hisle out there anyway. Hisle said he understood, but still he carried his outfielder's glove with him, ready should an emergency arise when he could come off the bench to save the day.

Indeed, Hisle rarely did more in Sun City that year than take his swings (he demonstrated his great power to right center field, too, hitting 6 home runs in the exhibition games), run his laps in the outfield with his earphones on his head and his inspirational tapes playing on the recorder in his pocket, and tell anyone who asked that he was "fine, just fine," earnestly nodding and smiling, the furrows in his brow making him appear almost apologetic that people had to be so troubled as actually to worry about him. In the off-season, he had gone home to Portsmouth, gathered together some old buddies, and had them help get his batting eye and his timing back. In a Portsmouth gymnasium, Hisle had his friends — obviously not able to throw as hard as major league pitchers — take turns pitching a rubber ball to him from only forty feet away. In that gym, he saw his dream of returning to his pre-injury status fulfilled.

When the team went north in 1981, Hisle was the regular DH. Ben Oglivie, who had had his chance to show he could hit left-handed pitchers when Hisle was first injured in 1979, was ensconced in left, with Molitor and Thomas firmly occupying the rest of the outfield. Hisle had some soreness early on, and missed some games. Then, when Molitor was hurt in Anaheim, Hisle, unbidden by Rodgers or anyone else, thought he'd be needed. He picked up a ball, and began to stretch out his arm, throwing against a wall. Two days later he couldn't lift his arm, and he was gone for the rest of the season. Rodgers told Dalton, "What could I do, assign a coach to follow him around the field?"

When Sun City saw the Brewers arrive in 1982, Hisle was in yet a new circumstance. He had played in only 70 games during the three preceding seasons. Rodgers and Dalton could not count on him; even the postsurgery shoulder was, clearly, undependable. Rodgers said, "Last year, we were counting on Larry, and were disappointed; this year, if he's sound, it's an unanticipated plus." This time, Hisle arrived in Sun City in a different mood; his wishful approach to the '81 season had ended sadly, and he finally admitted, "I'll do anything to help the team, but I'll have to do it hitting and running." Ceremoniously, he gave his gloves to old friends and accepted that he had become a one-dimensional ball player. Again, he hit some drives that soared through Arizona's light atmosphere; on other days, he was swinging the bat with one hand. When asked about his health, he was "fine, just fine." And less than six weeks into the new season, the godawful pain came back, and Dalton placed Hisle on the disabled list for the fourth, and obviously last, time. At 35, his bearlike body still hard as stone, his legs powerful, his wrists quick, his career was through. Just as the reality of it became clear, he got a call from a friend in the organization. On the phone, Hisle cried.

The impact of Larry Hisle's painful four seasons was apparent on the field as Milwaukee went out for the top of the fifth. Though he had played one of the least skill-intensive defensive positions, left field; though, after that, he was viewed strictly as a hitter, readily replaceable by a platoon of Don Money and Roy Howell; though he was now 35 years old, with only two seasons left on his long-term contract, his ordeal had had a profound impact on the nature of the Milwaukee roster as one looked around the field.

In left stood Ben Oglivie. Until 1979 he had been firmly typed as a platoon player, unable to hit left-handed pitchers. He said, looking back, "I believed it myself. These were people" — his managers and general managers in Boston and Detroit — "who knew baseball. They had spent a lifetime studying the game, and they said I couldn't hit lefties." But Oglivie was there in 1979, ready to step in for Hisle, and he hit 29 home runs, then tied for the league championship the following year with 41.

Gorman Thomas, on June 10, was in center. Had Hisle not been hurt, the Brewers' strategy going into the winter meetings at the end of 1980 would have been radically different. Their outfield would have been loaded, with Hisle, Oglivie, Thomas, and the power-hitting Sixto Lezcano, the stylish Puerto Rican right fielder who had hit .321, with 101 runs batted in, in 1979. Dalton went to those winter meetings with the specific goal of obtaining a top-quality relief pitcher. In Dallas, planning to move Molitor to center, he had offered Lezcano or Thomas to the Chicago Cubs for Bruce Sutter. With a healthy Hisle, the club would have been able to trade both men in the same deal for the relief pitcher of their choice, plus change.

In right, Marshall Edwards was starting because Charlie Moore was substituting behind the plate for Ted Simmons. Not only would Edwards conceivably not have been on the roster were Hisle still able to play both ways, but if Thomas and Lezcano had both been traded for a relief pitcher, Simmons would not be a Brewer — and Moore would still be the regular catcher.

Look, then, to the infield: could Milwaukee, loaded in the outfield, have resisted Oakland's 1980 offer of pitcher Steve McCatty for Jim Gantner, at that time still a reserve? Would that have left Molitor perpetually at second? Or would they have held on to Gantner, installed him permanently at third, and ignored the free-agent availability of Roy Howell?

The Milwaukee lineup was by no means a house of cards built on the shoulders of Larry Hisle. But the roster manipulations that Harry Dalton engaged in daily had in many ways taken their particular color from Hisle's physical plight. Strangely, Larry Hisle's unavailability had *decreased* Brewer needs by forcing Dalton to look longer at Oglivie and to find a new position for Molitor. In a way, it made possible the trade that brought Fingers, Simmons, and Vuckovich to Milwaukee, and gave the Brewers a real shot at winning the championship of the American League's Eastern Division.

Advertisements for DiGel and the Yellow Pages allowed Bob Uecker and Dwayne Mosley to segue into the top of the fifth. Paul Molitor stood at third base, chatting amiably with Cal Ripken Sr.; Jim Gantner, on the other side of the infield, engaged in conversation with umpires Rocky Roe and Durwood Merrill. The score was 6–3, Milwaukee, when the younger Ripken came to the plate.

Ripken had failed to reach base in his first two at-bats June 10, after ravaging Milwaukee pitching in the first three games of the series. He had come into Milwaukee struggling, not nearly living up to the press notices that had preceded him to the major leagues. He stood 6'4" and weighed 200 pounds. He had flourished in the minor leagues to such a degree that Baltimore traded third baseman Doug DeCinces, a regular for six years, to California. As the Orioles' third base coach's son, he had been readily accepted by his teammates, and was spared the icy reception still afforded so many rookies. Pete Vuckovich said his own professional kinship was first with his own teammates, second with other major leaguers, and last with minor leaguers, even those in the Milwaukee system: "They want my job," he said. Pitcher Randy Lerch remembered his first spring training with Philadelphia, when Tug McGraw, one of the more congenial men in baseball, approached him, said, "You're a left-hander, aren't you? No way you get *my* fucking job," and walked away.

But accepted as Cal Ripken Jr. was, he was simply not hitting — not, that is, until he got to Milwaukee. His bat had shown sudden life in County Stadium, and Kuenn and Dobson had determined that it was necessary to pitch Ripken inside; his line drives had come off pitches over the outside corner of the plate.

Ripken's fifth-inning at-bat said something about the nature of pitching and hitting and baseball strategy. Ripken had not been swinging at the first pitch, and he didn't know Slaton and what he threw. With the Orioles down three runs, it also made sense for Baltimore hitters to be patient, and to try to work for a walk. Slaton had excellent control, and the situation indicated he could sneak a critical first strike past the batter. So he threw a fastball over the outside corner, and Ripken, predictably, let it pass. Now the batter was set up for the inside pitch, with which Milwaukee's strategists thought he had trouble. Slaton had forced him to concentrate, even more than otherwise, on the outside corner; further, down in the count, Ripken was more likely to swing at a marginal pitch that he might otherwise decline. So Slaton, clearly in control, fired a fastball high and inside. Ripken, for his part, punched at it defensively — and dropped a fortuitous single over shortstop. Robin Yount had earlier seen his career ineffectiveness against Sammy Stewart extend to 0 for 16, on a Stewart mistake pitch that Yount sent soaring into Al Bumbry's glove deep in center field. Now Cal Ripken, outmaneuvered by Jim Slaton, had started off his career against the Milwaukee pitcher 1 for 1, on an excellent pitch following a superb one.

But Slaton's ill luck did not extend further in the inning. Pitching admirably, he next humiliated Dan Ford with a "slurve" on a 1-2 count, which Ford flailed at, his swing letters high even as the pitch dipped precipitously when five feet from the plate, finally to be caught by Moore inches off the ground. Also going to 1 and 2 with the next batter, Eddie Murray, Slaton threw a low fastball that Murray pounded into the ground and that Gantner and Yount turned into a double play.

Earl Weaver disappeared into the dugout runway for a cigarette. The Milwaukee groundskeepers, in their improbable yellow tunics and blue lederhosen, came out to sweep the infield. Dennis Martinez, who would start Baltimore's next game, sat at the far end of the dugout, keeping the pitching chart. Next to Martinez, Jim Palmer — pitcher, underwear model, dinner speaker (his $4,000 fee was as high as any ball player's) — sunned himself, soaking up the fine sunshine of a rare June afternoon.

	1	2	3	4	5	6	7	8	9	R	H	E
Baltimore	1	2	0	0	0					3	8	1
Milwaukee	2	0	4	0						6	10	0

Upstairs, Bud Selig paced. He never watched a game from the stands, out among the paying customers. On his occasional road trips with the team, he sought the seclusion of one of the enclosed boxes provided for the visiting executives of other clubs, or the company of the home team's own brass in their private enclaves. At County Stadium, he traveled between the press box, a folding chair near the first base end of the press-level terrace, and his own enclosure, his peregrinations directly proportionate to the tenseness of the game at hand. He said he couldn't sit still long enough to occupy a seat in the stands. Also, though Selig personally answered every complaining letter from Milwaukee fans, and though he often took his lunch at a nearby drive-in where fans would approach him with thanks, queries, and occasional curses, he was clearly uncomfortable with too much direct contact with the customers. Generally good-natured, Selig was nonetheless somewhat stiff when he was out of his element — that is, his fellow investors in the Brewers, the owners of other big league clubs, the business elite who took it upon themselves to provide the bread-and-circuses entertainment of major league baseball for the sports-mad masses. Selig was well liked among the owners; his only real enemy in baseball councils had been Bill Veeck, the imaginative and informal Barnum who had owned the White Sox until early 1981. The two men were as far apart philosophically as they were stylistically, and Selig was glad Veeck was no longer a member of the 26-man club that owned the game. He chafed at Veeck's popularity with the press and the public, and one sensed that such popularity was, in Selig's cosmos, a transgression of sorts.

Selig was passionate in his Milwaukee boosterism, and still more so in his belief that the presence of a major league club in his hometown enhanced its stature. For eighteen years — from the time it first became clear that the Braves were off to Atlanta — he had given himself over to baseball, first to the acquisition of a team and then to the running of it. Through those eighteen years, he had also continued to operate Selig Ford (the family dealership that became Selig Chevrolet during the auto slump of the early '80s), but his heart (if not the growth of his personal fortune) was in baseball. He also had an interest in Jake's, a delicatessen on Milwaukee's north side, a neighborhood once Jewish and now black. Ben Barkin, a Selig partner in both the ball club and the deli, said they made more money from Jake's. From the days of Teams, Inc., the civic group that waited hat in hand for a major league team to return to Milwaukee in the late 1960s, Selig had become, in his city's eyes, the living embodiment of major league baseball in Milwaukee. Since the frantic spring of 1970, when Selig and his partners wrenched the club from bankruptcy in Seattle, the players, of course, had come and gone; so had the executives, a string of four general managers in the club's first eight years, before the arrival of Harry Dalton at the end of 1977. Through those years, Selig was the one constant, the face of the Brewers. The team's financial vice president, a young accountant named Dick Hoffmann, thought the club's two greatest assets were its franchise from the American League and Selig himself: he was, Hoffmann said, "the moral sword of baseball in Milwaukee."

But more than any other way, Selig exercised his authority through his wielding of one decidedly nonmoral sword: the budget by which the team operated. He believed the CEO of a baseball club was, in actuality, a financial officer. Unlike most teams at the time Selig's group bought the club, the Brewers from the very beginning operated on a budgetary system of surpassing exactitude. Experienced baseball people told him that the business defied budgetary logic, so unpredictable a team's performance, or the weather, or the mood of the fans; in fact, it wasn't until the late 1970s that the commissioner's office bothered to encourage the various clubs to install a uniform chart of accounts to help monitor expenditures and revenues. Unbusinesslike practices were endemic in both leagues, the various owners either so wealthy they could ignore practical reality (in 1982, when *Forbes* magazine published its list of the 400 wealthiest individuals in the country, the ownerships of 12 of the 26 clubs were represented); so desperate to win at any price they chose not to heed that reality; or so self-involved, so focused on the personal publicity that accrued to a ball club owner, that they felt that operating a baseball team was cheap at any price.

The Milwaukee partnership (it reorganized as a regular corporation in 1981, when the tax benefits of unprofitability appeared no longer to be germane) represented a great deal of money: the meat-packing Mayers and the beer-making Uihleins were both on the *Forbes* list. But watching expenditures was of such concern that at the first partners' meeting following the club's founding, Ed Fitzgerald, an heir to an insurance fortune who would become the club's board chairman, suggested, "Bud doesn't need the money," and proposed that Selig's initial salary of $45,000 a year be reduced by $5,000 (Selig later denied the story, but two other owners confirmed it). Feeling at least a little more flush than that, though, the partners let Selig's salary stand.

For his own part, the club president was ever mindful of the pennies. The original 23 partners had together anted up $10.8 million to buy the club, $5.1 million of it in cash and $6 million in notes (the total sum provided a thin bank account for working capital) carried by Sportservice, Inc., the food concessionaire, and Northwestern Mutual Life Insurance Company. Conveniently, six other partners in the ball club were Northwestern Mutual trustees, including Brewer board chairman Fitzgerald. (He was called "Young Ed," to distinguish him from his father, the insurer's retired chairman.)

The debts were secured only by the right to play baseball in the American League, and not by the personal holdings of any of the partners; if Selig and his partners failed, and decided not to ransack their personal fortunes further, Northwestern Mutual would have found itself in the baseball business, much as the Ford Motor Credit Company and the General Electric Credit Company found themselves in possession of the defaulted Houston Astros in the late 1970s. For Sportservice, to which the broke Seattle Pilots were badly in hock, it was a matter of necessity to carry the loan; for Northwestern Mutual, it was the sort of "civic investment" the Milwaukee-based firm found worthy.

Like most clubs new to a city, the Brewers drew fairly well their first year, counting 933,690 paid admissions. (The American League, at the suggestion of Oakland's Charles O. Finley, counted tickets paid for, whether used or not, as admissions; the National League, more conservative in a score of ways, did not consider a season ticket left idle in a drawer in some company's personnel department as an admission.) But as the woeful reality of the team's ineptitude sank in, Milwaukeeans became rather tougher to entice, and in their second year, 1971, the Brewers sold only 731,000 tickets. With baseball still in the attendance doldrums to which it had sunk in the late 1960s, Selig was forced to call on his partners for an additional $3.5 million in operating capital, yet faith was such that not one investor failed to meet the overcall. In 1972, attendance dropped to a catastrophic 600,000. But, with a minuscule payroll and every possible economy in force, the team managed to lose only $717,000. For "Budget Bud," the numbers were bad, but could have been far worse.

As the club struggled on the field and at the gate, Selig continued to force adherence to the budget. As each fiscal year drew to a close at the end of October, department heads were required to come in with figures that showed the barest inflation. Marketing, run by Dick Hackett, was the closest thing to a sacred cow. From his cheaply paneled office beneath the stands in County Stadium, its walls dotted with plaques and certificates from Kiwanis and Rotary clubs, army recruitment offices and civic associations, Hackett sought to put people in the seats, an especially daunting task in the years when even many of his office employees didn't bother to attend the games, so charmless was the ball club. Selig felt each dollar spent on promotion would continue to pay off for years, as the bonds between club and fans were strengthened. At the same time, a succession of dismal finishes in the standings was earning the Brewers preferential amateur draft choices, and the players who would form the core of the successful teams of the late '70s and early '80s were thus acquired, most notably Robin Yount and Paul Molitor.

But, as Selig often said, "they changed the rules on us in 1975." On December 23 of that year, arbitrator Peter Seitz decreed that Los Angeles pitcher Andy Messersmith, who had played the previous season without a contract, was freed of further obligation to the Dodgers. Seitz's decision, later upheld on two appeals to the federal courts, in effect abolished the reserve clause, that phrase in the uniform player contract that bound a player to a specific team for his entire playing life, unless the team chose to trade or sell those contractual rights to another organization. Initiated in the 1870s, the reserve rule at first allowed only 5 players to be thus bound by each club; recognizing a good thing, the owners jumped the limit to 11 in 1883, to 14 in 1887, and finally to all players under contract. Seitz took the clause literally — that it bound the player to one "option" year of service beyond the year for which he was under contract. The owners said — had been saying for nearly a century — that a contract renewed under the option became a new contract, with *its* accompanying option. The game had been exempted for decades from antitrust action, ever since Justice Oliver Wendell Holmes wrote that "personal effort not related to production is not a subject of commerce," and so defined baseball. But the Players Association had finally got the owners to settle disputes by arbitration, and had consequently been able to maneuver the reserve clause out of the courts (where Holmes' dictum held, seemingly impregnable) and into the arbitrator's office. Seitz, on issuing his thunderbolt, said that he was merely "interpreting the renewal clause as a lawyer and an elderly arbitrator." The Seitz decision, and its subsequent modification in the negotiations for a new Basic Agreement between baseball and the Players Association in 1976, triggered a variety of activities that were consistent with the behavior patterns of the various club owners. On the one hand, Dodger owner Walter O'Malley, the Brooklyn lawyer who had amassed an immense fortune in Los Angeles — in the late 1960s, he placed his individual net worth at $24,000,000 — said to his fellow owners that he would refuse to sign free agents, broadly signaling that if other clubs vowed the same, there would be no escalation in players' salaries. On the other, the desperate desire to obtain high-grade free agents sent most clubs into a bidding frenzy that bent the game's salary structure into a new, radically distended shape.

Yet it wasn't only the money paid free-agent stars that inflated player payrolls; it was, as well, the tacit acknowledgment, as established by the free-agent salaries, that baseball players indeed were worth the kind of money the owners were paying. Two years before free agency was established, a salary arbitration procedure negotiated in the previous contract talks went into effect, whereby players with more than two years' tenure in the major leagues could assert their own value before an arbitrator who had also heard the club's evaluation of the same player. (In one such hearing, recalled arbitrator Richard Mittenthal, "a player claimed his errors were because the infield hadn't been properly maintained, and the club presented bills to show the infield had been maintained well.") Bound to choose either the player's figure or the club's, arbitrators determined salaries *based on what players of comparable talent and tenure were being paid.* In the first year of arbitration, the highest salary awarded a player was the $135,000 granted Oakland's Reggie Jackson. But once the first free baseball market in more than ninety years was created in 1976, arbitration figures began to reflect player values established by the bidding for free agents. By 1980, when Chicago Cubs pitcher Bruce Sutter was awarded $700,000 by an arbitrator, it had become clear that the ripple effect from the first few years of free-agent signings had reached every player in the game who had two years' major league service (the minimum necessary for arbitration eligibility), free agent or not. If one owner wanted to pay an outrageous salary to a free agent, every other owner would feel its effects in arbitration, or in negotiations that could conceivably culminate in arbitration. In these negotiated contracts, raw sums soared and bonuses — based on Cy Young and MVP Awards, on plate appearances, games played, innings pitched, even a player's "making weight" — proliferated. Early in the century, American League president Ban Johnson had discontinued the original Most Valuable Player award because it gave the players who won it an edge in negotiations. Now such honors were *built into* the negotiations. Finally, it was not ability that determined a player's value but the *scarcity* of ability — the sort of thing that, by most classical economic definitions, makes a market work.

For Bud Selig, the bottom of the fifth inning saw his organization deploy talent that well represented the financial realities of the free-agent era. What made this a particularly telling representation was the fact that none of the men who would bat for Milwaukee in the fifth had ever played in the uniform of any major league team but the Brewers. Each had arrived at his financial level not because of a mad auction among greedy owners but because of the *threat* of such an auction — because of the presence of a marketplace.

Charlie Moore led off. He was a solid, unexceptional ball player whose negotiating leverage derived from his utility as both a catcher and an outfielder. It brought him a five-year contract that averaged out at $330,000 a year, escalating from a $215,000 base in 1982.

If he were traded before the middle of 1983, his new team would automatically assume a further salary burden of $30,000 a year. He was guaranteed a single room on the road. He grounded out.

Marshall Edwards, who followed Moore, had no leverage. His presence at the tag end of the roster made him a movable piece, readily replaceable in ability (if not in spirit) by any number of Triple A players. But with the major league minimum of $34,000 providing a floor, the spare-part Edwards was able to earn $40,000. The minimum was part of the Basic Agreement negotiated by the Major League Players Association, and it applied only to members in good standing — that is, men in the major leagues. When Rodgers sent Edwards to the minors in April, the player had to leave his major league salary behind. So long as he was with the big club, Edwards did have a chance to improve, however slightly, on the $40,000 — largely through opportunities presented by the injuries and temporary infirmities suffered by his more celebrated teammates. If he appeared in 50 major league games in 1982, Edwards would receive a $2,500 bonus; if he had 125 plate appearances, he would be similarly rewarded. But if he should miraculously bat .350, and steal 100 bases, his reward would come in future seasons. On June 10, he advanced 2 percent of the way toward the first goal, a little more toward the second, but realism prevented anyone from thinking his flukish two-hit day — he singled over third here in the fifth — would shove him even an inch toward the last.

With $40,000 in unguaranteed salary on first, $300,000 of assured money came to the plate in the body of Jim Gantner. In 1979, Gantner had earned only $27,000; in the subsequent two years, his earnings jumped first to $60,000, then to $127,820, bonuses included. But he was now eligible for arbitration; he was approaching free agency; he was an established player. The contract he and his agent had won from Dalton in the spring was a three-year deal that would provide him with a bonus of $50,000, a first-year salary of $300,000, a second year at $350,000, a third at $400,000. If he appeared in 145 games, he would receive an additional $10,000; a like amount would be his if he was named to the All-Star team; a further $5,000 would accrue for winning the Gold Glove. His agent could not extract for Gantner a no-trade contract, but the full three years were guaranteed — as was a single room on the road. Before he popped out to Ripken in foul territory, Gantner watched Edwards steal second and move on to third on Rick Dempsey's throwing error.

Paul Molitor's salary had gone from $65,000 in 1979 to $210,000 (in his first year of eligibility for arbitration), to $320,000 and, now, $360,000. Before the year was out, he would earn an additional $75,000 in performance bonuses. He also was promised the coveted single room. Most of all, he would enter the next season — the last before his free-agent eligibility — poised to triple his salary, at the least. If he were to stay in Milwaukee, he would come to terms long before that final year ended. If he contributed what the club thought him capable of, he would surely extract an offer that would be more than competitive if he were to test the open market. The double that scored Edwards, making it a 7–3 game, helped.

And finally, Robin Yount. By 1979, at age 23 when the season began, Yount was already earning $470,000 annually, as part of a guaranteed long-term deal signed before he, too, could reach free agency. His next agreement, which began in 1981, brought him $546,500 a year, through 1983. At the beginning of 1984, he could choose to accept three further guaranteed years from Milwaukee at $521,000 a year or, declining to do so, he would play that 1984 season for $546,500, in order to earn his untrammeled freedom at year's end. Over the three set years of the agreement, he could earn another $150,000 in bonuses. Yount always liked having roommates, so the ubiquitous single room — the most grantable of perks — didn't appear in his contract; instead, the club was obliged to extend to him a $300,000 loan.

After Yount struck out to the end the inning, Bud Selig watched his expensive talent emerge from the dugout to take their defensive positions. The five players who had appeared for his team in the fifth were — in 1982 alone, irrespective of the coming escalations built into their contracts, or of the bonuses each received on signing, or those they would earn over the course of the season — earning a total of $1,461,500. For one game, the five men were earning the equivalent of $9,021.60. For one half inning — one eighteenth of a game — they had earned $501.20.

If Bud Selig were asked whether he was willing to pay $501.20 for the run the five men had produced, would he have obliged? As he looked at the happy crowd that sunned itself in the stadium's seats, or at the radio commentators up in their booth; as he emerged from his comfortable box to twit his friend Ken Nigro of the *Baltimore Sun,* over in the press box; as he puffed on his cigar and contemplated his position as the president of one of only 26 major league clubs in the country, provider of entertainment for a city, companion and partner of some of the wealthiest men in the country — as he absorbed all this, and saw these talented young men wearing *his* uniforms, playing in the name of *his* company, how could he have possibly refused?

In Milwaukee, Bud Selig saw his player payroll escalate from $1,360,875 in 1977 — an average of $54,435 a player — to more than $8,250,000 in 1982, or more than $330,000 a man. This 600-plus percent increase, in the city that comprised, by most standard measurements, the smallest market in the major leagues, could easily have spelled catastrophe for the Milwaukee franchise. But a number of factors not only saved the club from bankruptcy but actually saw it become truly profitable beginning in 1979.

First, of course, was Selig's reliance on budgetary controls. Putting his operating officers through the annual budget wringer kept nonessential costs down; the problem was that nonessential costs made up only a small fraction of the operating budget. More important, Selig saw revenues grow at a rate that kept apace with expenses. In 1976, the last year before free agency, the Brewers ran their business on an operating budget of $5 million; although it had more than doubled (to $10.6 million) by 1979, the club still managed a handsome profit of $1,527,388.

Obviously, the greatest single factor that enabled the Brewers to see profits mushroom while expenses soared was the winning team they had put on the field, which drew a ticket-sale take of some $8.75 million. (In 1972, when the club lost $717,000, *total* gross revenue, from all sources, was only $2.5 million.) On the Saturday night in November 1977 when he fired his general manager, the director of the farm system, and his field manager, Selig was expressing a frustration paradoxically derived from the club's marketing success; while the club continued to lag on the field, Hackett's efforts had paid off to the extent that the Brewers were drawing, from 1975–77, roughly 1.1 million paid admissions annually. "What, I wondered, could we do if we could put a good team on the field?" Selig sought to answer his question by hiring Dalton.

Yet the years between Dalton's hiring and 1982 saw a number of other developments, largely independent of the action on the field, that also enabled income to expand along with expenses. For one thing, a variety of factors had made baseball more popular throughout the country: the front-page news that free-agent signings afforded baseball in the off-season; the galvanizing 1975 World Series between Cincinnati and Boston; the return to on-the-field prominence of the New York Yankees, baseball's keystone franchise. For another, the simple maturation of several years of aggressive marketing to community and business groups throughout the state was paying off. And, for a third, Selig had simply got smarter, or at least more determined in his effort to squeeze the stone as fiercely as possible.

In perhaps his most naive expression of civic cheerleading, Selig had for years failed to regard broadcasting as a true revenue center. Not once was the radio contract put up for bids, automatically granted as it was to WTMJ, itself a pillar of the civic establishment. Invariably, at a time when broadcasting income began to skyrocket for other clubs, the Brewers were dead last in *Broadcasting* magazine's annual survey of radio and television income for major league teams.

Immediate responsibility for broadcast relations was delegated to Gabe Paul Jr., whose father had been the chief executive of the Cincinnati Reds, the New York Yankees, and the Cleveland Indians. Though Paul had grown up in baseball, he had little broadcasting expertise. His other responsibilities included stadium maintenance, the usher crews, and certain other operating areas; radio-television was simply one more area that needed attention. It was Selig himself who called the broadcasting shots, and though he might justify his approach with grand statements about the joint community effort that baseball entailed, he was making a costly mistake.

At the end of 1980, Selig finally righted broadcast matters by hiring from WTMJ Bill Haig, the station's general manager. Haig was an exceedingly adept and sophisticated professional whose knowledge of the inner workings of WTMJ and the radio industry placed the Brewers on an equal footing with the broadcast community, and enabled the club to squeeze the stone for a better deal.

On hiring Haig, Selig asked him, "Do you think anyone else would want us?" To Haig, it appeared that WTMJ had made Selig feel the station had been doing the ball club a favor in broadcasting its games. Immediately thereafter, Haig notified WTMJ and every other radio station in Milwaukee that the rights were up for grabs.

The management of WTMJ took umbrage at the Brewer announcement; they had regarded theirs as a special relationship — as indeed it had been — and they did not chase the Brewer account with nearly the energy of John Hinkle and his colleagues at WISN, the Hearst-owned station. Hinkle, who said after he won the business, "I wasn't a baseball fan before, but I sure am now," dazzled Selig, Haig, and Hackett with an elaborate and expensive promotion plan (Hackett's involvement in these discussions was an expression of the club's belief that broadcasting was, still, a critical part of marketing). WISN also displayed a determination to sign up as many outlying "network" stations as possible throughout the Midwest. And, finally, they backed up their earnestness with a cash offer of more than $1,100,000. Between 1976 and 1980, the club's expenses had more than doubled; broadcasting income had tripled.

Selig had, in twelve years, learned what was possible in the business of baseball, and what was not. There was no question that the Milwaukee franchise's net worth had increased from the $10.8 million it had cost to purchase the Brewers: the club was now profitable; its debt had been retired; the line of wealthy individuals and groups waiting to purchase baseball franchises had not run out. Yet neither had baseball become, as it had been decades earlier when fortunes were made in the game more often than they were lost, a sensible investment, at least not in a city as small as Milwaukee. The club's longstanding status as a limited partnership had enabled the investors to write off losses against their personal income tax in lean years, but the dividends paid out in profitable years just covered the tax liability incurred by those profits, as in 1979 (when $750,000 in dividends were paid on profits just above $1.5 million). Partners who left, such as former board chairman Ed Fitzgerald, were bought out by other partners or by the club itself, and though they realized a capital gain, it was barely better than what one could get from a regular savings account. And, most telling, the original $10.8 million investment translated — when one figured in an annualized inflation rate of 6 percent over the years since 1970 — to $21.7 million in 1982. That was barely less than the comparably computed value of the New York Mets, which Doubleday, the privately held book publishing company, and some partners had purchased in 1980 for $21.1 million (those partners also threw in some $5 million of working capital). The Baltimore Orioles, purchased in 1979 by Edward Bennett Williams, had gone for only $12.2 million, in a market much larger than Milwaukee's. Not counting the $7 million value of the thirty-some acres of land owned by the Chicago White Sox, that franchise, in the nation's second largest city, had been sold in 1981 for only $13 million. Each successive sale made Selig's deal look worse and worse.

6

	1	2	3	4	5	6	7	8	9	R	H	E
Baltimore	1	2	0	0	0					3	8	2
Milwaukee	2	0	4	0	1					7	12	0

Harry Dalton's was a relatively familiar name to baseball fans. In his more than a decade and half as a general manager, Dalton had become a favorite of the nation's baseball writers. First, he gave them good and interesting teams to write about, back in Baltimore. In California, he had been particularly aggressive with Gene Autry's money in the first two years after the establishment of free agency. And since his arrival in Milwaukee, Dalton had put another competitive team on the field.

But his popularity with the baseball press was merely made possible by his actual works and deeds; what iced it was his very nature, somewhat at odds with that of most men in his position. Dalton had an easy affability, and a constant approachability, that endeared him to reporters. He was, as well, a phrasemaker, mindful of a reporter's need for a pithy comment, a quotable one-liner. Unlike many of the former ball players who held general managers' jobs — men like Houston's Al Rosen, the Chicago Cubs' Dallas Green — Dalton never dodged questions or criticisms by cloaking himself in the garb of expertise: he made his decisions, he said, on what his staff people told him, insisting he himself knew nothing mysterious about the inner life of baseball. His Amherst education and his witty and engaging wife, Pat, made him appear in some ways *above* baseball, a man who could put the game in perspective and remain aware that it was not all there was in life.

Although Dalton was careful and circumspect about his players' salaries, about pending trades, and about the other internal matters that affected his team's fortunes and success, his approachability

and his apparent well-roundedness made him a sought-after commentator on matters pertinent to baseball at large. After serving,
with Sal Bando, catcher Bob Boone (then with the Phillies), and
Met vice president Frank Cashen, on the "study committee" designed as a stalling maneuver in the months before the 1981 players'
strike, he became one of the first people reporters turned to for
perspective on baseball's wrenching labor situation. The *Boston
Globe*'s Peter Gammons, probably the most respected beat writer
in the nation, called him frequently, as did other writers whose
interest in (if not knowledge of) the game extended beyond balls,
strikes, and home runs. A single observation by Gammons alone
often served to disseminate Dalton's words (or those of others the
reporter interviewed) across much of the baseball nation; the writer's
Sunday column in the *Globe* was the linchpin of a series of similar
columns of gossip and quotation that made up an unofficial baseball
news service. Gammons, who wrote with more enthusiasm about
baseball than any other member of his profession, was at the heart
of a group of writers who formed the network — Phil Hersh of
the *Chicago Sun Times*, John Lowe of the *Valley News* near Los
Angeles, Tracy Ringolsby of the *Seattle Post-Intelligencer*, and, until
he became a general columnist and moved away from the baseball
beat, Randy Galloway of the *Dallas Morning News*. They were
all good reporters, with excellent connections in the sport, and they
talked to one another constantly, sharing the tidbits and rumors
they encountered in their daily travels; come Sunday, their papers
often shared the same items, mutually pooled from their distant
locations.

In the spring of 1981, Dalton offered Gammons, and thus his
network, a number of well-stated if uncontroversial judgments about
the labor situation. With Gammons, and a few other reporters he
trusted, he would also at times slip deftly off the record and offer
opinions rather more provocative, especially if they had reached
the ears of his fellow members of the baseball establishment. Informed and articulate as he was, Dalton was thus able to influence
coverage of the impending strike in a positive way, granting his
auditors ideas and perspectives that enabled them to do a better
job in the unfamiliar territory of labor reportage, a field in which
they were all over their heads, save perhaps for Jerome Holtzman
of the *Chicago Tribune* and Murray Chass of the *New York Times*.
("He's one of the two or three best," owners' negotiator Ray Grebey

said of Chass, "even though he's Marvin Miller's mouthpiece.")

Another reporter, also in the elite of the field, to whom Dalton spoke that spring was Tom Boswell of the *Washington Post*. Boswell, who shared Gammons' enthusiasm but was able to convey it in a glittering and elegant prose style more akin to first-rate literary criticism than to traditional sports reportage, had the advantage of working for a paper that did not have a home team. Although he covered the nearby Orioles in more detail than he did other teams, Boswell was basically free to range over baseball as he saw fit, traveling this week with the Dodgers, the next with the Reds, and so on. He picked and chose his subjects by their newsworthiness and their appeal to him; he had freedom.

During the months leading up to the strike, Boswell wrote frequently about the clouds that lay ahead. In February, gathering material for a stoutly opinionated piece about what was afoot, and what its consequences might be, he talked to Harry Dalton. When his article appeared — not just in the *Post* but in a wide number of papers that pick up material from the *Post*'s news service — it detonated an intense reaction inside baseball officialdom. Dalton, according to Boswell, said he felt that the owners wanted a strike, and that common sense could settle the labor issues easily.

There was nothing shocking about Dalton's apostasy; he was a noted dove in the management-labor wars, and had made similar statements to Gammons and a number of other reporters that spring. But he was always careful to step off the record before sharing such views, which was not only his nature but also a prudent path, mindful as he was of a gag rule imposed by the owners (and ardently supported by Selig, Dalton's boss) as they headed toward confrontation with the players.

The gag rule became known late in March when the *Times*'s Chass reported that Dalton had been fined $50,000 by the Player Relations Committee for his indiscretion.

Operating independently of the commissioner's office, the PRC was a separate corporation charged with representing baseball ownership in all labor disputes. Its board of directors consisted of owners representing both leagues, including Ed Fitzgerald, chairman of the Brewers' board through 1981. Its chief executive was Ray Grebey, a labor relations specialist who had prepped for the job in a long career with the General Electric Company, a firm noted as much for its hard-line labor policies as for its toasters and irons.

Although the PRC never collected Dalton's fine — after the '81 strike was over, a post-settlement clemency was issued — the very fact that it levied the fine was the first public indication of a sea change in the management of baseball's business affairs. Further, as the players and the owners hurtled toward the seven-week strike that rent the '81 season, the primacy of the PRC became clearer and clearer.

For what was obvious in the spring and summer of 1981 was the absence from the labor front of Bowie Kuhn, the commissioner of baseball. In the months leading up to the strike, Kuhn took a poor-mouth stance in public whenever he could, citing consolidated (and unexaminable) financial data that purported to show that the great majority of baseball teams were losing great sums of money. As the strike deadline approached — and then during the strike itself — he stated in rare interviews and speeches that as commissioner of "all baseball," he could not side with either owners or players. It was a patently specious claim, hired and paid as he was strictly by the owners. But at no time during the many months — years, even — of player-owner fencing that preceeded the strike did Kuhn visibly involve himself in negotiations; nor was Kuhn in evidence when Harry Dalton was fined, despite the specific responsibility for issuing fines granted the commissioner in the Major League Agreement, the document that binds the 26 clubs together.

Kuhn's distance from the labor front, though, was not a matter of diffidence — Kuhn was almost aggressively nondiffident — nor was it a smokescreen thrown up to disguise noble behind-the-scenes effort. He was on the sidelines of the negotiations simply because he had been banished to them by the owners, his employers. For in 1976, after arbitrator Peter Seitz freed the players from the reserve clause, after players and owners could not come to agreement on a modification of Seitz's unilateral emancipation proclamation, the owners locked the players out of training camp. But Bowie Kuhn, citing the "best interests of the game," opened the camps. From that day forward, Kuhn became something less than a commissioner: the game's most important off-field issue, relations with the players and their union, was fought in a venue closed to Kuhn and open to the owners' new creation, the PRC, an independent corporate entity not under Kuhn's jurisdiction.

The commissioner's office had come into being following the 1919

Black Sox scandal, when public faith in baseball's integrity was shattered by evidence that the 1919 World Series was fixed. Seeking a white knight who could cleanse the stains of scandal, the baseball owners turned to federal district judge Kenesaw Mountain Landis; in Will Rogers' words, "Somebody said, 'Get that old boy who sits behind first base all the time. He's out there every day anyhow.' So they offered him a season's pass and he jumped at it."

Although the immediate cause of the creation of the commissioner's office was certainly the Black Sox scandal, this was merely the event that ensured any commissioner an utterly free hand in governing the affairs of baseball. Burned by a hideous collapse in public faith in the game, the owners were effectively forced to give over control to an apparently "disinterested" party. Fortuitously, Landis had demonstrated such disinterest when he presided over the suit growing out of the war with the Federal League in 1915–16. In that case, Landis had effectively said, "The law be damned, let's settle this mess *right*." Such sentiment surely appealed to a group of sixteen businessmen who preferred not to have their affairs settled among the potentially inhospitable walls of federal courts or congressional hearing rooms.

Still, it was not the Black Sox scandal that created the *need* for an omnipotent commissioner. Rather, the historical National League antagonism toward the newer American League; the remnant robber-baronism of certain owners (investing in each other's clubs, raiding the putative property rights of other of their brethren, and the like); and the near-universal habit of deciding virtually every common question on the basis of the narrowest self-interest — these were the reasons for the necessity of the owners' signing over their rights of capital to an outsider. When the Black Sox spread their stain over the public perception of baseball, the owners tied themselves to the mast of Landis, and let another determine their course.

Throughout Landis's autocratic, capricious tenure, the owners behaved like children cowed by a stern and unforgiving schoolteacher. Landis had insisted on absolute authority before he took the job, and he demanded its retention through the various renewals of a contract that proved to guarantee him a lifetime job. Though rebellion among the owners would manifest itself periodically, the members of the lodge didn't dare curtail Landis's power for fear he would take his case to the public. A constant grandstander and a brilliant manipulator of the press, Landis could have undone the game's immense progress since the Black Sox days simply by telling the American public that the owners no longer wished to ensure its integrity. Landis, in his own eye, was the anthropomorphic representation of the game, and the owners rightfully feared the ticket-buying public agreed with his self-appraisal. But when Landis died, in 1944, all bets were off.

The owners hired as the judge's successor Albert B. "Happy" Chandler, a Kentucky politician with a penchant for singing "My Old Kentucky Home" at the drop of a shot glass. It became immediately clear that Chandler would not have the unfettered freedom Landis had enjoyed, and he was notified he would not be rehired as he approached the end of his first term, in 1950. The Cardinals hated Chandler because he had refused to allow them to play a Sunday night game; the Yankees wanted him out because he had invalidated a player deal the New York team had made; several other clubs opposed him because he had exonerated the Pittsburgh Pirates of their putative wrongdoing in the signing of a heralded high school pitcher, Paul Pettit; and rumors persisted for years — in part fostered by Chandler himself — that not a few clubs refused to forgive him for allowing the Brooklyn Dodgers to integrate baseball by signing Jackie Robinson to a professional contract.

Whatever the specifics, it was clear in the Chandler firing that a hand so free, and so active, as Landis's would not be allowed again. The search committee appointed to locate a successor proposed Ford Frick, a former newspaperman who had been president of the National League since 1934, and Frick served two timorous terms, being led as much as leading. He was in turn succeeded by a retired Air Force lieutenant general, William D. "Spike" Eckert. The most forceful thing about Eckert was his nickname. He knew little about baseball, and baseball knew less about him: after his election, two owners confessed they thought they had been voting for former air force secretary Eugene Zuckert. (The fascination with men with military backgrounds wasn't new; when Frick was elected in 1951, other finalists included Generals Douglas MacArthur, Dwight Eisenhower, and Maxwell Taylor; in 1965, Taylor was again a candidate, as was retired air force chief of staff Curtis LeMay.) Eckert was as ineffective as he was anonymous, and he did not last a full term. His firing in December of 1968 was announced with great sanctimony in a statement that read "General

Eckert has just delivered his resignation effective with the appointment of his successor. We have decided to accede to the general's wishes."

Leonard Koppett of the *New York Times,* writing about Eckert's firing, summarized with great accuracy the issues that had dominated the choice of commissioners since Landis's death: "Eckert was a victim rather than a failure. The office for which he was chosen . . . in 1965 was already an anachronism. The men who run baseball with such absolute power — the owners of the major league clubs — would have preferred no commissioner at all, but they could not face the public relations consequences of abolishing the office that stood for baseball's integrity. . . . Conscientious, sincere but totally uninformed and unqualified for baseball's so-called highest position, Eckert was as powerless as any puppet for the years it would take him to become familiar with even the rudiments of the business — and powerlessness was exactly what the owners sought." He was fired, Koppett wrote, because "he could not give the illusion of vigorous leadership — the illusion the owners wanted — and when he did involve himself in a few problems of substance, the owners considered his honest efforts to be meddling."

The owners struggled to elect a successor to Eckert, dividing pretty much on league lines between Chub Feeney, the genial San Francisco general manager who would later become National League president, and Mike Burke, the modish president of the New York Yankees. Other compromise candidates failed to attract the nine votes necessary in each league, and the owners went searching for someone who was familiar with baseball, someone who hadn't the public following of a statesman, someone who didn't incite the negative passions of rivals within ownership circles. When they realized that there was one class of person who fit all these requirements — an employee — they seized on the ablest of them, Bowie Kuhn.

Kuhn was not *precisely* an employee. As a Wall Street lawyer, he had served as counsel to the National League, on retainer; it was in that capacity that he represented the National League in the lawsuit brought against it by a young Bud Selig and his colleagues at Teams, Inc., when the Braves left Milwaukee for Atlanta. Kuhn fit all the requirements. He was intimately familiar with the litigation history of baseball and had played a role in some labor matters. He demonstrated his knowledge of the game's past by reciting the starting lineup of the 1944 St. Louis Browns at an early press conference. He certainly had no public following to use as a lever against the owners. And, ever lawyerly, he had no specific rivals among the owners: he had been paid for years to do their bidding. Thus did he ascend to his imperium, the sixteenth floor of 75 Rockefeller Center in New York City, the home of an institution formally known as "Baseball — the Office of the Commissioner." Yet Kuhn never became a do-nothing in the job, or a toady to the owners. In fact, he consolidated his power by using individual owners as whipping boys, uniting the other owners behind him as he punished renegades — the unrepentant Charles O. Finley, the unconventional Ted Turner, the uncontrollable George Steinbrenner. With enemies like those, Kuhn had many friends.

Perhaps Bowie Kuhn's best friend in ownership was Bud Selig. The Brewers' president was an inveterate committee member, meeting goer, and plan maker, and his earnest belief that what was good for baseball was good for Milwaukee made him a natural ally of Kuhn's. Kuhn called Selig "Buddy," as his oldest friends all did, and the two men's wives got along well, too. Louisa Kuhn was a stately, somewhat formal woman with an acid, cutting sense of humor; Sue Selig (she had worked in the Brewers' publicity department before she married Bud, six months after he divorced his first wife), short, energetic, and slightly cynical, was a good foil.

"Nobody realizes what this man has done for baseball," Selig said. "Bowie may not project an image of warmth or friendliness, but he is a fine, decent, extremely intelligent and capable man." Selig acknowledged that Kuhn was something of a public relations disaster — aloof, imperious, stuffy — but that the truly important work he did made him invaluable to the owners.

What Kuhn did, whenever his work became public, was cite the "best interests of baseball," as he did when he opened the training camps, against many owners' wishes, in 1976. The phrase appeared in Article I of the Major League Agreement in slightly grander form — "the best interests of the national Game of baseball" — and Kuhn's intepretation of the authority granted him under the clause was like a conservative's view of the Warren court's interpretation of the Fourteenth Amendment to the Constitution: it enabled him to do whatever he pleased. Yet the very fragility of his power, and the owners' ability to work around it, was made abundantly clear when they kicked him away from the negotiating table with the creation of the PRC.

Still, as much as Kuhn tried to help the game during his steward-ship, he concomitantly handicapped it by the self-important, humor-less way he proceeded in his job, which led the wife of one Milwau-kee official to refer to him as "a waste of American food." His celebrated coatless attendance at wintry World Series games, his stupefying appearance behind a slapdash wooden podium built on a minute's notice so he could properly announce the postponement of a World Series game in rainy Boston in 1975, were characteristic of Kuhn's stuffed shirt style. Virtually no one on the commissioner's staff gave an interview without one of Kuhn's three staff publicists present, earnest young men hovering like gargoyles, taking notes as if for history (or for lawsuits). Telephone calls to people in Kuhn's office went unreturned, except by the same palace guard. When Bob Wirz, the commissioner's chief PR man, held a press briefing at the 1981 winter meetings to report on what had gone on at a meeting of owners, his answers were so evasive, so lacking in any usable information, that he might have been the commissioner's Tass.

Kuhn was also, of course, burdened by the job itself, especially by having to contend with the peccadilloes of his various employers. Probably his greatest thorn was Ted Turner of the Atlanta Braves, an unpredictable and rather bizarre millionaire who fought with Kuhn often. The transcript of a 1977 Turner-Kuhn confrontation, published by the *Atlanta Constitution,* reveals both the oblique turn of one club owner's mind and how this commissioner dealt with it. At issue was Kuhn's one-year suspension of Turner for irregulari-ties in the Braves' signing of outfielder Garry Matthews:

> *Turner:* Give us a way out of this thing, if you can, as the guy who is supposed to be the Big Chief of baseball. The little Indians. I am like the little Indians out in the West. You hear about the Big Chief back in Washington, the Great White Father who says, "You've got to move off your reservation." We kept moving the Indians back and back and back until they had to fight. A few of them had to fight. I do not want to fight. Great White Father, please tell me how to avoid fighting for what little we have left. The buffalo are gone. The white man came and killed off all the buffalo. . . .
>
> I am very contrite. I am very humble. I am sorry. I would get down on the floor and let you jump up and down on me if it would

help. I would let you hit me three times in the face without lifting a hand to protect myself. I would bend over and let you paddle my behind, hit me over the head with a Fresca bottle, something like that. Physical pain I can stand.

Kuhn: I think you have said some very statesmanlike things. . . .

C. Raymond Grebey, the GE alumnus who ran the PRC, had a public image barely better than Kuhn's. He too had to contend with a bruisingly short leash granted him by the owners. He clearly was not the primary decision maker on labor matters but instead was merely pushed on camera by the owners, there to mouth their pieties. During the heat of the labor negotiations, he appeared to the players to be a union buster, to writers an obfuscator, to much of the public the symbol of the labor troubles themselves.

With the owners passing their no-leaks edicts, and struggling to maintain the appearance of a united front when there was none, Grebey was unable to manipulate the press as successfully as his Players Association counterpart, Marvin Miller. Miller was eternally accessible, agreeable, and frank, and it was not surprising that the players' perspective on the game's labor dispute got a wider airing than the owners' did. Grebey, for his part, was affable and engaging when he wished to be, the trappings of his office belying his bellicose public posture: his right hand and general counsel, Barry Rona, was a former organizer for the ILGWU; Grebey's office walls boasted an inscribed photograph from baseball's most visible rebel, Bill Veeck; another prominently displayed picture showed a young Grebey with two men, officers of the supermilitant International Union of Electrical Workers, whom he ranked among his greatest influences. Still, Grebey appeared to the world to represent the embodiment of the seigneurial, players-be-damned attitude of the PRC itself.

It was more, though, than a matter of public relations; it had to do as well with the structure of the PRC and of the PA. Grebey's group had an inverted structure — at the top were 26 owners, who had delegated oversight on labor matters to their appointees on the PRC, who in turn gave orders to their man at the bargaining table, Ray Grebey. (One baseball official reported that, in December 1980, the owners gave Grebey the authority to make a settlement — and when they saw he might, they took the authority away.) The players, though, chose player representatives (in many cases, unwilling souls who merely attended meetings and reported back), who constituted an executive board that took its leadership from Miller. Grebey was at the bottom of his chain of command, Miller at the top of his.

Also, where Miller's constituents were, by and large, men who had invested their talents in physical expression, the owners were men who had placed theirs in the accumulation and manipulation of wealth. In many cases, they were free-market buccaneers, men who had operated their businesses unfettered by union pressure. There were no unions at Marion Labs, the pharmaceutical firm operated by Kansas City owner Ewing Kauffman. There had never, ever been unions at the Wrigley Gum Company, whose ruling family also ruled the Chicago Cubs until 1981; nor had there been at Du Pont, of whose controlling family former Philadelphia owner Ruly Carpenter was part. Eddie Chiles, of the Texas Rangers and the Western Company, knew no unions. Nor did attorney Edward Bennett Williams, who owned the Orioles; nor McDonald's chairman Ray Kroc, owner of the Padres; nor Mrs. Jean Yawkey, whose money had placed former catcher Haywood Sullivan atop the Red Sox; nor the Mets' Nelson Doubleday, proprietor of the nation's largest nonunion publishing firm. The owners, by and large, were not used to back talk from the hired help, and not even Grebey's years of preparation at the hard-line GE could possibly have prepared him for getting into the trenches with his own troops, as it were, firing at him from behind.

On the other hand, no army ever so loved a general as the players loved Marvin Miller. Miller was brought to baseball from the United Steel Workers in the mid-1960s by Philadelphia pitcher Robin Roberts, chairman of a three-man search committee that also included Harvey Kuenn; he was then endorsed by Bob Rodgers, who was a member of the association's executive committee at the time. Miller was selected over, among other candidates, New York lawyer Richard M. Nixon, and from the very first he took an aggressive posture, not least because he called the organization what it was: a union. The Players Association, founded in 1954 under the leadership of players Ralph Kiner and Allie Reynolds, was the fifth such cooperative organization in baseball history, but not until Miller's arrival did it begin to use the power inherent in collective unionism. Not once, unlike his various part-time predecessors, did Miller buy the owners' line that the commissioner was guardian of both labor and capital within the game. Most important was the fact that Miller was an extremely smart man who was able to play the owners' individual self-interests against one another.

At no time was this clearer than in 1975, after arbitrator Seitz's Messersmith decision. The timing couldn't have been better; the Basic Agreement, the document that governs owner-player relations, was about to expire. Seitz's grenade blew the progress of negotiations into a different shape, and the various court appeals engaged in by the owners retarded the progress of the talks, while every player in the game had the legal right to walk from his contract a year after its expiration. Miller later acknowledged that he had been prepared to accept a severe modification of the Seitz decision, and even at the time of its issuance he proposed negotiation. But the owners, wrongheadedly confident they could overturn Seitz in court, retreated into a no-win adversarial relationship with the union, writhing in fanatic opposition to any modification of the reserve clause.

Finally — with the help of Kuhn, who ended the spring training lockout — Miller settled with the owners on a brilliant "compromise," which allowed a player his freedom only after six years in the major leagues. Pitcher Mike Marshall, in fact, at Miller's private invitation, publicly threatened a lawsuit against the Players Association if Miller bargained away any of the players' just-won freedom. Miller was thus able publicly to take a "middle path" that got the players precisely what they wanted: a regulated flow of free-agent talent into the marketplace. Thus were Miller and the union able to keep supply short of demand, fundamentally forcing the owners to fall over one another in frantic competitive bidding for the small amount of talent available each year. It was certainly doubtful that a somewhat better than average outfielder like Atlanta's Claudell Washington would be earning more than $700,000 a year on a five-year contract if *every* outfielder were available the year Washington had to negotiate. And it was even safer to assume that one particularly bizarre aspect of Washington's contract — a four-year college scholarship — wouldn't have been part of the deal.

The Milwaukee Brewers had stayed fairly clear of the washing-the-laundry-in-public aspect of salary negotiations that was common in the game. For one thing, the Milwaukee press corps wasn't terribly aggressive on financial matters; for another, Dalton and Selig were solidly, and consistently, close-mouthed on salary questions. And, frustrating whatever interest in the matter that the Milwaukee papers had, and helping to keep Dalton and Selig secure in their discretion, the club simply hadn't been involved in the sort of situation that leads to salary leaks: they had not lost to free agency any player they had wished to keep; they had not, since 1977, signed a key player out of the free-agent pool; they had never, under Dalton, gone to arbitration with a player — although, furious with Jim Gantner and his agent, Tony Pennachia, in 1982, Dalton came close. "They were trying to gouge me, trying to squeeze that last, unreasonable amount from me," he said. In an uncharacteristic display of spleen, Dalton said, "I was itching to give it back to them." But he settled Gantner's contract at the eleventh hour.

The Brewers were paid well. All told, they were in 1982 the fourth-best-paid team in baseball (Selig liked to point out that his club usually ranked higher in won-lost percentage than in salaries). But the salaries were notably balanced. Only Fingers, Simmons, and Thomas had managed to get their annual compensation over $600,000, and only Thomas among those was a home-grown Brewer locked in, without pressure, to a long-term contract. Dalton had inherited Simmons' $640,000 annual contract (half of it deferred) from St. Louis, and when Fingers came over in the same trade, he had but one year left before free agency; logic — getting full value in the trade — compelled Dalton to sign him to a long-term agreement shortly after he arrived in Milwaukee. Pete Vuckovich, who reached just short of the $600,000 figure under the same circumstances, had made it clear that if Dalton hadn't signed him by the beginning of the 1981 season, his first in Brewer uniform, he would leave at the season's end. Convinced there was no way he would get what he wanted, especially from a team for whom he had not yet thrown a pitch in competition, Vuckovich spent much of his first Sun City spring training anticipating what he might draw on the free-agent market — anticipating, as he put it, "finally learning what I'm worth." It was Vuckovich's reasonable goal never to have to work again after his career ended, and off-season labor during his career held no allure for him. It posed a sharp contrast to an earlier generation of players: in the winter of 1951, Robin Roberts, who had won 21 games for the Phillies that year, sold cardboard boxes at $75 a week, and the Yankees' Yogi Berra and Phil Rizzuto reported daily to a clothing store in Newark, selling men's pants.

It was a different financial world that the post-Seitz player —
and general manager — lived in. Dalton was annoyed by players
who sought to renegotiate, or who publicly complained about their
salaries in the newspapers, but by and large he had learned to live
with the operative realities of the modern baseball market. Like
most general managers, he was more troubled by guaranteed contracts than by the pure dollar amounts of those contracts. But,
like most general managers, he signed them. There was no choice,
really; the guaranteed contract, which entitled a player to his specified salary no matter what his performance, was insisted upon by
virtually every player who had any leverage. By the summer of
1982, 48 percent of all major leaguers would continue receiving
salaries, valued in the aggregate by the PRC at more than $400
million, even if they were unconditionally released. (There were
even 69 major leaguers whose salaries could not be suspended even
if they suffered incapacity in the course of committing "criminal
or felonious acts," in the PRC's words.) Insurance policies covered
physical incapacitations, but there was no recourse for the ball club
if talent, or even will, suddenly evaporated. It was a difficult, high-
stakes poker game for Dalton and his colleagues, but supply, demand, ownerly ego, and, in the end, public tastes determined what
risks a club would take, what salaries it would pay. Player agent
Randy Hendricks summarized the heart of the matter: "When a
schoolteacher can sell out the Astrodome, I'll give *her* two hundred
grand."

The team that took the field in County Stadium in the top of
the sixth on June 10 was, fundamentally, what Harry Dalton wanted:
a club of balanced salaries and balanced personalities. He and his
lieutenants in the Dalton Gang placed much stock in good citizen-
ship, off-field behavior, and other homely virtues; they felt that
how talent disported itself was as important as talent alone. The
Uniform Player Contract, which all major leaguers signed, read,
"The Player represents and agrees that he has exceptional and
unique skill and ability as a baseball player." It also said, "The
Player . . . pledges himself to the American public and to the Club
to conform to high standards of personal conduct and good sports-
manship." Dalton took both dicta seriously. There were no blaring
tape decks on the Brewer team bus; most of the players were active
in charity work; they were generally agreeable and patient with
the press. Jim Slaton, pitching, was a solid, amiable Southern Cali-

fornian; his catcher, Charlie Moore, called "Munchkin" by his teammates, a polite and good-natured man endlessly tolerant of those who questioned his occasional mental lapses. Don Money, at first base, farmed in the off-season in southern New Jersey and spent road-trip afternoons watching television in his hotel room. Gantner, at second, was an apple-cheeked boy from small-town Wisconsin. Yount, the shortstop, made perhaps his most controversial utterance when he learned that Dwyn Castle, a short, dumpy woman of early middle age who called herself "personal photographer to the Milwaukee Brewers players" and who was president of a Robin Yount Fan Club, had "ROB19" (19 was Yount's uniform number) on her license plates; said Yount, "But what if I wanted it for *my* license plates?" Molitor, the third baseman, "captained" the Pepsi Fan Club, signed autographs forever, and led the team's Baseball Chapel. In the outfield, there was the earnestly agreeable Edwards, the quiet and dignified Oglivie, and — well, there was Gorman Thomas, but his idiosyncrasies were the all-American, good ol' boy sort, and 30-plus home runs a year could easily make one forget several inches of beer belly. And despite his tough guy posture, Thomas's most intense avocational passion was his devotion to Peter Sellers' *Pink Panther* movies. On the road, Thomas, Moose Haas, and equipment manager Bob Sullivan never missed a *Pink Panther* film. When Sellers died, Haas wore a pink memorial armband.

Arrayed against the Baltimore Orioles, the Brewers on this day saw a team that was, in personality if not in the nature of talent, a mirror image of itself. The Orioles, too, were gentlemen, solid citizens; their leading delinquent was probably Weaver, the manager with a record number of umpire-directed game expulsions and a history of drunk driving citations.

Weaver drank a lot, and managed to disarm his critics by acknowledging his frailty and by managing to issue the perfect response in the most embarrassing situations. At his most recent arrest, which resulted in the suspension of his driver's license, the arresting officer had asked if Weaver had any physical disabilities. "Only Jim Palmer," he said, referring to the cranky nonpareil of the Baltimore pitching staff.

Harvey Kuenn had determined that the game was Jim Slaton's "to win or to lose," and that he would be sticking with him until he lost his effectiveness, that there was no reason that Slaton, a starting pitcher through most of his career, and himself a reasonably fast and tidy worker, would be unable to complete the day's work.

Kuenn was no less confident when Al Bumbry began the sixth with a single to center field, on Slaton's second pitch. On a team deeper in relief pitchers — a team, say, like the 1979 World Champion Pittsburgh Pirates, which had 322 relief appearances over the season, or almost precisely 2 per game — Slaton would be in some peril now; but on the Brewers, his job was to last until he no longer could, to last at least until the game reached the eighth or ninth: until Rollie Fingers could come in. Still, the prospect of Fingers' imposing presence in the bullpen gave Slaton — gave all the Milwaukee pitchers — the opportunity to go all out, not to pace themselves so deliberately. Ted Simmons said he called for more sliders from Brewer pitchers from the fifth inning on than he had with the Cardinals, because the presence of Fingers meant he could ask the pitchers to endure additional pain.

Slaton could work without worrying about Bumbry over on first; a four-run deficit made it highly unlikely that Weaver, not much of a proponent of the running game under any conditions, would allow his center fielder to risk himself for just one of those runs. Weaver swore by the trinity of "pitching, defense, and three-run homers," and if his defense was off somewhat this year, what with the aging outfield and uncertain left side of the infield, then he needed those three-run home runs all the more. The next three batters — Roenicke, Singleton (especially batting left-handed now), and Dempsey — all had home run potential, and Bumbry was on first, waiting to be delivered.

Until the third inning today, Slaton had never before faced Roenicke. Roenicke's second full year in the majors had coincided with the year of Slaton's disability with his shoulder injury; also, as a right-handed batter usually platooned by Weaver, Roenicke never started in those games Slaton had pitched against Baltimore. The batter could proceed on his own knowledge of situation pitching, on divining what made sense for a pitcher to throw at a given juncture in a game: he could, in a word, be a guess hitter, as so many major leaguers were. The problem with guess hitting, Cecil Cooper said, is that one is "trying to outguess two or three people — the pitcher, the catcher, maybe the manager." Yet guessing was the application of experience, and his own experience as a hitter was all Roenicke had to go on.

Slaton approached Roenicke by the book, with a fastball up and in followed by a slider low and away. But both pitches missed, and Roenicke was comfortable in the count at 2 and 0. Yet Slaton managed a fastball that Roenicke fouled back, a slider for a ball, and another fastball, which an overeager Roenicke sent rocketing into the upper deck in left field, foul by 30 feet. Pitcher had now offered batter a classical sequence of fastball-slider-fastball-slider-fastball. The count was 3 and 2, and it was for Roenicke to decide whether Slaton would adhere to the sequence and come forth with another slider or whether the pitcher was perhaps fearful for his control — both sliders had been out of the strike zone — and would go with the easier-to-control fastball. Baseball truism has it that in the American League, pitchers are fairly likely to throw an off-speed pitch with 3 balls in the count. Yet the one time today a Baltimore batter had taken the count to 3 balls — Dempsey, in the fourth — Slaton had come in with a successful fastball for the strikeout. But that pitch was so far off the plate that no one in the park but the umpire thought it was a strike, and perhaps Morrison, the umpire, would now take the outside edge of the plate away from Slaton. If indeed Morrison still had amends to make, it would virtually require Slaton to eschew the less-manageable slider. Yet, like everyone else, ball players, no matter how studious and careful, remember most vividly what they themselves have experienced. Only once before had Gary Roenicke batted against Jim Slaton, and that was in the third inning today when Slaton's artful slider produced a pallid pop-up behind shortstop.

Roenicke set himself for the slider, and swung four inches under the ball as Slaton's fastball held its plane.

It was one out, still a man on first, Baltimore trailing 7–3, aching for the sweep of the Brewers. Slaton, as he had with Roenicke, began Ken Singleton, whose thirty-fifth birthday it was, with a fastball-slider-fastball combination, and the count reached the same 2 and 1 it had after three pitches to the previous batter.

Singleton, with his bothersome elbow, had been batting only .178 right-handed for the season, but the different physics of hitting left-handed had enabled him to keep his average against righty pitchers at .283. At 2 and 1, he fouled off a low fastball. Singleton was deadly on off-speed pitches, and had seen few today. Charlie Moore then set himself up on the inside part of the plate and called for another fastball, but Slaton was six inches wide of the target. Singleton had what Moore called "a slow bat." "That's not a knock,"

Moore explained. "It just means he's not a true pull hitter. It forces you to bring the fastball in. If you get it out, you allow him to extend his arms, and it's good-bye." And thus did Singleton meet Slaton's fastball directly over the middle of the plate, waist high, and send it 420 feet into the bleachers in right center, a suitable birthday celebration.

It was now a 7–5 ball game, and Slaton was still five outs from getting his team and Harvey Kuenn to the point Kuenn wanted to be: to the eighth inning, which was Rollie Fingers territory. In the dugout, Kuenn remained relatively unperturbed. "Ken Singleton can hit any pitch out," he reasoned, "and now there are three straight righties coming up." None of the three — Dempsey, Dauer, and Sakata — was especially fearsome, and had Kuenn checked, he would have learned that they were, together, lifetime .231 hitters against his pitcher. It was not, though, the sort of information Kuenn consciously stored, as Weaver did on his hundreds of index cards. He knew only that the home runs each of the three had hit earlier today were off McClure, the lefty; that Slaton had been sharp, at least until the bad pitch to Singleton; that his other bullpen arms — lefty Jamie Easterly and righty Dwight Bernard — had been used up in the previous days' losses to Baltimore; and that it was still five outs from Fingers' time.

Gorman Thomas, in center, and Ben Oglivie, in left, shaded Dempsey over toward the right side, his opposite field. When Dempsey got his pitch, he was a pull hitter; when he didn't, especially against a right-handed pitcher, he was overmatched. And on Slaton's fifth pitch, a good fastball toward the outside of the plate, Dempsey barely managed to dump the ball into right field, but too far in front of Marshall Edwards for him to make the catch.

It was Baltimore's eleventh hit of the day, and on Kuenn's instruction, Pat Dobson called the bullpen and told Rollie Fingers to warm up.

As much as Kuenn didn't want to use Fingers before the eighth inning, the tying run had now reached the plate — and if a manager could be said to operate predictably, Kuenn was that manager. It wasn't that he had developed set patterns, for he hadn't been in the job long enough for that. But unlike men who have pointed their entire careers toward particular jobs, with firm notions of how they would perform them, notions they had nurtured and refined and made personal over the many years of waiting — unlike, say, Bob Rodgers — Kuenn had become manager by default. He had once wanted to be a manager, hoping to be named when Del Crandall was fired by Selig in 1975, but after he was passed over then, his series of physical ailments banished the possibility from his mind. He spent the Alex Grammas years, the George Bamberger years, and Bob Rodgers' brief tenure content as a coach and devoted as an employee. It was not simply that Kuenn was grateful to Selig and Dalton for sticking by him during the crises of his illnesses; more, Kuenn was *proud* of his gratitude. He would, he said, do anything for the Brewer organization; if they wanted him to manage, that was great, and if they wanted him to take tickets, he'd probably do that, too. "I'm an organization man," he said, and when he said it, one could almost hear organ music. His generally laconic voice lifted as he said the word "organization," as if it were the name of some deity. It was something Bob Rodgers — an independent thinker, a man not as accustomed as Kuenn to subsuming his will to some other entity — would not say so easily. George Bamberger would say it, but it would have been impossible for Bamberger, so utterly unselfconscious, to say it without modifiers: "I'm a fuckin' organization man," Bamberger might say; then, he'd likely follow it with, "How 'bout a fuckin' beer?"

Suddenly confronted after his almost too successful first week on the job with a three-game losing streak, a thinned-out bullpen, and a pitcher in trouble, Kuenn felt compelled to warm up Fingers, the best relief pitcher in the league. He hadn't pitched for three days (losing streaks, particularly those in which the games aren't close, conveniently preserve and protect the arms of ace relievers). And Kuenn needed, his team needed, his organization needed, to win this game.

For his part, Fingers was moderately surprised. As he had the spring before with Rodgers, he had told Kuenn he'd do anything for him, but he asked that Kuenn not get him up in the bullpen unless he planned to use him. Over his long and distinguished career, Fingers had cared for his arm by using it only when necessary, saving the pitches that were in it for the moments when they'd be needed. Daily, he'd tell his manager how much he felt he had in his arm, and the manager would confidently plan pitching strategy with Fingers' sound self-appraisal in mind. Like many outstanding relief pitchers, Fingers was at his best when his best was necessary. Given a four-run lead, Fingers might give up a couple of runs, but in a tied game, or a one-run game, he was nearly unhittable. The first situation called for him to throw; the second insisted he *pitch,* insisted he save nothing at all.

As Fingers began his warmup in the bullpen, he proceeded slowly, just playing catch, really. Like other pitchers who have remained outstanding into their middle thirties, Fingers had survived because he was intimately familiar with the tolerance, the quirks, the *personality,* of his arm. Thus the 15 hard pitches — 7 in the bullpen, 8 out on the mound — that he needed to warm up: simply putting his right arm through the familiar exercise told it, as it were, that it was time to work. Watching Fingers in the bullpen during the late innings of a game in which the Brewers were leading, one could see him paying rather more attention to the game than most relievers do; as soon as the hit or walk that would chase his predecessor from the game was registered, Fingers would suddenly pivot toward his warmup catcher and fire the ball with ever-increasing energy. By the time his manager reached the mound, and by the time the home plate umpire came out to force the manager into the obvious decision, Fingers would be nearly done. Then, after arriving on the mound, he'd use his 8 allotted pitches to fine-tune the engine. By the time the batter stepped in, Fingers was ready.

On June 10, he was still only playing catch when Rich Dauer stepped in against Jim Slaton, assuming his peculiar, pulled-back, somewhat mincing stance at the rear of the batter's box. Standing back as if against an invisible wall at the box's far end, Dauer thus gave himself the longest possible look at each pitch, the best possible chance to see how the pitch moved. (Some batters don't want that opportunity; Chicago's Tom Paciorek usually stood at the very front of the box, hoping to intercept the pitch *before* it moved.) Dauer's specialty was bat control. Despite his second-inning home run, it was not his game to swing for the fences but rather to punch and poke balls over the infielders and in front of the outfielders. Charlie Moore felt Dauer was as tough to pitch to as any Oriole, able as he was to adjust to any pitching strategy. He had some trouble with fastballs up and in, but the third or fourth time a team tried that approach, Dauer would adjust his stance and his swing and thereby reduce his vulnerability. He struck out only once every five games, one of the best figures in the league.

Slaton and Moore chose to give Dauer off-speed breaking pitches; the first, a slider, was a ball, low. Then, on the second pitch, Rick

Dempsey, who had stolen only 14 bases in his lengthy major league career, broke for second. Slaton's high change-up floated in (relatively speaking: major league change-ups travel as much as 70–75 mph, or more) toward the plate, and Dauer reached virtually over his head for it, in vain. By the time Dauer's bat had cut through the air where the ball wasn't, Moore was out of his crouch. He quickly took one step into the left-handed batter's box and fired a straight overhand throw toward second base. Jim Gantner had broken for the bag as Dempsey did, and when Moore's throw arrived just barely to the left field side of second, Gantner caught the ball and in one motion swept it across his body, onto the straining Dempsey, and jerked it in the air, appearing as if a Samson brandishing the jawbone of an ass. Optimally, a ball thrown from pitcher to catcher to second base travels its course in 2.9 seconds, and Dempsey simply hadn't the speed to get to second that quickly. His dash was rendered futile the instant Dauer swung and missed. Two pitches later, Dauer singled.

But now there were two out, and for the least likely of reasons: first, Earl Weaver had called for a hit-and-run, a play he disdained even more than the bunt; second, the Brewers were caught totally unawares by the play, as Slaton had thrown a change, which was hardly called for in the circumstances; and, third, Rich Dauer had swung and missed on a pitch he had been ordered to make contact with.

Lenn Sakata followed Dauer, and went down swinging at another Slaton change-up, the fifty-ninth pitch the Milwaukeean had thrown. Weaver's failed hit-and-run was immeasurably costly, not merely because its success would have left men on first and third rather than just Dauer on first. What it had truly cost was one of the 27 precious commodities a team was allowed to consume in a game: an out. Weaver hated to bunt because he preferred to get three chances to score a man from first instead of two chances to score him from second. More, he knew that the odds of scoring *more* than one run in an inning were sharply reduced by the sacrifice of a batter. The same logic applied to the hit-and-run: it needlessly risked an out. Yet Weaver would try it, however rarely, when Dauer was batting, because Dauer virtually never missed the pitch and because his own slowness afoot increased the likelihood of a double play. After the game, Weaver said, "That's what's wrong with the goddamn hit-and-run; the guy's only human, and he's gonna miss one now and then, or maybe line it to the shortstop. Sometimes it'll work, and the other guy'll be on third." But, today, it hadn't worked. "I don't care if I'm four runs down," Weaver went on. "Richie Dauer can get the bat on the ball with anyone in the league."

Still, Weaver's attempt to milk some production from the weakest part of his batting order — the part that generally produces neither the long ball nor the high on-base average — was typical of him by its very untypicality. Kuenn knew Weaver almost never bunted, almost never hit-and-ran. But one of Weaver's edges came from the "almost" — came from the fact that several times a season he would intentionally step out of his long-established patterns and call for the unexpected. But, "The guy's only human, and he's gonna miss one now and then."

Harvey Kuenn's batters were, by one definition, *not* human. His was the most devastating offensive roster in the major leagues. Every batter in his regular lineup, save Gantner, had genuine home run power, and even Gantner was capable of the occasional blow into the seats. This convenience was yet another factor that allowed Kuenn to remain within his own patterns — which is to say, the established patterns of decades of managers whose actions had defined the shape of modern baseball. Bill James, the eminent baseball analyst who was able to squeeze brilliant and fluid theories from rock-hard columns of statistics, maintains that baseball strategy is governed by a Law of Competitive Balance, which dictates that lesser teams, and lesser men, are forced to make compensating adjustments to overcome their deficiencies. Thus, if X is not working, but a team is still winning, they will stick with X; a losing team will have to try Y, and then Z, and keep on looking for the small edge that will enhance their chances. Through such determined and (at times) desperate efforts, new strategies and new refinements of old strategies are constantly being developed. And, after more than 100 years of professional baseball, the number of options available to a manager or a general manager are enormous, but *those that work* are relatively few, and relatively well established. Perhaps the game's most recent refinement of any great impact, in fact, has been the use, in the past few years, of good pitchers in the long-relief role. What had once been a slot assigned to the weakest pitcher on a team is now being occupied by men of more and more notable accomplishment — for instance, men like Jim Slaton.

Bob Rodgers had not rewritten the strategy book when he gave that job to Slaton in the spring, and Kuenn surprised no one when he kept Slaton there. More notably, though, Kuenn did not fiddle with the Brewer batting order, with that string of musclemen capable of hitting home runs by the handful. In fact, he consciously took a step back from Rodgers' approach, intentionally allowing his batting order to harden, as it were. Today, Cecil Cooper was injured, which placed Don Money in the lineup, and, though Money was a right-handed hitter, and not a high-average hitter, Kuenn plopped Money into Cooper's number three spot in the order and disturbed the rest of his lineup as little as possible. He gave Ted Simmons the day off, too, and simply moved Ben Oglivie and Gorman Thomas up a notch.

	1	2	3	4	5	6	7	8	9	R	H	E
Baltimore	1	2	0	0	0	2				5	12	2
Milwaukee	2	0	4	0	1					7	12	0

Storm Davis began the bottom of the sixth facing those three: Money, Oglivie, and Thomas. Jim Palmer sunned himself at the far end of the dugout as his teammates went to the plate in the top of the sixth. Mike Flanagan, another Baltimore pitcher, called Palmer "Cy Old," in honor of Palmer's three Cy Young awards and in deprecation of his senior position on the Baltimore staff; Flanagan also called teammate Scott McGregor, a slight, guileful pitcher with unprepossessing speed and unerring control, "Cy Future." Later in the summer, he would begin to call Storm Davis "Cy Clone," so faithful an adherent of Palmer's the young pitcher was. He was poised and confident on the mound, tall and lean, like the older man; mostly, though, he went about his work quickly, rarely pausing between pitches long enough for the plate umpire to reassume his stance. He had been effective against Milwaukee, as he had in the previous fourteen and a fraction major league innings he had pitched this season, and his speedy procession through the Brewer lineup had rushed the game into those innings where managers would begin to make their strategic moves. It was likely, with left-hander Tippy Martinez and right-hander Tim Stoddard in the bullpen, that Milwaukee would get only one more crack at Davis.

Though Davis's style was itself suited to Palmer's tutelage, and his personality such that he could sit for hours with Palmer, listening to the more experienced man's readily offered advice — Palmer was, save for Weaver, probably the most determinedly opinionated man in baseball — though Davis and Palmer fit by logic, they also fit by quirk: habitually, Palmer befriended the least celebrated of his teammates. When catcher Dave Duncan was hanging on by his fingernails to the twenty-fifth spot on the Baltimore roster, Palmer, who was one of baseball's true celebrities, was his closest companion on the team.

While Davis took his warmups, and Palmer took his sun, and Rollie Fingers continued a desultory game of catch in the bullpen, Cecil Cooper invited Marshall Edwards to sit with him on the Brewer bench. Cooper felt he was ready to pinch-hit if necessary, but he knew as well that Paul Jacobs, the team physician, was right in suggesting that *should* he pinch-hit, Cooper's athlete's instincts made it extremely unlikely that he would be able to jog lazily to first base and not imperil his agitated hamstring.

Cooper was physically unprepossessing, though certainly not unathletic. He was tall and slender, his skin the color of coffee ice cream, his hairline receding rapidly. He spoke quietly, with occasional intensity; usually he was considered, in his statements, almost professorial. He kept largely to himself, although he clearly had a bond with Simmons. The catcher was the same age, and similar enough in tastes and worldview that he, like Cooper, would have been out of place at the clubhouse card table occupied by those more conventionally manly men, Thomas, Money, and Caldwell. Too, Cooper had befriended the timid Marshall Edwards, also out of place in the clubhouse, though in different ways. One thing Cooper liked about Edwards was that he was the rare teammate who openly sought advice about hitting, advice Cooper wanted to give but for which few others asked. "If they don't ask for it, they don't hear what you say, anyway," Cooper said. Kuenn, the former batting coach, said much the same thing, but players harbor no jealousy for a batting coach. Cooper, on the other hand, was teammate, but rival, too.

There was no question Cooper had sound advice to give. He had an excellent batting eye and quick reflexes, but his great strength lay in his rigorously analytic approach to hitting, which enabled him to perform far beyond his merely physical capabilities.

Cooper came from Brenham, Texas, a small town in the central part of the state most celebrated for the ice cream manufactured there. As a youth, he never harbored thoughts of playing professionally. But, at Blinn Junior College, and later at Prairie View A&M, Cooper hit well enough to attract the attention of scouts. He was drafted into the Red Sox system in 1968. Later, left unprotected from the professional draft, he was picked up by the Cardinals, but they weren't impressed enough to put him on their roster and instead sent him back to the Boston organization. Cooper worked his way through the minors, eventually becoming Boston's regular first baseman in 1974. After three years, a virtually anonymous member of a star-laden team, uneasy in the strutting atmosphere of the Red Sox clubhouse, wary as a black man in a city that rarely takes to black athletes, Cooper found his deliverance when he was traded to Milwaukee. At first, he hated the very idea of Milwaukee: a last-place team, he thought, going nowhere. But he warmed to the trade soon enough, as both he and the team matured.

The breakthrough came for Cooper when, after years of experimentation, he finally found a comfortable and productive batting stance. Up to that point, Kuenn said, "Coop had as many batting stances as times at bat." Upon settling on a basic attitude at the plate, and upon earning the recognition in the game that his performance justified, writers began to say he hit "just like Rod Carew." Without gainsaying his respect for Carew, the best hitter for average of the 1970s, the constant comparison irritated Cooper, who was intensely proud of his self-improvement and of the effort and time and intellection he had applied to achieve it. True, like Carew, who was also a left-handed hitter, Cooper placed his weight heavily on his rear foot, and bent his body into a crouch that made it appear as if his bat, held flat, were being pulled backward by the umpire. He said of the bat position, "It makes it easier for me to get my hands started." He lifted his front foot up so that he barely grazed the dirt with his toe. At the approach of the pitch, his weight suddenly shifted forward and his bat came around at terrific speed, on an even plane, especially brutal to pitches on the low-inside corner. Line drives jumped from it. Like Carew, he stuck to this stance in its basic elements but adjusted to suit the pitcher, the situation, and, it sometimes appeared, the phases of the moon. Cooper might move away from the plate an inch or two, or up or back in the box, or he might close the wide spread of his legs a bit. He always stayed low, though, so he'd be less tempted to swing at high pitches. They were his one weakness, and pitchers often worked Cooper "up the ladder," tempting him into the territory in which the pitcher had the advantage. (Asked what he did when he faced a pitcher whose strength was the high fastball, Cooper said, "I walk.") In essence, despite his protestations and his variations, Cooper's stance *was* much like Rod Carew's.

Yet there were critical differences. For one thing, unlike Carew, Cooper generated from his crouch-and-lean considerable power. In each of his last three full seasons, he had hit at least 20 home runs; in 1979 and 1981, he led or tied for the league lead in doubles. As he grew more confident in his hitting prowess, Cooper became convinced he could hit 30, 35, or more home runs in a season if he tried to. It was a characteristic ball player's view of reality, like Gorman Thomas's notion that he could easily trade his home runs for a .300 batting average. But Cooper was probably correct.

For what distinguished Cecil Cooper from other hitters was that unrelentingly analytical approach to baseball. He knew his capabilities, both at bat and afield. In his brief spring training stay with the Cardinals, he was targeted for a move to the outfield. It was a move that he knew would enhance his chances to escape the minors, but Cooper rebelled. "I knew I couldn't master the throwing," he said. "I had a first baseman's arm, a popcorn arm." He always had faith in his hitting, though, and a sense of how he could improve it further. In the off-season, he would do a little jogging to stay in condition, but in the age of Nautilus he stayed away from weight machines, fearful for his flexibility. He did some light arm curls with small weights — never more than 10 pounds — and he engaged in some finger exercises to strengthen his hands. He was self-deprecatory as he spoke about his training regimen — how slight it seemed next to Yount's weight work or the racquetball of any number of players or the ceaseless running pitchers often engage in — but he became serious, firm, almost defiant, when he explained *why* he trained as he did. Holding his arms the way a surgeon does after scrubbing, waiting for the nurse to pull his gloves down on his hands, Cooper said, "This is my game, right here." He dropped his arms, and ran his right hand along his left forearm, from his elbow past the wrist to the tips of his fingers. "This is where I earn my living."

Cooper used his miraculous fingers, wrists, and forearms carefully, studied their capabilities, experimented with their deployment. In batting practice, while so many other players would try to break seats in the bleachers off the fat pitches of the coaching staff, Cooper would put his analyses into practice, and simultaneously provide a tutorial in hitting to anyone who was watching. One hit would go on a line to left field, the next high in the air deep to right. Then, a ground ball up the middle, another behind an imaginary runner dashing from first to second. Finally, a home run to left, a home run to center, a home run to right.

In Sun City one morning in March 1982, he told a bystander what he would do with each pitch just as Sal Bando, on the mound, went into a windup. "Line drive to left," Cooper said. A line drive to left followed. "Fly to right." And then came the fly to right. If, on occasion, he miscalled his hit, he'd dig in and do it again, and do it right.

The advantage, Cooper felt, was not only that he kept his precious tools well oiled but also that he could employ the same discipline during a game. From the dugout he studied pitchers tirelessly, and in the on-deck circle he was enrapt in concentration, his hands clutching the special bat he favored, a Louisville Slugger Model C243. Originally designed by Hillerich & Bradsby for Detroit first baseman Norman Cash, the C243 has the narrowest handle the company produces, and the widest barrel. Rex Bradley, H&B's vice president for professional and amateur services, marveled at the refinements players sought in their bats; his company produced bats for most major leaguers, each hand-turned on a lathe to individual specifications of length, weight, conformation, finish, knob size. Bradley remembered when ball players simply said "I want a 35-inch bat, and make it heavy." Now his firm produces 300 different models for major leaguers.

When he was in the batter's box, crouched in his bent-kneed pose, Cooper would flex his C243 in slow circles as the pitcher stared in for the sign. Rolling his wrists, he'd loop his bat over the plate, perpendicular to the ground, and at times bring it to rest momentarily in front of him, as if it were the vertical hair in a gunsight — bring it to rest momentarily as if he were aiming his bat, his weapon, aiming it at the man who would soon throw a hard, spinning missile at him. Then he would bring it back, waggling it slowly in its flattened attitude, lift his weight off his front foot, and — while he waited — determine where he would hit this pitch.

On June 10, temporarily disabled by his hamstring pull, Cooper was unable to exercise his abilities. Instead, he sat on the bench with Edwards, his pupil, and Edwards listened intently as Cooper motioned out toward Storm Davis, noted the movement on his fastball, the drop on his curve. As he was instructing Edwards, though, Cooper was also tutoring himself: it wouldn't be today, but in time he, too, would face Storm Davis.

Money, Oglivie, Thomas — Davis's bottom-of-the-sixth opponents couldn't have been more dissimilar from Cooper. First Money, the right-handed pull hitter, dead still in the box, probably the slowest runner in the American League. Years of occasionally disabling, always annoying injuries — years of torn knee ligaments, recurring back spasms, a hernia, a perpetual bruise in his groin from the pressure of his protective cup — had diminished his offensive arsenal. He had endured a long career of making way for others. He started with the Phillies as a shortstop, and was moved to third when Larry Bowa matured. Then he was shuttled to second to accommodate Mike Schmidt, then shipped to Milwaukee, where he played virtually everywhere, capable at most positions but because of his injuries and his eternal peregrinations, stellar at none. He had survived in the majors because he adapted well, because he had unerring baseball instincts, and because he was, still, a powerful hitter.

On Storm Davis's first pitch, a fastball that stayed on the outer edge of the strike zone, Money (who stood practically on top of the plate) nonetheless got around fast enough to rip the ball down the third base line. Cal Ripken reached for it, his leading, left foot kicking up the base-line chalk, his right foot following his body's momentum well into foul territory. Turning more than 180 degrees to right himself, he released a pure overhand throw — a rarity for a third baseman — and just caught Money at first, the ball beating the runner to the bag by a nanosecond, enough of a margin for Rocky Roe, the first base umpire, to make an instant judgment and jerk his hand in the air, signifying the first out.

There was no protest from Money or from Ron Hansen, coaching at first. If Money were not so notoriously slow, there might have been at least the pretense of an argument, but Don Money simply didn't beat out infield hits. American League umpires in the forties and fifties often said that if Ted Williams didn't swing at a pitch, it had to be a ball — his eye was that highly regarded. Conversely, today, if an infielder got a ball to first around the same time Don

Money arrived there, it had to be a putout. If Ripken's throw and Money's foot reached first base at precisely the same instant, he'd still be out, by the same combination of logic and presupposition. Besides, the hoary playground rule — "tie goes to the runner" — didn't apply at County Stadium: no such dictum exists in the major league rulebook. There *are* no "ties"; to a major league umpire, somebody has to win. Rarely was it Don Money. Of course, had Money hit the ball marginally more softly, Ripken would not have had time to right himself and make the full-overhand throw, and it would have been a hit. Had Money been a year younger, or his body one injury less hobbled, it would have been a hit. Had Milwaukee's infield grass, kept intentionally long near the base lines by Harry Gill to enable Milwaukee's abundance of good bunters to deaden their bunts more readily — had the grass been shorter, or the afternoon drier, or Ripken's reach an inch or two less, Money would have had a hit.

Ben Oglivie, the next batter, might have become a more analytic hitter than he was. He certainly had the intelligence. He also had the exposure: Oglivie grew up in the Boston system with Cooper, who remembered Oglivie, pencil-thin and trembling, showing up at Jamestown, New York, at the lowest level of Boston's minor league empire, carrying his clothing in a carpetbag. But Oglivie was quickly typed as a platoon hitter, and the wisest of his coaches recognized that his steel-cord arms, and his free, almost wild swing, were the assets that would keep him in the major leagues. Though Oglivie could hit for average, his power hitting, his vicious line drives, were his rare attributes. At times Oglivie would overthink his periodic slumps at the plate and start trying to go to left, as he had the week before in Oakland, as Baltimore's defense was daring him to do today. At his best, though, he would sort of zone out, stop thinking of situations and responses, and allow his fine instinct to take over. He needed, Kuenn felt, to retain his aggressiveness; he needed not to second-guess himself. Without his own second-guessing, his analyzing, his mastication of every situation and every pitch, Cooper was a lesser hitter; without the same cogitation, Oglivie was a better hitter: his gifts were manifest, and needed their outlet. His off-field nature was much unlike that of the typical major leaguer: he was quiet, introspective, pacific. His hobbies — martial arts, electronics, reading philosophy — were as consuming as they were varied. One day in 1981, he drove from the spring training complex in Sun City to his home in Mesa, clear across Phoenix's metropolitan sprawl, while reading — as he drove — a biography of Jean Jacques Rousseau. The year before, he left the shower on in his hotel room as he departed for the ball park, and the hotel lost a good deal of floor and ceiling during the course of the evening; Oglivie said he did that "all the time."

On the field, he was also singular. His "Spiderman" outfield style, which had his glove hand shooting up from his shoulder to catch the ball, rather than waiting for the ball to come down, made it seem as if he were unsure that it *would* come down. He was a fast runner, but often negated his speed with his dreadful sliding; once, he injured a wrist while sliding, and thereafter approached the act with dread. At the plate, though, he was anything but tentative, a free swinger with terrifying bat speed and an undeniable joy in deploying it, in swinging at anything that happened to be round and white.

So far on June 10, though, Oglivie had been cautious. In two at-bats against Sammy Stewart and one against Davis, he had seen 15 pitches and had swung his bat but once, for his third-inning single. Of the 14 other pitches, 10 were balls and 4 were called strikes. He had not succumbed to his greatest weakness, chasing bad balls. He had established that the Baltimore pitchers would have to throw him strikes.

Yet the gap between Davis's desire to throw strikes and his ability to throw them was real, and was made more so by what appeared to be a fear of challenging Oglivie. For each of the first three pitches to Oglivie in the sixth inning, Rick Dempsey set a target at the bottom edge of the strike zone, and each time, Davis was a shade lower. Three straight fastballs had missed, and Oglivie stared out at the pitcher, his big bat oscillating madly behind his left shoulder. From the third base coaching box, Harry Warner picked up the hit-away signal from Kuenn and relayed it to Oglivie; a two-run lead, a strong hitter at the plate, an inexperienced pitcher on the mound — it was a characteristically predictable call on Kuenn's part. He was the manager, after all, who told his players when he took the job to take their licks, to enjoy themselves.

But Davis's pitch, a knee-high fastball, wasn't the cripple that lesser pitchers throw when they're down 3 and 0 in the count; Oglivie fouled it back off the screen. At 3 and 1, Davis was still disadvantaged, yet the very sequence of pitches he had thrown —

four straight fastballs, all at the bottom edge of the strike zone — forced Oglivie to puzzle what would come next and prepare for the necessary adjustments he'd have to make if he were to avoid swinging under yet another low fastball. One couldn't really *think* about the adjustments, unless one approached hitting the way Cecil Cooper did, and even Cooper would have a task on his hands. A Davis fastball, which would travel roughly 90 miles an hour, would take less than half a second to reach Oglivie; when it was still more than 20 feet from home plate — after it had traveled but .15 seconds — the batter would have to begin his swing. If the pitch were a curveball, the elapsed time would be somewhat greater, but so would the adjustments — the discernment, given the ball's arc, of the height at which the pitch would intersect the vertical plane of the strike zone. And Oglivie had, in two at-bats, seen nine Davis pitches, all of them fastballs. But this next *was* a curve, and as it came slicing in on Oglivie's hands, he was overcommitted and struck the ball with the handle of his bat. It jumped into the air, rapidly gained altitude, and soared into center field, where Bumbry, Roenicke, and Sakata all converged. For a moment, the three men froze; no one called for it. Then both Roenicke and Bumbry accelerated, and saved the play through the instinctive application of outfielding's "rules": Bumbry, the center fielder, the captain of the outfield, reached to catch the ball low, and Roenicke, the wing man, the subordinate, reached to catch it high. The two men, attempting to intercept Oglivie's fly at two different places in its flight, thus passed each other without collision as Bumbry snatched it at hip level. Two out.

Then came Thomas. He pulled at his collar, tugged at his pants, adjusted his hat; he planted his feet in the batter's box and repeated the routine. On the mound, Davis stood still, his right foot on the white pitcher's rubber, his left foot a pace back. He looked, in repose, so utterly unlike the burly, thick-waisted, unshaven, endlessly fidgeting Thomas that it was hard to believe they were participants in the same sport. Davis's stance made him appear, despite his 207 pounds, bladelike; his enormous, basketlike fielder's glove, cupped in front of him at the end of his long, slender arm as if it were a bushel basket, made him appear even more fragile. It was a deceptive appearance, though, for Davis had the physical attributes one sought in a pitcher — height, strong legs, large hands. He was a Baltimore type, the product, said George Bamberger, of the team's scouting system. "Baltimore's scouts know pitchers, just like Minnesota's scouts know hitters," he explained. Always, it seemed, there was a Davis bubbling up from the Orioles' system — strong, smart, capable.

As Gorman Thomas settled into his wide-legged stance, Davis manipulated his right hand in his glove, making his grip. The determination of what his first pitch would do — provided, that is, that his mechanics were sound — was being made as Davis's fingers gripped the ball. Each baseball has a distinct "personality," a shape and feel all its own. Jim Palmer once submitted to a test posed by a reporter, feeling a dozen new balls for roundness while blindfolded. The writer marked those Palmer had rejected on the first pass, mixed up the balls, and had the pitcher appraise them again. The results were identical. Even a seemingly "round" ball has distinct characteristics. Lamarr Hoyt of the Chicago White Sox told *Sports Illustrated,* "Balls are never perfectly round. I throw mostly fastballs, but sometimes you have to go with what's given you. A ball with a high seam is easier to grip: I throw curves. A high mark on the narrow part: slider. A generally uneven ball: sinker."

Once a pitcher decides what pitch to throw, he then has to be sure that his intentions are not telegraphed to the hitter. An alert hitter can "read" a pitcher's grip, or his stance, as tip-off to the pitcher's intentions. Even such outstanding pitchers as Warren Spahn and Sandy Koufax would, at times, telegraph their pitches. Spahn, scourge of National League hitters for twenty-one years, gripped his fastball in such a way that the white of the ball showed between his index and middle fingers as he brought his left arm up. Koufax, at the height of his career, also gave away a bit of his game. When pitching from the stretch position, he'd hold his elbows against his body before throwing a fastball but keep them akimbo preparatory to throwing a curve. Even this foreknowledge didn't appreciably help Dodger opponents, though: first, they had to get a man on base before Koufax would pitch from the stretch; second, even *knowing* Koufax's curve was coming, they still had to hit it. A lesser — far lesser — pitcher like Milwaukee's Jerry Augustine was much more seriously handicapped when, pitching from the stretch, he'd bring his hands to his chin as he prepared to throw a fastball, to his chest on a curveball.

As attentive as Gorman Thomas might have been, though, there were no clues in Storm Davis's delivery, and Thomas was not one to alter his batting style. To be sure, Thomas could go to his shorter, two-strike swing, trying more for contact than for power. But with two men out, no one on, and the Brewers still holding a two-run lead, Thomas was looking for one of his precious "bumps." Dempsey had Davis give him nothing but curves, though, knowing that the fatter the curve, the more tempted Thomas would be to swing wildly. Even Thomas admitted, "Hanging breakers are too juicy, and I overswing." On the sixth curve, the count at 3 and 2, simultaneously tempted and frustrated, Thomas tried to check his swing, and tipped the ball into Dempsey's waiting glove.

7

	1	2	3	4	5	6	7	8	9	R	H	E
Baltimore	1	2	0	0	0	2				5	12	2
Milwaukee	2	0	4	0	1	0				7	12	0

Ted Simmons, who, wrote Roger Angell in *The New Yorker,* "looks very much like an Ivy League football player from the eighteen-nineties," had spent the afternoon in the shade of the bullpen. He was a blocky, solid man with legs one could build a skyscraper on; he became a catcher, he said, "because I looked like one." In uniform, he looked squat and unathletic, especially when compared to his larger or sleeker teammates. In his traditional, Brooks Brothersy street clothes, the illusion no longer held; Simmons then revealed large, strong hands, broad shoulders, and muscular thighs that strained at his tailored chinos. He was clearly too fit to spend his days in a deskbound occupation.

Someday soon enough, Simmons knew, he would leave his bats, his spikes, and his catcher's mitt behind on some ball field and move behind a desk, probably in the financial community. He had served for several years on the board of the Mark Twain Banks of St. Louis, and had just spent an off-season as a bank management trainee. He was an informed and active collector of American furniture, and his interest in the subject, along with his prominence in St. Louis, where he played for the Cardinals for eleven seasons, got him a seat on the board of that city's art museum.

Simmons grew up in the Detroit suburb of Southfield, a community that didn't really exist until the J. L. Hudson Company, Detroit's largest department store firm, opened its Northland Mall in 1954. Northland was the first large-scale suburban shopping center in the nation, and as it prospered, so did Southfield.

By the middle 1960s, Southfield, a largely Jewish community, looked much like hundreds of other instant suburbs that had grown up around the nation's big cities. Large thoroughfares crisscrossed its breadth and length, separating subdivisions thrown up to meet the demands of a suburb-bound population. In the subdivisions, streets curved arbitrarily across a treeless plain, harboring ranch houses, mock colonials, and two-car garages. Near the center of Southfield, the town's high school grew rapidly, almost too fast, becoming an enormous educational factory that accommodated a student population that could easily have filled two or three high schools in a city that had grown more slowly, more organically.

Ted Simmons was perhaps the most prominent person the city and the school produced. He was a running back in football, not terribly fast but extraordinarily strong, and determined and talented enough for the University of Michigan to offer him a football scholarship, which he accepted. In baseball, though, Simmons' star shone even brighter, and the Cardinals drafted him in the first round in 1967. In addition to offering "more money than my family had ever seen," the Cardinals agreed to let him continue (at their expense) his college education while playing in the minors. Simmons signed with St. Louis and gave up his football scholarship. But he enrolled at Michigan that fall and embarked on an academic program. Summers he spent in the St. Louis farm system, and only in the first of three-plus minor league seasons did he hit less than .317.

September to April, Simmons was in Ann Arbor, until he reached the majors. In the late '60s, Ann Arbor was one of the four or five campuses in the country most influenced by the anti–Vietnam War movement and the general rebelliousness of the age. Simmons was no radical, but he was in many ways affected by the campus life that swirled around him; not playing intercollegiate athletics, by dint of his professional baseball contract, he was not isolated by the life of training tables, practice schedules, and athletic dorms that sequestered so many other athletes. He might carry his catcher's mitt around ᶠʳom class to class, but as he got older, as he got a sense of himself, and of the self he wished to create, he was determined not to be perceived as merely a jock.

The Cardinals called Simmons up to the majors to stay in 1970. "I was 20 years old, and they told me I was going to play every day," he remembered. "At the time, I had no basis for understanding how to be a big league catcher." Immediately, though, he made an impact. In 1971, his first full season, he batted .304 while playing in 133 games. He also made an impact with his appearance: this was before he had acquired the Pudge Heffelfinger haircut, parted in the middle, that struck Roger Angell so forcibly, and before he adopted his off-field uniform of pinstriped suits, or blue blazers and cuffed chinos. Simmons wore his hair long, on his shoulders, back when such a coiffure was meant to denote something about its wearer. And his outspokenness confirmed the impression his haircut made: he was against the Vietnam War, determinedly so, and he was in sympathy with his contemporaries on the campuses in more general ways having to do with the direction of American culture, and the generation gap, and that whole bundle of issues and poses that characterized the politics of the day.

At the same time that Ted Simmons emerged from his collegiate life, still brandishing the flag of youthful rebellion, he met a man, fourteen years older, named Robert Gibson. The boy from the suburbs stood in awe of Gibson, as all his St. Louis teammates did — indeed, as the entire National League did. He was a pitcher of uncommon talent, and the talent was made matchless by his preternatural ferocity.

"Gibson as a person was as impressive as Gibson the pitcher," Simmons said in 1981. "He was aggressive, intimidating, awesome. For me, being 20, it was difficult. He wouldn't stand for foolishness. Subtlety wasn't his strong suit. He was the same when he pitched — when he said 'no' to a pitch I called, he'd make it clear why he said 'no.' He taught me how to catch; he taught me how to be a professional baseball player. He also taught me that you can't separate physical talent from emotional talent in baseball."

Bob Gibson had grown up in Omaha, in a four-room wooden shack without heat or electricity. He was one of seven children, their mother a laundress; there was no father in the house. Before his family moved into public housing, Gibson was bitten on the ear by a rat. He struggled throughout his boyhood, in desperate poverty, but finally he, like Simmons, went to college. Indiana University, his first choice, declined to offer Gibson a scholarship; their letter read ". . . an athletic scholarship for Robert Gibson has been denied because we already have filled our quota of Negroes." So Gibson ended up at Omaha's Creighton University, a Jesuit institution, where he played basketball and baseball.

By the time Ted Simmons reached St. Louis and the Cardinals, Gibson's career was at its peak; in 1970, he won 23 games. Catching 133 games for the Cardinals meant Simmons caught for Gibson. "He was the most intimidating player in the league," Simmons recalled. "He'd stare in at the batter, and I could feel his eyes burn. Every pitch was a war for him, every hitter a threat. He never gave in and never gave up. He won by force of his personality, and by his concentration."

Simmons found it hard to explain the actual techniques of calling a game he learned from Gibson; despite his articulateness, and his general willingness to talk, he saw baseball as something that did not reveal itself, except to participants. "It's so subtle," he said, "and so beautiful. You've really got to be out there to understand it, or to appreciate how many different things are going on. Gibson sort of condensed his lifetime into a single pitch; how do you explain that to someone? When you're catching, and you see everything there in front of you, you don't just see batting averages and pitching statistics. You get to the best part of baseball — the mental application of physical skills. You see personalities, and what they think and how they think and how they react in certain situations. Take a guy like Fingers; he's done it all. There's no situation that should be new to him, after all these years, and each time he pitches he's thinking about it like he's never been in this situation before. He just calls on that competitiveness of his, and gets into that game, really into it. It's why he's great."

Off the field, it was hard to see Rollie Fingers as a great competitor, or a great concentrator, or even a great pitcher. His most distinguishing characteristic was a well-waxed handlebar mustache, an appendage that surely denied Fingers any right to complain about autograph collectors' stopping him on the street or interrupting his dinner in a restaurant; through his long major league career, especially through his five appearances in postseason, prime-time action, millions of Americans had come to recognize Fingers as readily as any other major leaguer simply because of their repeated exposure to his singular upper lip. He was affable and approachable, but it was clear that he retained his affability by failing to make any effort to distinguish among all these new faces — reporters, fans, broadcasters, equipment representatives. He always seemed to be somewhere else, always removed, in some way, from his body, which was going through the motions of social convention and ritual while his mind was off in another place.

Fingers was a smart man, as smart as any on the team, but his was an intelligence called upon only when necessary. Reporters who met him for the first time were astonished by the blandness of his comments, the predictability of virtually everything he said. Fingers actually didn't give a damn, one way or another, about reporters. He was always cordial, always willing to stand still for yet another question, but he answered every question with almost a determined vacuity. He had been asked everything so many times, the answers were all lined up as if he had a Rolodex in his skull, the cards flipping automatically to the right place, providing the predictable response.

What struck one most about Fingers was, first, his apparent placidity — and then, on closer examination, the tension it disguised. He could be loosy-goosy, unconnected, apparently unconcerned. He used to say of Bob Rodgers, "All I want from a manager is that he shouldn't get me up when he isn't going to use me," and then he'd grin and go off to some clubhouse card game or ragging session. In the game of "flip" — a sort of tag with a ball that major leaguers engage in after they are in uniform and before the fans are admitted to the stands — Fingers would stand, open-faced and a little geeky, in the heart of things, amiably taking part. He was rarely serious, never earnest, endlessly jokey, even goofy.

But in other moments, the Fingers who could stand on the mound with the winning runs on base and the count 3 and 0, the icy Fingers who appeared a fearless gunfighter behind his mustache and beneath his narrow, squinted eyes — at other moments, this Fingers became visible. When he arrived in Sun City in '81 for his first Brewer spring training, he brought with him a steel device — it looked like something a dentist might roll out if his mere drill failed him — and daily twisted and pulled parts of it to strengthen or make more flexible his shoulder, his arm, his wrist. (Fingers called the device "Jaws," and within a day or two of his unveiling of it, the rookies and extra pitchers were fiddling with it, thinking that in this simple isometric device was the clue to Fingers' accomplishment.) He'd stand in front of "Jaws," twisting a handle to relieve the tightness wrought by fifteen years of throwing sliders, and his face would set into hard lines of determination.

In a quiet clubhouse, he'd often sit alone in front of his locker, anxiously gulping great quantities of milk, trying to calm a nervous stomach. Doctors who had treated him in San Diego and Oakland said he had a very low pain threshold, and that few pitches — especially the elbow-wrenching slider — were easy for him to throw. He struggled with his cigarette habit, fighting his addiction — and his fear of what the addiction represented, why he *needed* to smoke in the first place. He was a nervous man, and a serious one; he simply seemed not to want his teammates, or his opponents, to know the former, perhaps not wanting himself to know the latter.

To those who traveled with the Brewers, there were in 1982 — after Fingers had been named not only the Cy Young Award winner for the American League in 1981 but also the Most Valuable Player (the first time a relief pitcher had ever won that prize in the league) — two incidents that revealed that Fingers' apparent placidity was either crumbling or had been affectation in the first place. The first occurred on May 29, when the Rodgers-led Brewers were struggling along near .500, making little headway. Fingers was brought into a close game against the Angels, and when he gave up a hit that broke Milwaukee's back in the midst of a California rally, he angrily tossed his glove in the air, 20 feet up, in midplay. As Angels raced around the bases, Fingers quickly regained his composure and ran to back up the catcher — barehanded. No one could believe he had done it, not in the middle of the game; that night, at the bar at the Hyatt in Anaheim where the team was staying, two of the coaches who had been in the dugout when it happened swore that it *didn't* happen — that their drinking companions who had seen it must have been imagining things.

Later on the same road trip, something happened that was even more stunning to those who thought Fingers was the least excitable of ball players, a professional who simply went out and did his job, uncomplaining, never asking to renegotiate, content in his work. When the club reached Seattle, in the process of being consumed by the ill will that occupied the gap between Rodgers and his players, Fingers was warming up during a close game, and Rodgers bypassed him in the ninth inning when Bruce Bochte, a left-handed hitter, came to the plate for the Mariners. Bochte was a good hitter, but Rodgers was aware that he had been having terrible difficulty with left-handed pitchers this year, and that he had but a .238 lifetime average against Mike Caldwell, who was between starts and thus available to Rodgers. Nevertheless, Bochte reached Caldwell for the hit that tied the game, which the Brewers eventually lost in the eleventh inning.

In a depressed and dispirited clubhouse afterward, Fingers exploded in unwonted rage. "That fucking idiot! This is one more nail in the coffin!" he screamed. "Doesn't he think I can get left-handers out? I get paid a lot of money to do that!" When Rodgers was fired less than forty-eight hours later, Fingers was — along with Simmons, and Caldwell, who had always detested Rodgers — among the most gratified Brewers. But he was also perceived, among the fans, as the villain in a drama that had daily been reported in the Milwaukee papers, a story of the war between a manager and his team. The drone of the call-in shows was punctuated by telephoners who felt that Fingers had cost Rodgers his job, and though Rodgers was no folk hero to the Milwaukee fans, he was perceived as being the victim of a spoiled, underachieving group of overpaid athletes.

On June 10, around 3:45 in the afternoon, Rollie Fingers took the mound for the seventh inning. It was rare for Fingers to be appearing in a game so early, and rarer still to hear a handful of boos. Harry Dalton, the man who had fired Rodgers, was upstairs in his box. Dalton had for a week been telling reporters that Fingers' outburst had had nothing to do with the firing, that he, Dalton, had been on the West Coast trip and had come to realize that the team was simply not in good shape. He had been especially upset by the team's behavior on the flight from Anaheim to Seattle.

Dalton put a high value on dignified comportment in public. The players were required to wear coats and ties while traveling, and Simmons, for one, had once been fined for wearing jeans with his blazer. Howell, Molitor, and Cooper, as well as Simmons and a few others, looked comfortable in their stylish clothing, but to most of the players, coat and tie were alien uniforms. Thomas and Money always wore the same brown leather jackets cut like suit coats, and Caldwell wore various ill-fitting costumes. Vuckovich was a sartorial catastrophe, his sharkskin-type suits, white-on-white shirts, and wraparound sunglasses making him look like a cross between a movie gangster and an overgrown teenager still trying to squeeze into his youthful church-and-wedding suit.

Dalton expected his manager to enforce the dress code, and to control his players' public behavior. The late-May trip to Seattle was made by commercial flight, and members of the team had indeed been behaving badly. Rodgers was either disinclined or unable to do anything about the rowdiness and profanity emanating from the rear cabin. When he rather gently admonished Mike Caldwell for swearing loudly, the pitcher said to his seatmates, "Fuck him. I hope we lose the next ten games so we can get rid of that fucker." Cecil Cooper, sitting nearby, said, "You don't mean that." Caldwell said he didn't, but the intensity of his feeling was clear.

But whether or not Fingers had had anything to do with Rodgers' dismissal, his presence in today's game was indicative of the role he played on Harvey Kuenn's team. Rodgers, too, used him whenever he could, but Kuenn was offering his team on Fingers' altar: if they might need him, they'd use him. Kuenn believed in using Fingers only (and always) when the Brewers were tied or barely ahead — the so-called save situation.

Earlier in the development of the use of relief pitchers, managers used their best bullpen arms to keep their teams in close games in which they were trailing — and a man like Pittsburgh's ElRoy Face, in 1958, could win 18 games in relief. Back then, the standard of measurement of a pitcher, relief or otherwise, was victories; the later recognition of the save as a meaningful statistic actually changed pitching strategies (credit for promulgating the save statistic goes to Chicago writer Jerome Holtzman). In the National League in 1958, there were .32 saves per game played (using the standards of measurement that were established later); twenty years later, there were .43 saves for every game played, an increase of more than 33 percent (in 1938, there were but .18 saves per NL game played, back in the days when managers generally put their least reliable pitchers in the bullpen). With the heralding of the new statistic came an award — the Rolaids Relief Award, licensed by Major League Baseball to an antacid manufacturer — and with the publicity afforded the statistic, and the award, accrued a new regard for the men who came in to shut the other team down. Foremost among these men was Rollie Fingers.

The fact that Fingers hadn't pitched since his one-inning tour against Oakland the previous Sunday was cause for some concern; like most relief pitchers, he thrived on regular work. But he still had a two-run cushion to work with, and today, Milwaukee bats were as alive as Baltimore's. Kuenn had earlier thought the game was Jim Slaton's to win or lose, and Slaton still stood to get credit for the victory if Fingers could pacify Baltimore. The act of bringing him on in the seventh, earlier than he normally would like, and knowing Slaton had the stamina (if not the stuff) to last longer, showed how much Kuenn felt it necessary to win this game and keep the Orioles from capturing four straight victories. "He's always ready for me," Kuenn said later. "You never have to worry about him. In return, I try not to make him get up twice in a game."

Fingers' brief warmup in the sixth had got him ready enough, he felt, and he took his time when he strolled into the infield from the bullpen at the top of the seventh. He handed his warmup jacket to a batboy, walked casually to the mound, and began to groom the area just in front of the pitcher's rubber, digging a proper toe hole with his spikes, smoothing out the excavations of the other men who had pitched today, tidying up his office. He was in no terrible hurry to take his allotted warmup pitches; his effort in the bullpen was, he felt, sufficient. He had been going through this ritual in the major leagues for fourteen seasons now. Baseball careers stretch long for men of great talent, like Fingers, as well as for men of lesser talent who care for their bodies and work to refine their skills. The California Angels had a pitcher named Steve Renko who was 37 when the 1982 season began — old, but by no means ancient in baseball. Yet by the standards of, say, football, Renko hailed from the prehistoric age: a quarterback at the University of Kansas, he had been a teammate of the great running back Gale Sayers. In the intervening years, Sayers had gone on to an outstanding professional career, retired, been elected to the Football Hall of Fame, and in the minds of football fans was a symbol of a long-ago era. And Steve Renko was still pitching in the major leagues.

Fingers had changed as a thrower but not as a pitcher. The distinction is a cliché, but like most clichés, it is grounded in reality. Like prizefighters who are either boxers or punchers, pitchers live by their skills or simply by their arms. Kuenn thought Fingers was "above average with just his stuff" — which is to say, his arm alone made him a valuable major leaguer. "Add his concentration, though," Kuenn continued, "and he's great. With Rollie Fingers' concentration, anyone would be a better pitcher."

Concentration: it was, in a way, what Ted Simmons thought distinguished Bob Gibson, in his case concentration as it manifested itself in Gibson's ability to focus his energies, his mind, his talents, on a given pitch. It was certainly Cecil Cooper's strength as a hitter, his use of careful analysis and the applied science he brought to every confrontation with a pitcher. Ray Poitevint spoke often about a prospect's "lower half," that part of his makeup that was not visible from skill evaluation lines at the top of scouting forms.

Concentration was a major element of the lower half, and confidence was perhaps the other most important element. Some superb natural athletes may be able to get by on the latter alone — in the sense that, as Yogi Berra reportedly said, "you can't hit and think at the same time." Apart from recognizing that if Yogi Berra actually said everything that has been attributed to him, *Bartlett's* would need a separate edition just to contain his *mots,* there is some wisdom in the comment. There are athletes whose natural skills are so extraordinary that analysis — thinking — can get in the way of innate confidence. The old National League first baseman Buddy Hassett remembered that Hall of Fame hitter Paul Waner "said he just laid his bat on his shoulder, and when he saw a pitch he liked he threw it off." But, on the whole, in the world of major league baseball, which contains only 650 athletes out of a nation (indeed, a hemisphere) of ball-playing boys — in such exclusive territory, few men are so gifted that they can rely solely on skill, and instead need to think, to concentrate, to focus their attention on the athletic problem at hand, season after season, game after game, pitch after pitch. This mental application is, some players maintain, far more grueling than the purely physical aspects of baseball.

Kuenn called Fingers' arm "above average" — meaningful praise but hardly an appraisal that one would expect for one of the two preeminent relief pitchers in all of baseball's history (the other was the old knuckleballer Hoyt Wilhelm, but knuckleballers are a breed apart, freaks in a way, and endlessly downgraded in discussions of greatness conducted by baseball men). But Fingers' knowledge of his own skills, and his limitations, had led him to adjust his game. He had, like most young pitchers, attained prominence on his fastball. He learned to make the fastball more effective by developing a slider. And when he recognized in 1980 that age and innings had taken the sheen off his fastball, and that hitters could afford to concentrate on the slider (especially lefties, who batted .314 against him that year), he developed a forkball — a pitch that ran straight up to the plate and then dropped precipitously. The forkball, popularized in the 1940s by Allie Reynolds and Tiny Bonham, was a good pitch on its own, but not something a pitcher could rely upon exclusively. For Fingers, the threat of the forkball made his fastball more effective with hitters who were ever on the lookout for surprise pitches; and once the fastball was thus reestablished, the slider was renewed.

Over his career, Fingers had pitched 94 innings against the Orioles, with a superb 1.82 earned run average, 7 victories, and 9 saves. But June 10 was the first time he had faced Baltimore in 1982, and in 1981 he had seen the team only twice, for a total of 3⅔ innings. Before 1981, he had for four seasons been in the National League. So his experience against these particular batters was limited, and the first man he would face — the rookie Cal Ripken Jr. — was someone totally new to Fingers.

He relied on his catcher, Moore, and he relied on what he had learned from the other Milwaukee pitchers and from the coaches. Mostly, though, Fingers relied on the generic fact of *pitching* — that there was a certain way one did one's work. He started Ripken with a fastball, but this pitch, the first young Ripken had ever seen from the great Rollie Fingers, was low and inside. Ripken could expect the slider next, probably away — and he proceeded to lunge for a Fingers slider so far away that the end of his bat didn't come within six inches of the ball. He then saw two more Fingers fastballs, the first one up out of the strike zone but the second one a pitch that ran in from the middle of the plate. Ripken sent it on a line into the left field corner, where an alert Oglivie corralled it before it reached the wall and held Ripken to a single.

Dan Ford, he of the extreme, back-to-the-pitcher stance, was next. Fingers, and all the Milwaukee pitchers, knew that the only way to pitch Ford was inside, way inside. So Fingers gave him four straight inside pitches, eventually building the count to 1 and 2. A fifth fastball Ford tipped back toward Moore, who could not hold it. And then Fingers tried a fastball away, and Ford lined it past Money at first. Ripken went to third, where Paul Molitor said to him, "If you're going to keep hitting it down the line, let me know, and I'll play over a bit."

Of course, Molitor wasn't going to move over, not yet, not even if he thought every ball would be hit down the line, as Ripken's had been. Both Ron Hansen, who positioned the infielders for Kuenn, and Kuenn himself had been in baseball too long: you put your first and third basemen on the line when you're one run up and it's the eighth or ninth inning. Until then, it is prudent to give up the potential double inside the bag when one run couldn't hurt you, rather than sacrifice an inning-extending single in the hole between third and short.

By the time Eddie Murray, dangerous and imposing Eddie Murray, came to the plate, Fingers had begun to question whether he had his good fastball today. He had been having difficulty controlling it, and when he came straight with it, neither Ford nor Ripken had had trouble handling it. It was a dilemma, for Murray was one of the best off-speed hitters in the league; he could jump on anything that wasn't a fastball and with his sheer power propel it out of the park in any direction. Fingers determined to pitch Murray low and away, where the hitter would be least dangerous. And he'd leave his fastball out of it; his fastball wasn't doing the job.

His first pitch was a slider, in the dirt, which Moore blocked by moving his body in front of it. It was the sort of work that makes catchers weary, and also the sort of work that saves games; here, it prevented Ripken from scoring on a wild pitch, and kept Ford, the tying run, from moving to second, where Baltimore would have three chances to bring him home. (Ned Yost, the third-string Milwaukee catcher, had actually trained for his vocation by having his high school coach, his teammates, his neighbors — anyone he could corral — throw balls in the dirt to him for hours on end while he would throw his body at the pitches, keeping them in front of him.)

At 1 and 0, Fingers threw his first forkball of the day. It dropped suddenly, without warning, just as Murray swung, and it went directly under the blur of Murray's bat. Another forkball made it 1 and 2; Fingers was getting into his groove. Each pitch, he'd reach back behind his head with his elastic right arm, then whip through his motion, his arm coming three quarters overhand, then release the pitch — fastball, slider, forkball — at the same point, with the same arm speed, using the same motion he had used since he was a 17-year-old. Expecting a fastball, Murray couldn't adjust for the sharp drop; expecting a forkball, he risked swinging underneath the pitch and popping it up harmlessly. A first fastball — a throwaway pitch, just to show Murray he had one — was out of the strike zone, and Murray fouled it off. The next pitch was another fork, and Murray was too high on it, pounding it into the ground, toward

195

the right-side hole. Money and Gantner raced toward it, Gantner won the race, and Fingers was at first before Murray, to get Gantner's throw for the out. Ripken scored on the play, and Ford moved to second. There was one out, the score now 7–6.

Fingers performed the play perfectly, instinctively calling forth the endless spring training repetition of the pitcher-covers-first exercise. His delivery, which culminated with Fingers storklike and erect on his forward-thrust left leg, employed enough force to carry his weight toward first at its completion anyway. It left him vulnerable to the bunt toward third, or to the smash back at the mound, but these were minor concerns. Nolan Ryan, the outstanding fastball pitcher of the age, had so much force and momentum in his enormous delivery that he'd complete each pitch in an area in front of the mound, way off toward first, his head down, never once seeing a bat hit one of his pitched balls. (He also, not incidentally, fielded his position about as poorly as any pitcher in baseball.)

With their lead down to one run, the Brewers' concern became the man on second. But on Murray's ground ball, Ford came up lame. After calling time, he limped off the base toward the outfield; Cal Ripken Sr., the third base coach, raced over and spoke briefly with Ford. Ripken, now in his twenty-fifth year in baseball — he played in the minors six years, managed there for another twelve, then scouted for one year before joining Weaver's staff in 1976 — knelt down next to Ford and grasped the player's left hamstring in his own strong hand, an act he had undoubtedly performed dozens of times before. Earl Weaver came running out, followed by his close friend, the Baltimore trainer, Ralph Salvon, an obese man whose presence on any field but Baltimore's own invariably brought forth hoots and catcalls from the stands. After a few moments of the trainer's ministrations, Ford limped off the field between Ripken and Salvon, Weaver five steps ahead of them, calling for Jim Dwyer in the dugout, beckoning him onto the field to run for Ford. Weaver had asked after Ford's health, and that was that; he had work to do.

Dwyer, the pinch runner, was yet another of the pieces in Weaver's tool kit. He was 32, and had played for St. Louis, Montreal, the New York Mets, the Cardinals again, the Giants, the Red Sox, and now Baltimore. He had never been a regular anywhere. He had a degree in accounting, and he loved to play baseball, even if it was clear he would never amount to more than what he was —

a useful and fairly maintenance-free employee who could accept a limited role. He was called "Pigpen," for the usual reasons. He was a left-handed hitter. All of these things made him a perfect Earl Weaver player. That is to say, the sum of his parts was not terribly auspicious, but his parts, considered individually, had real value.

Baltimore continued to chip at Fingers. He tried his fastball again against Al Bumbry, who hit a ground ball that hopped over Fingers' head when he was in his erect-stork position and enabled Dwyer to move to third as Jim Gantner threw the batter out at first. There were two outs when Weaver reached into his tool kit for the last of his outfield parts, John Lowenstein.

If Dwyer was valuable because of his varied attributes, Lowenstein was priceless. If Dwyer was rare — because of his dedication, his itinerant career, his accounting degree, his uncomplaining willingness to adapt — Lowenstein was unique. He was a beak-nosed man of 35 and had played in more than 100 games only twice in his eleven-year major league career. When he was with Cleveland, the Municipal Stadium organist took to playing a different "theme" for each Indian player, and signified Lowenstein with "Hava Nagila"; instructed that Lowenstein wasn't Jewish, the organist switched to "Jesus Christ Superstar." By the time he had his three hundredth major league at-bat, Lowenstein had played every position but pitcher and catcher. He had a B.A. in anthropology from the University of California and was without question the wittiest man in the American League, the ready supplier of cogent and clever quotes for any desperate writer. And he had the engaging quality, desperately rare in baseball, of self-deprecation, ready to turn his wit on himself. In the middle 1970s, he had given an interview to the *Wall Street Journal* in which he made the case for mediocrity in baseball, citing himself as a model example. That was around the same time that Lowenstein, having discouraged some Clevelanders from forming a fan club in his honor, instead gave his blessing to a "John Lowenstein Apathy Club."

But Lowenstein was more than a pleasing ornament to baseball; he had become a fine player, too. He had always had speed, and had employed it well by mastering the walking lead off first base, enabling him to steal bases by surprise and to reach third on routine singles. He knew how to play the outfield, could fill in virtually anywhere else, and had become an able hitter. In 1979, his first

Baltimore season, he hit 11 home runs in only 197 at-bats. (By way of comparison, that 1-HR-in-18-at-bats ratio stood up well to, say, Gorman Thomas's 1:17 ratio in 1981, or to the fact that Eddie Murray had only once in his prodigious career exceeded a 1:20 ratio.) In 1980, Weaver used Lowenstein so well that he hit .311 in 104 games. And thus far in 1982, with the season less than one third over, Lowenstein already had 11 home runs while still serving as a platoon player.

In the third inning, when Baltimore had chased Bob McClure and Kuenn countered with Jim Slaton, the lefty-righty switch set in motion Weaver's batting order machinations, with Bumbry hitting for the right-handed Benny Ayala. With that one stroke, he had given the Orioles an offensive edge, and improved the outfield defense as well, placing the experienced and quicker Bumbry in center and moving the able Roenicke to left, where he was a marked improvement over Ayala. Weaver could have had Lowenstein hit for Roenicke then, another righty-lefty switch, a switch to Lowenstein's very hot bat (he was .375 lifetime against Slaton), a switch that would have been at worst a wash defensively. But when one used as many chess pieces as Weaver did, one also learned to save some for the end game.

In the sixth inning, when Singleton's homer halved Milwaukee's lead to 7–5, Lowenstein saw that he would likely have a pitch-hitting opportunity in the game's last innings. Either Slaton was going to settle down, maintaining his lead and getting the lefty-righty edge against both Roenicke and Ford, or, if Slaton crumbled, Kuenn would have to go to Fingers, and the same platoon advantages applied. Lowenstein had spent so much of his career as a part-time player he had learned how to stay in the game mentally, and he had learned as well how to loosen up on short notice. Sometimes Weaver would tell him to get ready; most of the time, he knew when to do so instinctively. He'd go into the clubhouse, or the dugout runway, and swing a bat, do some stretching exercises. By the time the batting order reached Roenicke's spot, Lowenstein was as involved, and as ready, as if he'd been in the starting lineup.

Fingers was less ready. He had allowed the gap to close to one run, and he had put the tying run on third. His fastball was still refusing to come under his control. And in Lowenstein he was facing a batter who, in Fingers' words, was "the toughest out on their team. I don't know why, but nobody for us gets him out. It just doesn't make any difference what you throw him. I don't want to give him anything to pull. I want to spot everything against him, one pitch inside, then outside. I want him to hit my pitch, but he always ends up with his pitch." Fingers might well have listened to Jim Slaton, who said, "I have no idea how to pitch him. I think I should have the catcher *tell* him what's coming — maybe that would make him think too much." And Moore, the catcher, was even more flummoxed: "Forget it — I haven't any idea what to do with him. I've been going against him for nine years. He killed us when he was with Cleveland, he killed us when he was with Texas, and he kills us now. It seems everything we try to do with him is wrong. Every year it's the same — basically, you just throw it up there and hope."

Lowenstein took a spread, knees-bent stance and stared at an outside slider before fouling off Fingers' inside fastball. Fingers then appeared to do what Moore had melancholically suggested — he threw a fastball up there and hoped — and Lowenstein, lifting his front foot with his swing, a curly-haired, mustachioed, modern Mel Ott, slapped a single into right, bringing Dwyer home. Baltimore had come from four runs back and tied the score. At last, Fingers knew for sure not only that his fastball was difficult to spot today but that it was, simply, "horseshit." His shoulders heaved noticeably, and he looked perplexed and somewhat beaten as he rubbed up the ball for the next batter, Ken Singleton.

Singleton was having a bad year, but in this series his bat had enlivened; he was 7 for 17 against Milwaukee pitching. Fingers now had to summon up his concentration, for the game was dangerously close to getting out of control. Wasting a fastball to start, he stuck with his slider, even though he knew Singleton was more vulnerable to fastballs; Moore, in fact, claimed that fastballs inside were the only way to get Singleton consistently. But Fingers was now going with the hoary dictum of "best to best," using his most effective pitch despite the batter's traits. It implied a macho approach, but that wasn't really it. Fingers knew he wasn't going to be able to "think" his way around Singleton. Now it was time for that other element of his "lower half": his confidence, his competitiveness. On the third straight slider, Singleton struck out, and Baltimore's inning was over.

Kuenn later said, "I was concerned. I saw he wasn't pinpoint sharp, and that his fastball wasn't working. But any given pitch can turn Rollie around and make him as sharp as you want him to be." He paused. "I try to keep an even keel, and it's easier to do it when I've got the best relief pitcher in baseball on the mound. I had to have faith in him." It recalled the comment of another manager, Johnny Keane, who said in 1964 about another pitcher, "I had a commitment to his heart." The pitcher was Bob Gibson.

	1	2	3	4	5	6	7	8	9	R	H	E
Baltimore	1	2	0	0	0	2	2			7	15	2
Milwaukee	2	0	4	0	1	0				7	12	0

At 7–7, in the middle of the seventh, Baltimore took the field with the sixth man in Milwaukee's order scheduled to bat. Around the infield, the lineup hadn't changed; Murray was at first, Dauer at second, Sakata at short, and Ripken at third. Dempsey, who was in the on-deck circle when Singleton struck out, was still in the dugout, buckling on his shin guards and chest protector. On the mound, replacing Storm Davis, was Felix Anthony "Tippy" Martinez, a left-handed Coloradan. And in the outfield, Al Bumbry took his place in center field, flanked in left by Lowenstein, in right by Dwyer. It was a total remake of the outfield — Ayala, Roenicke, and Ford — that had started the game for Baltimore.

Switching to Martinez was, obviously, an intermediate step for Weaver. Roy Howell, Charlie Moore, Marshall Edwards, and Jim Gantner were the next scheduled batters for Milwaukee — three lefties and Moore, who slapped the ball with approximately equal proficiency against right-handed or left-handed pitchers. By bringing in Martinez, Weaver could force Kuenn to turn his lineup around, bringing in pinch hitters at least for Howell and Edwards. He could counter then in the eighth or ninth with Tim Stoddard, his immense right-handed reliever.

Weaver's move to Martinez was an obvious one, especially given the nature of the Milwaukee team, which had fewer movable parts than did the Orioles. With Cooper hurt, what flexibility the team had was largely lost; Money, normally used as part of a left-right platoon with Howell, or as a right-handed pinch hitter for Edwards, was in the starting lineup. That left on the bench Mark Brouhard, a right-handed-hitting outfielder who couldn't play center; Rob Picciolo and Ed Romero, the reserves for Gantner and Yount and, today, because Money and Howell were both in the lineup, the backups for Molitor as well; Ned Yost, the third-string catcher, also a right-handed hitter; and Ted Simmons. Simmons couldn't run; as a catcher, he suffered from an inconsistent throwing arm; he was unable to play any other position with anything approaching real proficiency. Yet Simmons was the key to the bench today, just as he was the key to the team: it took its personality, it had acquired its shape, and it in many ways derived its identity from this thick-set trainee banker from St. Louis.

Simmons had not become a Brewer by any grand design of Harry Dalton's. In fact, his acquisition by the team was accidental, unduly expensive, and in many ways awkward. But through the machinations of Whitey Herzog, then the general manager as well as manager of the St. Louis Cardinals, Dalton found himself forced, in a way, to make Simmons a Brewer.

Dalton's arrival in Milwaukee after the 1977 season was the moment Bud Selig first began to believe his woeful expansion team would someday contend. An outlandish string of bad luck, and the perceived meddling of Angels owner Gene Autry, had enabled Dalton to emerge from his California experience with his reputation only barely tarnished. Buzzie Bavasi, a lifelong baseball man whose critics claimed had risen in the game through the obsequious behavior he offered his various employers, joined the Angels' staff as an aide to Autry, and Selig saw that Dalton was the likely loser in California's interoffice warfare. Selig brought Dalton in to run the baseball operation, Dalton brought in his old Baltimore employee George Bamberger to manage the club, various products of the Brewer system reached major league maturity, and in 1978 they suddenly became a contending team. The most games the Brewers had ever won in their bleak history was 76, in 1974, when they finished 15 games out of first. In 1977, they won only 67, 33 games behind the division-winning Yankees. But in 1978, the Brewers won 93 games; they were but 6 games out of first; they finished third.

In 1979, they were even better, winning 95 games, but the Orioles won 103, and the pennant. There was slippage in 1980, to 86 victories, but still the Brewers finished third. What was clear to the Milwaukee fans, and clearer still to Dalton and his colleagues, was that the Brewers had gone about as far as they could with a team that was notably bereft of one critical element: quality relief pitching.

Thus did Dalton set out in the 1980–81 off-season to search for the relief pitcher who could make his team a genuine pennant contender. It seemed simple enough: he would have to trade one or more of his established players (Gorman Thomas was the prime candidate) for such a pitcher, for a man, say, like Bruce Sutter, the outstanding right-hander who labored in vain for the lowly Chicago Cubs.

Dalton arrived in Dallas on December 6, 1980, for the annual ritual of baseball's winter meetings. He and the eight men who made up his brain trust — the Dalton Gang — gathered that day to plan their attacks on whichever baseball vaults contained pitching, especially relief pitching. In addition to Dalton, those present included Bob Rodgers; George Bamberger, by then serving as a special assistant to Dalton; scouting director Ray Poitevint, and his assistant, Bruce Manno; assistant general manager Walter Shannon; and scouts Dee Fondy, Ray Scarborough, and Walter Youse. Dalton assigned each man a list of clubs with which to maintain communication in the days ahead. On Monday, December 8, after a day and a half of renewing old acquaintances, trying to squeeze information from the competition, and generally taking the pulse of the meetings, Dalton and his colleagues convened in his suite at Loew's Anatole Hotel at nine o'clock in the morning. The previous Sunday afternoon, an anxious and distracted Dalton had told his wife, Pat, "This is one of the biggest weeks of my career." She took it as a signal to keep her distance. By Sunday evening, the Cardinals had announced they had acquired Rollie Fingers as part of an 11-player trade with San Diego.

At the Monday morning meeting, Walter Shannon spoke first. Well into his seventies, Shannon had spent nearly fifty years in baseball front offices. He had ended his playing career, still a minor leaguer, in 1934, and started a free baseball school in St. Louis. He went to the old Browns for help, and they gave him a few free balls. He then went to the Cardinals, and Branch Rickey gave him uniforms, equipment, and a salary.

Shannon stayed in the Cardinal front office until 1962 and then spent three years scouting for Cleveland. When Dalton became Baltimore general manager in 1966, he hired Shannon to run the farm system, and they had been together ever since. In Dallas, Shannon was responsible for following the maneuvers of the Cardinals, among other clubs. He had not yet learned whether Herzog, who was for the first time functioning with the free hand of a general manager, was still trying to get Sutter from the Cubs or whether he was content to proceed with the newly acquired Fingers as the mainstay of the Cardinal bullpen. "If St. Louis gets Sutter," Dalton said, "we should talk to them about Fingers." Shannon spoke as well about Cincinnati, San Francisco, the White Sox, and the Mariners; there was the possibility of the Giants' left-handed reliever, Gary Lavelle, but Seattle — who had pitchers Milwaukee liked — was a "complete zero" right now. The Mariners, trying to stock their expansion club roster with several usable players for the one or two truly talented men on their team, wanted far too much, Shannon said.

The conversation proceeded methodically around the room. George Bamberger said, "Boston needs what we need." Dee Fondy, a former big league first baseman who looked and talked like a slightly older Clint Eastwood, hadn't turned up anything with the Phillies. Rodgers said the Angels were asking for either Paul Molitor or Robin Yount for Mark Clear, which was patently out of the question. Walter Youse, the Eastern scouting supervisor, reported that a friend in the Orioles' organization was saying that Dennis Martinez's arm was sound. (It was information to be weighed carefully; Walter Shannon had learned from Branch Rickey never to say negative things about one's own players to people in other organizations, precisely *because* you might want to trade them later.) Baltimore had an abundance of pitchers, and although Martinez was a starter, he had an arm to envy, and in Youse he had an important backer. Shannon called Youse "the Godfather," a term of respect and a little awe. He was one of the most sagacious scouts in baseball, a short, portly, decidedly unathletic man who lived on a hilltop in Maryland and ventured down to pass usually unerring judgments on the abilities of high school boys and major leaguers alike. Dalton turned to Bruce Manno, Poitevint's assistant, and told him to call scout Felix Delgado. Delgado was in the Caribbean, and could give Dalton an appraisal of Martinez's performance in winter ball.

There were other players discussed, starters as well as relievers, players who might improve Milwaukee's pitching. Oakland might part with Steve McCatty, a starter, but they wanted Jim Gantner, and it was Gantner's promise that enabled Rodgers and Dalton to plan Molitor's 1981 shift to center field. Texas had relievers Jim Kern and John Henry Johnson — both of whom, it turned out, would slide precipitously downhill in the years immediately following — and there appeared to be an outside chance to get Joe Sambito from Houston. Then the talk returned to the Cards, who had Fingers and might soon have Sutter; then, the topic was the Cubs, who still had Sutter.

The month before, at the general managers' meeting in Florida, Cub executive vice president Bob Kennedy had been ready to trade Sutter to Herzog for outfielder Leon Durham and third baseman Ken Reitz. But he told Dalton that he'd prefer to trade Sutter for Molitor. Dalton countered by offering Gorman Thomas, who was being shunted out of center field anyway; Kennedy declined, insisting on Molitor. Now, in Dalton's suite in the Anatole, Ray Scarborough spoke. Scarborough, called "Hook," as much for his nose as for the curve he threw for various American League teams in the '40s and early '50s, was a special assignment scout. He was a heavy man, with thinning hair, a Carolina drawl, and a knack for the discursive anecdote. But he was also remarkably direct when he chose to be. Of Kennedy's Sutter-for-Molitor offer, he said, "Do we want to do it?" Dalton polled the room; the brain trust was split, 4-4. Even those who wanted to make the trade said, "It'd be very unpopular," or "You're going to have to answer the mail, Harry." Dalton said he'd think about it some. In the meantime, he wanted his people to find out what was the best deal they could make for Molitor, if they decided to trade him.

While the Milwaukee staff pursued hard intelligence in the lobbies and corridors of the hotel, Herzog continued with his hyperactive role at the meetings. In addition to the San Diego trade, which had brought him catcher Gene Tenace in addition to Fingers, he had announced on Sunday that he had signed Darrell Porter, the Kansas City catcher, to a free-agent contract. Herzog had managed the Royals before he arrived in St. Louis, and Porter had been one of his favorites. History and sentiment made the Porter signing logical. What was less so was Herzog's resulting stockpile of catchers: Porter, Tenace, and Ted Simmons.

Herzog also used his Sunday press conference to confirm that Ken Reitz, his third baseman, had invoked his contractual right to veto his trade to the Cubs, as part of a Sutter deal. Speaking to Reitz, and his agent LaRue Harcourt, through the medium of the reporters gathered for a press conference, Herzog said, "I like Kenny Reitz, I really do, but next year I'm playing Ken Oberkfell at third, and the first guy in my office is going to be Kenny Reitz, saying 'Get me out of here.' "

And thus did LaRue Harcourt fly into Dallas, to look after the interests of Reitz, one of his 25 major league clients. Harcourt thought he would resolve things with Reitz, the Cubs, and the Cardinals (resolution would come in the form of a $150,000 buyout of Reitz's no-trade rights, each club putting up half the sum), and return to California.

But Sunday night, when he heard Herzog had signed Porter, Harcourt had to change his plans: he was obviously going to have to stay in Dallas longer than he had expected, working in behalf of another client, Ted Simmons.

"I was totally stymied," Harcourt said later. "I mean, all these plans I had, the blueprint was all screwed up. I couldn't figure it out." His plans had been to see Simmons through the end of his current contract in 1983, and then move him to the American League, where Simmons' value as a designated hitter could be fully realized as he wound down his career.

Harcourt was a former college teacher who stumbled into sports agentry by accident back in the days before free-agency, when he helped a few players plan their investments. He was quiet, unassuming, decidedly unflashy, nearly clergylike: the antithesis of the popular image of an agent. He did not see his professional life as a war with general managers and club owners. He thought of himself as a conservator and enhancer of his clients' wealth, and as a planner of their futures. His "blueprint" for Simmons had been long in the planning, and looked, until that Sunday in Dallas, to be sound and secure. "Then I realized with Porter in here, that makes Teddy expendable; now St. Louis can get what they really need, maybe two starting pitchers." The blueprint was shot, and Harcourt changed his plane reservations and went looking for Whitey Herzog.

On Monday afternoon, with his men fanned out, chasing down as many cul-de-sacs as potentially profitable avenues, Harry Dalton took stock. He struck Toronto from his list. St. Louis was still alive, once Reitz agreed to the buyout and Sutter was shipped southward. Texas was still a possibility, and the Cubs, already stripped of their top reliever, were now dangling their number two man, Dick Tidrow. Dalton also had a meeting scheduled with Baltimore's

Hank Peters, to see if two of Baltimore's stockpile of pitchers could be pried loose for Sixto Lezcano, then the Milwaukee right fielder. Lezcano had had a bad year — .229 batting average, 18 home runs, 55 runs batted in — in 1980, but in '79 his numbers had been .328, 28, 101.

Houston had removed Joe Sambito's name from consideration, nothing had developed in Oakland, and Seattle was still holding out for too much. And Paul Molitor, Dalton had decided over lunch, was not available. "The long-range risk," he said, "just isn't worth it." He had in Molitor a player he thought could be a genuine star for ten, fifteen years.

On Tuesday morning, the Anatole lobbies were full, men in open-collared shirts rocking on their heels, smiling, slapping backs; others, also dressed for play, were in tighter, more earnest conversations, clumps of conspirators doing the business of baseball. The Anatole, tucked into the elbow of a freeway northwest of downtown Dallas, has twin lobbies that soar ten and fourteen stories' worth of atrium space to the skylit roofs; reporters on the balcony outside the mezzanine press room could keep an eye on the door to a general manager's suite and watch who was coming and going. Stories were started that way.

The official business of the winter meetings consists of innumerable sessions for the minor league clubs, meetings of rules committees, meetings of trainers and team doctors, meetings of traveling secretaries who convene with hotel and airline representatives, meetings of the owners, of course, and of every other imaginable grouping of nonuniformed baseball people. In the Batik Room, on the mezzanine, a perpetual meeting was held for job seekers — scores of supplicants, mostly young, mostly men, looking for their first baseball job. Donald Osik, 27, who had come down from Connecticut, was trying to find the job that would someday land him in the back-slapping crowds down in the lobby. Osik had sent letters to every major and minor league club earlier in the fall; only half bothered to reply, and of those, only one offered him so much as an opportunity to be interviewed. There were experienced job seekers, too. One, looking to catch on as a trainer, a position he had occupied before too much drinking had cost him his last job, was there to help himself, but also to shatter the illusions of those who saw baseball in a particularly noble light. "Remember Harry Agganis?" he asked, speaking of the one-time Boston Red Sox prospect, the so-called Golden Greek, who had died suddenly as his career was just getting started, and who had since been lionized in Boston. "Well, I knew Harry Agganis, and he was a *prick.*"

Among Tuesday's meetings for the employed was the annual managers' luncheon, where the 26 club leaders sat for a meal with the press. Midway through the meal, Bob Rodgers was called out to join Dalton, Scarborough, and Bamberger for an impromptu meeting. Discussions centering on Dick Tidrow had progressed, and while Tidrow was not nearly of the caliber of Sutter or Fingers, he was available, he was better than anyone the Brewers had, and he'd make an excellent number two reliever if Milwaukee managed to land one of the prime targets. It was now simply a matter of haggling with the Cubs over which prospect the Brewers would have to give up for Tidrow.

Dalton had given the Cubs a list of five young players, all but one of whom had spent at least some time in the major leagues. Rodgers, whose role in the week's decision-making was second only to Dalton's, expressed concern that one of the players on the list — David LaPoint, a left-hander the Brewers had brought to the major league brink — could turn into a 15-game winner. Bamberger said, "Good luck to him. Don't look back." A deal for Tidrow seemed imminent.

But Dalton had a meeting scheduled for three o'clock that afternoon with Herzog to pursue the possibility, first, of Rollie Fingers and, second, of Pete Vuckovich. It was two months earlier that Herzog had called to ask Dalton if he would trade right-handers even up, Lary Sorensen for Vuckovich. That call was prompted when Herzog heard from Bob Woolf, Vuckovich's agent, that he was looking for a long-term contract that Woolf described as "similar to Bob Forsch's." Herzog had just signed the latter pitcher to a deal reported in the area of $3.5 million over six years, and hadn't the will to go as far for Vuckovich. The Cardinals were not yet a contender, and Herzog saw no reason to plunge. It was a variant of the situation Bill Veeck, then owner of the St. Louis Browns, had found himself in twenty-nine years earlier, when 20-game winner Ned Garver had asked for a raise. Veeck told him, "We finished last with you. It's a cinch we can finish last without you."

Dalton had said no to Herzog's Vuckovich-for-Sorensen offer in October, and he said no again at the general managers' meeting in November — but he did have Dee Fondy do the sort of detective work that Dalton deemed critical in player evaluation. Fondy and other Milwaukee scouts admired Vuckovich's wide variety of pitches, and they liked his on-the-field composure as well; Ray Scarborough said, "He loves that mound." They felt, too, that Vuckovich could start or relieve, although had they asked Vuckovich they would have learned he detested relieving. He had been in that role once before, with the White Sox, playing for manager Paul Richards, a tactician celebrated for his knowledge of pitching. "I'll tell you what he knew about pitching," Vuckovich said. "He made me a reliever, and he made Goose Gossage a starter."

Dalton assigned Fondy to check whether the rumors of arm trouble that hovered around Pete Vuckovich were true, or whether the celebrated tales of Vuckovich's high times off the field were serious enough to merit staying away from him. Calling on his St. Louis contacts along the baseball grapevine — in Dalton's words, "Anyone from the guy you roomed with in Double A ball who might be coaching now, to the visiting clubhouse boy in Atlanta, to ushers who see a lot of games and hotel personnel who see a lot of ball players off the field" — Fondy learned nothing that would dampen Brewer interest.

In Dallas, at 2:30 Tuesday afternoon, St. Louis began to loom ever more prominent in the Brewer game plan. The Cubs had just informed Dalton they wanted two prospects for Tidrow, which gave Dalton pause. Yet he did not approach the St. Louis meeting with terribly high hopes. "They sound too eager," he said. But Dalton was kept waiting nonetheless, as Whitey Herzog and LaRue Harcourt met for most of Tuesday afternoon. Herzog had earlier told Harcourt his plans for Ted Simmons, and they did not involve a trade. Instead, Herzog said, he was going to put Darrell Porter behind the plate, switch Simmons to first, and move first baseman Keith Hernandez to left. Herzog told Harcourt he had talked with Simmons, "and it was fine with him."

Now, though, on Tuesday afternoon, this was less clear. Harcourt had called Simmons, and Simmons insisted he had never thought it was "fine": it was, he said, putting a peculiar semantic point on it, "fine, *but* . . ." Ted Simmons did not want to play first, at least not in St. Louis, where he worried he would embarrass himself by replacing Hernandez, the most adept first baseman in the league.

So as Dalton waited, Harcourt told Herzog it was not fine, that Ted Simmons wanted to catch 100 games in St. Louis or be traded —

to the American League ideally, to a contender if possible. Herzog, who had earlier determined that he didn't particularly want the headstrong, stubborn Simmons on his team, told Harcourt he'd try.

Walter Shannon had already carried conversations with St. Louis to the point where a Fingers and Vuckovich for Sorensen and Lezcano deal was on the table. But Herzog had had his own staff poll all the American League contenders after his meeting with Harcourt, and he had learned that only Milwaukee was interested in Simmons as a catcher. As Simmons had the right to veto a trade — he had ten years in the major leagues, at least five with the same club, was a so-called five-and-ten man — Herzog had to deal with Milwaukee, if he felt Simmons and Harcourt were serious about his desire to catch. So Herzog said to Dalton and Shannon at their afternoon meeting, "Okay, if you guys want to win a pennant, here it is: Ted Simmons."

The catch was the price. Dalton quickly agreed to add Dave LaPoint to the trade, and was trying to determine what else was necessary, when Herzog insisted that a young man named David Green, who had yet to play Triple A ball and had not even hit .300 in Double A, be part of the deal. St. Louis scout Angel Figueroa called Green the best prospect he'd seen in ten years. Had Dalton thought about giving up Green? "Never. He was never even discussed at a staff meeting. We had not even tried to assess his market value. He was even further out of the question than Molitor."

Ray Poitevint first saw David Green play when he was on a scouting trip to Nicaragua in 1976. Poitevint was the first American baseball executive to take an active interest in the Central American country; his first discovery there, when he was still in the Orioles' front office, was Dennis Martinez. "David Green was 15 years old when I saw him," Poitevint said. "He was extremely gifted, a kid playing in a league with guys 25 to 30, guys who would've made a pretty decent Double A club. Carlos Garcia told us about him." Garcia, who was in charge of Nicaragua's national amateur baseball program, was in 1980 serving a ten-year prison sentence meted out shortly after the Sandinistas overthrew the Somoza government.

"David Green," Poitevint continued, "is without a doubt the most talented prospect — physically and mentally — I have been associated with in the twenty-two years I've been involved in scouting. Any good scout can see physical ability. You sign a prospect if you think he has the physical tools to play in the major leagues. What stops the majority of those players is their mental makeup. Look at Pete Rose: he doesn't have the greatest tools, but he's got the number one mental makeup in the game. And David Green has Willie Mays's physical abilities and Pete Rose's mental abilities."

By Wednesday, St. Louis was the only club with whom the Brewers were still having productive conversations. Dalton didn't want to trade Green, and was hoping he could still make a deal that didn't include him. He wasn't wholly confident, though. Pat Dalton, who had attended eight other winter meetings with her husband, and had been married into the game for twenty-two years, said, "The strain on Harry was like nothing I'd ever seen before. I gave him as much space as he needed; I answered phones; I occupied myself. It was like outer space."

By Thursday morning, Herzog and Dalton knew a deal could be made. Although Herzog was still insisting there was no deal without Green, and although Dalton was "still trying to dodge that particular bullet," things had fallen into place; the Milwaukee staff vote on trading Green had gone 5–3 in favor. "I had given Whitey fourteen names, the best prospects in our system except David, and I said, 'Whitey, take one, take two.' But then Whitey said it was David Green or no deal."

Dalton had reason to believe Herzog was not bluffing. On Wednesday, he had heard from someone with another club that the Yankees were after Vuckovich. Early Thursday morning, one of Dalton's staff members overheard a conversation in the lobby among several Yankee officials. It was about Vuckovich, and a pending deal with the Cards.

So when they met early Thursday, Dalton asked Herzog if the Yankees were indeed making offers, and Herzog confirmed it. Not too long after, they shook hands, and Herzog gave Dalton two pieces of paper: one giving him permission to discuss contractual matters with Simmons' agent, LaRue Harcourt, and one informing Harcourt that this permission had been granted.

When Harcourt first met Ted Simmons, in 1971, it was still the paleolithic era of baseball representation. "At that time," Harcourt recalled, "the contract was the least important thing I did for the athlete. You learned to stand there with your hat in your hand and appeal to management's sense of reason and fairness." Mostly, Harcourt helped his clients with investment and tax problems.

Through the combination of his own negotiating skills, the changes in the game's financial structure, and Simmons' own considerable athletic achievements, Harcourt was able to guide Simmons from his first full-year contract of $22,000 to his current five-year agreement, which brought Simmons $640,000 a year. Harcourt was the first agent to negotiate a free-agent contract, when pitcher Bill Campbell signed with the Red Sox in 1976. "The free-agent explosion was the result of supply and demand," Harcourt said. "Here you were picking up a prime player with no development costs. That was instead of signing 20 kids, and having one of them reach the big leagues five years later — as an *average* major leaguer. The cost to the club for those 20 players would run half a million dollars; to develop an outstanding player, it might cost one or two or three million."

According to Harry Dalton, Harcourt's estimates were, if anything, a little low. He saw David Green's potential value as incalculable. Ray Poitevint remained opposed to the trade, but Dalton knew that his farm director would *have* to be against it — Green was his prize. Ray Scarborough told Poitevint that he, Poitevint, was going to be a general manager with some other club in a few years anyway; besides, as Dalton put it, "Not every phenom phenominates." Poitevint didn't argue with Dalton, but he continued to "feel more confident about David Green" than about any prospect he'd "ever seen."

Dalton and Harcourt met for the first time on Thursday afternoon. The agent — representing a player who had, three days earlier, asked his club to trade him — requested a payment of $1 million for the waiver of Simmons' right to veto the trade. "I was thinking, how bad do they want to make this trade?" Harcourt said. "Now, I reason Ted's worth 1 to 1.1 million dollars a year in today's market, especially in the American League. I wanted other considerations, too, because look what Milwaukee's getting: your right-handed DH, your left-handed DH, close to an outstanding catcher, and a backup at first base. He ought to be worth a ton." One million dollars added to the three remaining years of Simmons' contract would bring his annual compensation up to $973,000.

Harry Dalton, for his part, first asked that the nonfinancial considerations — covenants involving future freedoms for Simmons — be removed from the table. Harcourt agreed soon enough, and they began to argue about money. Dalton had no problem conjuring with the *idea* of buying a player's right to approve a trade; it was, he reasoned, not a precedent at all but rather "just like a free agent's situation," adding, "We are attempting to buy a player's acceptance of our employment."

So Dalton was prepared to spend — but on Thursday afternoon, he reminded himself that he might still have a shot at a smaller deal, one that didn't involve a recalcitrant Simmons and thus would not involve Green. Failing even at that, he could now turn to the Phillies, who Fondy had learned were willing to part with a pitcher or two for Lezcano. Dalton wanted Simmons, but he had come to these meetings for a relief pitcher. If he failed now, he reasoned, he could try again during the spring interleague trading period, which the clubs had initiated precisely to give them further maneuverability.

Until 1972, and the first Basic Agreement between the ball clubs and the Players Association, the no-trade contract was illegal — if not formally proscribed, then at least effectively prohibited by the two league offices, neither of which would assent to any such covenant. In that 1972 document, however, Marvin Miller, representing the players, was able to negotiate the right of a "five-and-ten man" to veto a trade. Clauses of a like nature began to appear in contracts as a result of negotiation, too — clauses inserted by the agents of players who simply did not want to move against their wishes. General managers and agents alike did not realize for several years that a five-and-ten right, or a negotiated no-trade proscription, had monetary value. The first five-and-ten man to turn down a trade, Ron Santo, did so in 1973 without the matter of money being raised by either side. The general manager who tried to acquire Santo remembered, "It didn't even occur to us to mention the possibility of money." That general manager was Harry Dalton.

By 1980, most agents had come to realize that a no-trade covenant was a fungible asset. The clubs were slower to realize it. The Cleveland Indians, in fact, had not too much earlier given first baseman Andre Thornton a no-trade clause instead of the additional $50,000 Thornton's agent was asking. But another club — the Orioles — realized the value of no-trade clauses so well they insisted, while negotiating with third baseman Doug DeCinces, that if agent Ron Shapiro wanted a no-trade clause, he would have to have in the contract as well a specified buyout fee, to prevent DeCinces from holding up a trade at deadline time by making tough demands. The DeCinces clause became a model for many other clubs, but in Dallas, LaRue Harcourt and Ted Simmons were not limited by any contractual encumbrances.

When Whitey Herzog and his staff had first begun to investigate American League possibilities for Ted Simmons, they were surprised to learn that Milwaukee was the only contender willing to put Simmons behind the plate. Although his arm was erratic, and though he had once allowed 28 passed balls in one season, just one short of the modern major league record, Simmons was difficult to dislodge on a tag play at home and was certainly adept — if a little cerebral — at calling a pitcher's game. But by Thursday in Dallas, the pending Milwaukee deal had become the chief topic of conversation and speculation in the Anatole's lobbies. Further, Harcourt's position — that Simmons did not want to catch fewer than 100 games in *St. Louis* — had now to be understood in a different way: with the designated hitter option in the American League, Simmons' distaste for first base was no longer so important. Among those clubs who realized this — and were fearful of one of their chief rivals' acquiring players of the caliber of Simmons, Vuckovich, and Fingers — was the New York Yankees.

"The Yankees came back to me," Whitey Herzog said later, "and I told them I had a deal with Harry Dalton worked out, and I wasn't going to do anything unless Harry called me up and said he couldn't sign Simmons. But the Yankees offered me a very good deal" — it included New York's best pitcher, Ron Guidry — "and I knew I could make that if Harry couldn't come to an agreement with Ted."

Thus, late Thursday afternoon, Dalton learned from Herzog that because of the New York offer, the Milwaukee fallback — a smaller St. Louis deal — was no longer possible. It was the seven players agreed upon or no deal at all. Meanwhile, Dalton and Harcourt were making little progress on the buyout of Simmons' right to kill the trade. Early in the evening, they broke off their talks until after dinner, and Harcourt and his wife, Alice, settled into one of the Anatole's lobby restaurants. They dined in the company of a number of reporters who kept dropping by, seeking the latest news on the Simmons negotiations. It was the Harcourts' ninth wedding anniversary.

While the Harcourts ate in, at the Anatole, Dalton ventured outside the hotel's artificial air for the first time since Monday. The Daltons, the Seligs, and fifteen other people connected with the Brewers celebrated their annual winter meeting dinner at the Chateaubriand, a Dallas restaurant. The party broke up fairly early, as Harcourt was waiting back at the hotel for Dalton and Selig, who had come into the negotiations because of the sums involved. The Brewers knew about the Yankees, lying in wait. It was, Ray Scarborough said, "nut-cutting time."

At the hotel, Harcourt and Dalton and Selig talked at each other until 2 A.M. Harcourt had brought his price down to $800,000; Dalton and Selig offered less than half that. Tom Flaherty of the *Journal* and Rick Hummel of the *St. Louis Post-Dispatch* teamed up and alternated calling Dalton's room and Harcourt's every fifteen minutes. Shortly after 2 A.M., back in his room, Harcourt told Hummel, "I think it's got a chance." Later in the same conversation, the long hours taking their toll, he said, "My gut feeling is it won't be made."

In Dalton's room, at 2:15 A.M., the Associated Press called. The reporter asked, "Can I go to bed now?" Dalton told him, "You can do whatever you want, but *I'm* going to bed now."

In the room adjoining Dalton's, Bud Selig paced the floor. He had struggled to wrench a franchise out of Organized Baseball, and then he had endured a laughingstock of a team for eight years. Almost as bad, for three years now he had suffered the frustration of coming close, seeing a pennant within reach, but seeing it at the same time slipping further away. He wanted Vuckovich and Simmons and especially Fingers in Milwaukee uniforms. Later, he remembered saying to himself, "If it's worth doing this, I'm going to have to find some other parts of the operation to cut to make it work. I knew that when we got home, I was going to put our whole organization through the most difficult budgeting process in the world, and cut enough money out to justify what we did in Dallas." It wasn't quite as serious as when Boston owner Harry Frazee sold Babe Ruth to the Yankees in 1920 for $125,000 and a $315,000 loan, for which Frazee put up Fenway Park as collateral, but this was a big move for Milwaukee.

In the morning, Bud Selig called his controller, Dick Hoffman, back home in Milwaukee and told him to get out his budget knives. Dalton, awakened at 6 A.M. by a phone call from a television station in Green Bay, turned phone duty over to his wife. Herzog had given Dalton until 1 P.M. Friday. Dalton instructed Dee Fondy to renew talks with the Philadelphia Phillies, who were offering various combinations of pitchers Ron Reed, Dickie Noles, and Bob Walk for Lezcano — a small deal, not a pennant-winning deal, but the only option left. The Yankees got back in touch with Herzog, and openly downgraded the Milwaukee players in the proposed Simmons trade. Herzog was somewhat insulted.

At 10:30 A.M. Friday, barely half a day from the interleague trading deadline, Harcourt told Dalton that Simmons would turn down the $375,000 buyout the Brewers had offered. Harcourt was convinced Dalton and Selig would have readily sent the four players and $800,000 to the Cards for the St. Louis Three; he was asking only that the money be sent to a different bank account. He knew Dalton was concerned with his salary structure. Later, Dalton — who had visions of Cecil Cooper, Gorman Thomas, and his other established stars trooping into his office — did not disagree.

Finally, around noon, Dalton got permission from Harcourt to call Simmons. He told the catcher about how Frank Robinson paved his way to the Hall of Fame when he joined the Orioles and led them to the pennant; he told him about Milwaukee, about the team, about how Bob Rodgers planned to use him. Pat Dalton spoke to Simmons' wife about the cultural opportunities in Milwaukee.

When Dalton got off the phone, he secured a deadline extension from Herzog. And when Harcourt walked into Dalton's room shortly after one o'clock, Dalton jumped the offer to $745,000, over three years. "That's quite a change in your position," Harcourt said. Dalton agreed, stuck out his hand, and asked, "Have we got a deal?"

Harcourt said he had to talk to Simmons, and after an eighty-minute conversation, in which player and agent chewed the options open to them — including waiting for the next interleague trading period, in the spring — and considered the reality of leaving the organization Simmons had been involved in since he was 18, after eighty minutes of gut-wrenching pacing and fretting in Dalton's room, Simmons said yes.

The trade soon became known as the Simmons deal — even if it had been initiated by Dalton's wish to get Rollie Fingers, even if it might someday become known (as Ray Poitevint predicted) as the Green deal. It added $875,000 to Milwaukee's annual payroll, and more than another million annually when Dalton negotiated new contracts with Fingers and Vuckovich the following spring. It raised Milwaukee's attendance break-even point to something in the area of 1,700,000, in the smallest market in the major leagues. It would lead to Bud Selig's periodically asking farm-department assistant Dan Duquette to "tell me something bad about David Green."

And so it was that in the seventh inning on June 10, 1982, with Baltimore and Milwaukee tied 7-7, with two outs and no one on (both Mark Brouhard, batting for Roy Howell, and Charlie Moore had grounded out off Tippy Martinez), Ted Simmons came to bat, hitting for Marshall Edwards. He grounded out to short.

8

	1	2	3	4	5	6	7	8	9	R	H	E
Baltimore	1	2	0	0	0	2	2			7	15	2
Milwaukee	2	0	4	0	1	0	0			7	12	0

When Earl Weaver brought in Tippy Martinez to pitch the seventh, to turn around the Milwaukee batting order, Harvey Kuenn had responded as expected. Playing for one run now, Kuenn was forced to yank his platoonable players (and, in the process, strip his bench). He had brought in the right-handed Brouhard to hit for his DH, the left-handed Howell. He had Ted Simmons, whose power potential was useful with two men out, hit for the left-handed Edwards. As Milwaukee took the field for the eighth, Simmons moved in behind the plate and Moore replaced Edwards in right. The Milwaukee bench was now down to Ed Romero and Rob Picciolo, the reserve infielders, and Ned Yost, the emergency catcher. Baltimore's bench was equally depleted.

The platoon offense had long been established in baseball. Tris Speaker, managing a pennant-winning Cleveland team in 1920, played lefty-righty platoons at three positions. And yet the strategy was not popularized until Casey Stengel shuttled hitters in and out of his powerful Yankee lineups of the early 1950s. The premise was that a right-handed hitter had a better opportunity to "see" a lefty's pitches, and vice versa; coming from the opposite side, a pitch was pre umably more readily trackable, its movement easier to discern. Most important, perhaps, a righty's curveball, when coming in on a left-handed hitter, did not have the disconcerting propensity to start its course aimed directly for the hitter's head.

In general, statistics bear out platoon theory, even if it can be argued that it is self-fulfilling. Lefty hitters see so few lefty pitchers, they can have difficulty with them simply because of unfamiliarity. Left-handed hitters, far more common in baseball than are left-handed people in society, attained that status not least because of the perceived advantage they had against the preponderance of right-handed pitchers. Simultaneously, as left-handed hitters became more and more common (Jim Gantner, for one, was a natural righty whose father taught him to bat left-handed, the better to enhance his baseball opportunities), so necessarily did the hunger for left-handed pitchers increase.

Yet, within the game, there remains, as a relic of those days of rarity, a view that left-handers are not merely mirror images of righties but somehow of a different species altogether. By far the most common baseball nickname over the years has been "Lefty," yet there has been not a single recorded instance of a player nicknamed "Righty." (Indeed, when Houston pitcher Vern Ruhle came up with the Detroit Tigers, his perceived peculiarities were such that his teammates called Ruhle — a right-hander — "Lefty": the term had taken on connotations of personality rather than physicality.) Left-handers are even supposed to pitch differently; conventional wisdom has it that a left-hander's ball "moves more." Even so astute an analyst as Earl Weaver acknowledged that this appeared to be so, even as he recognized that there was no sensible reason that it should be so. Weaver did stop short of citing the explanation offered by his former player, Merv Rettenmund, who said lefties' pitches move more "because they throw against the earth's rotation."

Roy Howell in 1981 batted .136 versus left-handed pitchers and .248 against righties, and Weaver knew Kuenn would not leave him in against Tippy Martinez, not while the right-handed Mark Brouhard was available. (At one point in 1981, Bob Rodgers had sought out Howell "to tell him I didn't think of him as a platoon player," and that he was using him the way he was "for a reason." As it turned out, the reason was — apparently — that Howell was a platoon player.) Marshall Edwards was similarly typecast. And as Ted Simmons was a switch hitter with power, capable of providing the winning run with one swing, out came Edwards. Weaver could also have guessed the sequence of Kuenn's moves. If Simmons had hit for Howell, leading off the inning, Kuenn would have likely had to pinch-run for him, using up yet another body on the bench

(Brouhard, though hardly a sprinter, ran well enough to remain in the game if he reached base). A two-out single by Simmons, though, would not have constituted enough of a head start toward a run to justify removing him from the game.

Weaver was also advantaged in plotting his pitching strategy. Presuming — fairly — that Brouhard had to bat for Howell, and Simmons for Edwards, he was protected by the onset of three right-handers in a row at the top of the Milwaukee order, and any threat mounted by the Brewers could immediately be countered by reaching into his bullpen for righty Tim Stoddard. There would be no pitcher's advantage against the switch-hitting Simmons, coming up third in the seventh inning, and Martinez would stay in at least long enough to face the left-handed Gantner, who followed Simmons. If Martinez could get that far, Stoddard could presumably come in to shut off anything Milwaukee started.

The men who scouted for Milwaukee, and for every other major league club, were mindful of a manager's need to respond to — or to force — the exigencies of platooning. Jamie Easterly, called "Rat," had come to Milwaukee because Dee Fondy learned that Montreal was willing to part with him, and because Dalton knew that his team, no matter how dependent it might become on a first-rate reliever like Fingers, would still have a need for a man who could "turn around the order." It became Easterly's job to come in behind a right-handed starter in the sixth or seventh, force the opposing manager to pinch-hit for lefties in the lineup, and leave him trapped with righties when Fingers came in. Marshall Edwards had been plucked away from the Baltimore system for his speed, and not less incidentally for his left-handedness. As Sal Bando and Don Money were aging, and as Milwaukee was seeking a solution to its third base problem, Roy Howell was deemed desirable because, hitting left-handed, he could hit pitchers Money or Bando might struggle with. Dalton had put a price tag on this last edge when he signed Howell to a contract in 1980 that guaranteed him $1,825,000 over five years.

Still, however clubs balance their rosters and their minor league systems by making sure there are enough left-handers to go around — pitchers and hitters — they look more closely, of course, at how well a player's physical attributes are deployed. Milwaukee scouts had two main "beats": the so-called free-agent talent (a term predating the days of Messersmith, McNally, and Marvin Miller, the term denotes the amateur ball players plucked out of high schools and colleges) and professional talent. Among the latter, the Brewers concentrated on players already in the major leagues, or in the Triple A leagues at the top of the minor league pyramid.

Dee Fondy and Walter Youse were by far Milwaukee's harshest judges, at least in the phrasing of their appraisals. One of Fondy's reports, concerning a team in the National League East, described thusly a one-time star now rather long in the tooth: "Slow bat, dead body. A liability on this club. If he had any class, he would retire." Youse, Harry Dalton said, could "say in ten words what another scout can say in a hundred." That was positively loquacious compared to the appraisals of the first great scout Dalton had known, Freddie "Bootnose" Hofmann. Hofmann, Dalton remembered, had two all-purpose comments: "He can play" and "He can't play." If pressed, though, Hofmann also talked about "primary abilities," "secondary abilities," and "thirdiary abilities."

All scouts are asked to grade players on a scale used as shorthand throughout the major leagues, rating them in various aspects of their games from 2 (poor) to 8 (excellent). In a lifetime of scouting, Youse had seen only one amateur ball player he considered an 8 — a young Pennsylvanian named Reggie Jackson. Youse thought David Green was the best prospect he had seen since Jackson, lacking only the power Jackson displayed at a comparable age.

Living on the road most of the summer, and making off-season trips to the instructional leagues in Arizona and Florida, to the winter leagues in the Caribbean, and to fortuitously placed schools in the nation's Sunbelt, scouts often travel in packs. Usually seated behind the screen in back of home plate, they wear sun hats and carry radar guns, stopwatches, and notebooks. Walter Shannon had been doing it so long he no longer used his stopwatch: he could recognize the difference between "5" (average major league quality) speed and "6" (above average) speed without mechanical aid. The scouts trust one another, too; it isn't uncommon for one, judging a prospect's curveball, to ask the man next to him, "Was that a four or a five?" and then use his companion's estimate as his own.

Ray Poitevint of the Brewers rarely relied on the judgment of others, and he didn't want his staff to do so, either. The Brewers subscribed, as did most clubs, to the reports of the Major League Scouting Bureau. Before Dalton's arrival, Milwaukee was almost totally dependent on the Bureau, employing only five scouts of their own; indeed, Bud Selig told Milwaukee reporters in 1976 that it was "impossible to afford more than that." One of the first things Dalton did, though, was to expand radically the size of the scouting staff until it reached 30 in 1982, such expansion made possible only by the sharp upturn in Milwaukee attendance starting in 1978. Dalton and Poitevint had fired almost all of the scouts and minor league managers in the Brewer system, and in their first two years in Milwaukee the club released 70 minor leaguers whom the two men found wanting. The Bureau, supported by a $100,000 annual fee paid by each subscribing club, was used only as an insurance system, a safety net, in case an amateur prospect was overlooked by Milwaukee's staff. Poitevint otherwise had little regard for the Bureau's judgments: answerable to no specific club, Bureau scouts had become, he felt, masters of the noncommittal. The men who worked for Poitevint were never that; they were generally as bold as they were intelligent. Poitevint — and Dalton — valued brain power highly in their associates, and in ball players. Walter Shannon said, "You don't have to be a great thinker to be a good ball player, but it helps. In the second part of Ben Franklin's autobiography, he describes the checkers players he'd watched in Europe. Those who were only interested in the outcome of the game usually lost, but the guy who was thinking analytically about each successive move would win. Same with ball players." And with good scouts, who seek out potential more than present talent.

At the professional level, Fondy, Shannon, Scarborough, and Youse carried most of the scouting burden, the first two in western ball parks, the latter two in the East. Among the men who specialized in amateur talent, Poitevint reigned supreme, with the others (as well as Julio Blanco-Herrera in Florida and the Caribbean, Felix Delgado in the Caribbean alone, Nelson Burbrink in the Midwest, Tom Gamboa in Northern California, and Roland LeBlanc in Southern California) helping to make final judgments on the variety of prospects scouted out by the troops in the field. These latter, who traveled from high school to sandlot daily for salaries that rarely reached $25,000 annually, included a wide variety of men, including Sam Suplizio, the banker–outfield coach in Colorado (who had his own subsidiary network of 250 tipsters, or "bird dogs"); Johnny Neun, an 81-year-old former major leaguer who was still Dalton's special sliding coach way into his late seventies (and who was the last man — before Ron Hansen — to execute an unassisted triple play in a major league game); and Bill Moffitt, who lived in Long Beach, California, coached minor leaguers in spring training, and had fathered two professional athletes: pitcher Randy Moffitt and a professional tennis player who, after she married, played under the name Billie Jean King.

Perhaps the most interesting of the scouts was Blanco-Herrera. The son of a Cuban brewery owner who had sponsored semiprofessional teams in Havana, Blanco-Herrera fled the Castro revolution and got a job working for the National Brewing Company, in Baltimore. A few years later, someone at National told its owner, Jerry Hoffberger — who also happened to own the Orioles at the time — that Blanco-Herrera knew something about baseball. He was made a scout and became an early member of the Dalton Gang, combing Latin America for Ray Poitevint. He was responsible for "opening up" Nicaragua to Poitevint and the rest of North American baseball, and had since extended his explorations to Guatemala, Honduras, Colombia, and Ecuador. He had even begun to go to the Dutch island of Curaçao, having become aware that transplanted Curaçaons dominated the professional athletic leagues in the Netherlands.

Poitevint had a clearly enunciated set of scouting principles. The first attribute he and his staff looked for was speed, "the one skill that can help you on both defense and offense and the one that can't be taught." Then he looked at a youth's physical qualities, his body type and the stage of his development. Like all scouts, Poitevint had to make judgments not merely on a player's present skills but also on his potential; the scouting report form asked for two ratings in every category (speed, hitting, power, arm, range, etc.), both for current ability and future ability. Poitevint could look at a 6'4", 185-pound 17-year-old and see a 6'4", 220-pound 26-year-old (just as Boston scout Dave Philley had seen a rail-thin, 6'1", 165-pound Cecil Cooper in 1968 and imagined a mature man with home run potential). Thick legs scared Poitevint; with age, they could become anchors, greatly reducing speed and mobility. A pitcher's hand size was critical if he was to master a wide variety of pitches. Stiff wrists often indicated that a pitcher would have difficulty developing a good curve. Walter Shannon almost automatically dismissed any high school hitter who struck out frequently, no matter how he hit when he connected. Shannon's half century of experience had convinced him that this was the surest sign of future failure. "A scout," Ray Poitevint said, "has to have a good imagination."

Everybody on Milwaukee's team (as well as Baltimore's, of course) had been through the scouting appraisal while still in his teens, and each one of them had progressed to the major leagues through a combination of skill and luck that made scouts look brilliant. LaRue Harcourt overstated the case slightly when he said it meant signing twenty players to get one to the major leagues; 8.9 percent make it, or 1 in 11, although the majority of those make it for only a handful of late season games. The process is slow and chancy; though every scout holds some hope for every boy his team signs, most are realistic enough to realize that the great majority of minor leaguers have virtually no chance to reach the majors. Indeed, most will serve out their minor league careers, at pay in the area of $1,000 per month for six months a year, merely as teammates and opponents — sparring partners, as it were — for the gifted and fortunate few.

It was the task of Poitevint's former assistant, Bruce Manno, to keep the Milwaukee minor leaguers — cannon fodder as well as prospects — both happy and hungry, to motivate them in a world where their high school or college greatness failed to distinguish them at all from the mass. When Manno took over the farm system, he kept Poitevint's rules intact: no facial hair (a freedom allowed as reward only upon reaching the majors); no walking — only running or jogging — from place to place in spring camp (to stress the importance of conditioning); clubhouse carpeting only in "AAA Country," as a sign described the loftiest part of the huge locker room at the spring training complex. Similar Pavlovian rewards awaited the eager young ball player at each rung of the organizational ladder.

Few young ball players can see the odds stacked against them, or the strain and privation in store for them, when they sign their first professional contracts. Up until that point, almost all have found themselves the objects of the most flattering attention, in their home communities, from their peers, then from major league scouts. But unlike their football- or basketball-playing counterparts, who have the attention of their college campuses, thousands of alumni, and millions of fans focused on them as they develop their skills, baseball players usually have four or five years of rickety ball parks, seedy clubhouses, and dull small towns — Paintsville and Pikeville, Stockton and Beloit — waiting for them.

Among the men who played for Milwaukee on June 10, there was a varied provenance. Rollie Fingers predated the major league draft, having entered professional baseball the year before the big league teams decided to halt the bidding wars for 17-year-olds by instituting a draft to the rights of high school seniors and college juniors (in the U.S. at least; Caribbean and Canadian players remained fair game at any age). Don Money was neglected in the first draft, in 1965, and later signed with the Pirates at a tryout camp in Washington, D.C. By and large, the rest of the Brewers confirmed the judgments of scouts and general managers. Molitor, Yount, Simmons, and Thomas were all major league stars, and all were first-round draft choices as well — in Molitor's case, the third player selected in the entire country, after outfielder Harold Baines of the Chicago White Sox and pitcher Bill Gullickson of the Montreal Expos. As Thomas told it, he became a first-round choice almost in spite of himself. Pitching when he wasn't playing shortstop in high school, he was suspended for intentionally hitting four straight batters just before a flotilla of scouts showed up to watch him. The scouts, Thomas said, paid one of his coaches $20 to lift the suspension; after the game, they paid the coach another $20 to let Thomas display his hitting abilities in batting practice. Duly impressed, the Seattle Pilots made him their first amateur draft pick. When his mother told him the Seattle Pilots had picked him, Thomas had never heard of the nascent expansion team. "I thought I had been drafted into the navy," he remembered. In 1974, Marshall Edwards, the overachieving "extra player," had gone undrafted, and was signed by Poitevint (still with Baltimore at the time) after the cream of amateur talent had been skimmed by the major league clubs. Pete Vuckovich was a third-round choice, and so confidently anticipated his selection that he compiled a 0.0 grade point average in his last semester at Clarion State Teachers College in Pennsylvania. Charlie Moore and Mark Brouhard, competent but undistinguished, were both fourth-round choices — Brouhard in the January draft, a far less fruitful (and prestigious) source of players than the regular June draft. Ben Oglivie was something of a surprise, making it to major league prominence despite his seventh-round origins, and Roy Howell had disappointed — he was picked in 1972's first round, fourth in the country, by the Texas Rangers.

The most stunning contradiction of expectations was Jim Gantner.

Gantner emerged from Eden, Wisconsin, a small community near Fond du Lac, itself the hub of a kind of rural Ruritania. The area is notable for its large Belgian population, and its historical isolation had bred a Wisconsinite popularly perceived as something of a hick, with an accent, peculiar to the region, that sounded a blend of French-Canadian English and Maine's Down East twang. Gantner's wife, Sue, was pure farm, a countrified girl who married the local hero. Gantner was his high school's best athlete, captain of both the basketball and baseball teams (he was primarily a pitcher and a catcher in high school). He went to college at the University of Wisconsin's branch at Oshkosh; while hardly a top-class baseball academy, UW-O did, in Gantner's years there, twice make it to the NAIA World Series.

Gantner was 20 when Brewer scout Emil Belich signed him. Like most clubs, the Brewers paid special attention to local talent: should a local boy make it to the big league team, it pays off at the box office. Even if he doesn't make it that far, a low-round draft choice, with his concomitantly low salary, is a fairly inexpensive way of generating good will.

Gantner, physically unprepossessing at 5′11″, had some virtues: he was a determined player, with a good glove and an above-average (by major league standards) arm, and he was an infielder who batted left-handed. But the attention paid to the Brewer draft class of '74, by people both in and out of the organization, was focused elsewhere. Since the institution of the first major league draft, in 1965, each club has compiled a private ranking of the nation's amateur baseball talent. (With the advent of the draft, the days were gone when a college boy could, as Harvey Kuenn had in 1952, instruct all interested clubs to submit a sealed bid for his services. Detroit won Kuenn's auction with a $55,000 bonus offer.) Reports from the Major League Scouting Bureau, and from a team's own scouts in the field, are appraised by front office personnel, and a pecking order is created. Certain high-ranking scouts — "national cross-checkers" — travel around the country to look at as much of the top talent as possible, thus helping to define the distinctions that make player X the 127th most desirable draftee in the country and player Y the 128th.

Milwaukee had, by virtue of its finish in 1973, the sixth pick in the draft. The best player available, in the estimation of scouting director Jim Baumer and his associate Tony Siegle, was a tall catcher from Oregon named Dale Murphy; the third best was a 5'9" outfielder from Los Angeles, Lonnie Smith. In 1982, these two would finish first and second in the National League voting for Most Valuable Player. Neither was available when Milwaukee picked; nor were second-ranked (pitcher) Tommy Boggs, and fourth-ranked (shortstop) Bill Almon, whom the San Diego Padres made the first pick, overall, in the draft. When Milwaukee's turn came, they opted for Claude "Butch" Edge, a right-handed pitcher who, before he gave up baseball, managed to appear in 9 games for the Toronto Blue Jays in 1979. In the second round, Milwaukee selected Bryan "Moose" Haas, another right-handed pitcher, who would enter the major league team's starting rotation in less than three years. After Haas, though, the names lose their ring of familiarity: Tom Van Der Meesche, Barry Cort (7 major league games, 1977), Gary Beare (23 major league games, 1976–77), Michael Denevi, Steve Bowling (236 major league at-bats, 1976–77), David Sylvia, William Taylor, Carl Pohlman, Paul Bain.

Finally, in the twelfth round, Baumer and Siegle selected Gantner, the local boy. He was the 270th pick overall. He was, to be sure, the first Wisconsinite the Brewers picked that year, but he did emerge in the local-boy rounds of the draft: Milwaukee selected, in the ensuing three rounds, three more players from their market area (including Jerry Augustine, in the fifteenth round).

Tony Siegle, who went to work for the Houston Astros in the late 1970s and moved from there to the Philadelphia Phillies in 1981, remembered, "We certainly didn't expect Gantner to make it to the majors; you can't *expect* anybody to make it. But I can't even say we thought he had a really good chance, which you can tell from the round we picked him in. The idea was to send him to our club in Newark, New York, that year, where we'd have a lot of players just out of high school. We thought he could help be a stabilizing influence." He was 20; he had been to college; he'd be a leader. Gantner accepted an offer of $3,000 plus incentives to sign with Milwaukee; the club had budgeted him for $6,000.

While the Brewer front office riveted their attention on the progress, in particular, of Edge and Haas, Gantner slowly made himself more than a sparring partner for his Newark teammates. (In addition to various North American high schoolers, the Newark team had a large complement of young Latinos signed independently of the draft; the opening day roster in 1974 included the names Silva, Ortiz, N. Rodriguez, J. Rodriguez, Ejarque, Sanchez, and Castillo.) Gantner had played shortstop in college, but Brewer scouts didn't feel he had the arm motion suited to the position, and they soon moved him to third base.

Out of 130 candidates in a full-blown farm system, Harry Dalton said, one hopes that perhaps 50 qualify as players with any chance at all of reaching the majors; the rest are merely filling out rosters, enabling their more gifted teammates to have someone to play with. By 1975, Gantner had been elevated to this "chance" category, even if the organization was unsure what his position might be. The minor leagues are intended for experimentation as well as refinement of skills, and players move from position to position according to their perceived abilities, and according to the expected needs of the major league club as well. Branch Rickey, when he ran the Cardinals, once held a special camp just to try players at new positions; he even tried changing Terry Moore, an outstanding defensive outfielder of his era, into a shortstop.

Playing for Milwaukee's Double A Thetford Mines, Quebec, farm team in the Eastern League in 1975, Gantner stayed pretty much at third base, making his final serious foray at short in midseason. His manager, John Felske, in July of that year filed a report that ended further experimentation with Gantner: "I don't feel Gantner can handle playing shortstop," Felske said, in one of the game reports a minor league manager files daily with a club's front office. "His arm action at second base on a double play is a long, drawn-back throw allowing the runner to get closer to him. Tonight he threw one in the dirt on that play. He has no range whatsoever to his right, and again he takes too long to get rid of the ball."

But Felske liked a great deal of what he saw of Gantner at third; he also liked his attitude — he was, in Tony Siegle's term, a "pepper-pot" — and his bat. Felske moved the boyish, rosy-cheeked, somewhat chunky Gantner up and down in the batting order, but generally had him batting third or fourth. He hit 12 home runs that season. It wasn't a particularly distinguished team Gantner played on, but it was probably representative of what one could hope for out of the Double A club in an expansion organization's sixth year. Lenn Sakata, whose pivots at second dazzled Gantner, played in the same infield. Dick Davis, a fine hitter who reached the majors with Milwaukee and then wandered around in the National League, played outfield and first base. (Davis never reached the heights others had predicted for him, and was traded early in 1981 to Philadelphia for pitcher Randy Lerch, who performed without distinction for Milwaukee. A few months earlier, Dalton had turned down Houston's offer of pitcher Joaquin Andujar for Davis; Andujar became one of the National League's most successful pitchers in 1982.) Beyond Gantner, Sakata, and Davis, though, the 1975 Thetford Mines club featured young men who would never make the majors, or who would leave terribly indistinct marks when they did make it: Sam Mejias, later an itinerant National League outfielder; Danny Thomas, a prodigious hitter plagued by terrible emotional imbalance, who lost his chance with the Brewers when he refused to play on Saturdays for religious reasons, and who later hanged himself in a southern jail cell; and pitcher Lafayette Currence, distinguished more by his euphonious name than by the eight games he appeared in for the Brewers. Together they labored in anonymity, known only to their families, their girl friends, and major league scouts and farm directors.

It was John Felske's job to nurture, babysit, and at times entertain the young men who played for him in Thetford Mines and, the following year, in Pittsfield, Massachusetts, to which the franchise was moved. He tried to win ball games; he tried to impart to his players the skills and the discipline that might enable them to rise above the middle minors; and he filed daily reports to the farm system office in Milwaukee. These reports reveal the nature of minor league life better than those of the big-city journalists who take an occasional weekend minor league furlough in midsummer:

"Tonight Clark got thrown out of the game in the bottom of the ninth inning with two outs, and his only comment was, 'That's right!' Soon after Clark left the game, yours truly left the game, being thrown out for calling the umpire a number of obscenities. . . ."

"In the first inning Dick Davis struck out [and] threw his bat, just missing Gantner in the on-deck circle. I took him out of the game immediately." (Felske's successor as Milwaukee's Double A manager, Lee Sigman, hadn't quite the same decisiveness: coming out to the mound to remove pitcher Dwight Bernard from a Triple A game in 1981, Sigman asked for the ball and Bernard said, "Fuck you, Siggy. Get lost." Sigman retreated to the dugout. At season's end, he was made a scout and minor league instructor.)

Felske again, near the end of the 1976 season: "Right now we are back in Pittsfield and it's been raining since five o'clock this afternoon. The ball park is under water. If we don't play the double header tomorrow we will be playing a double header on Tuesday against West Haven, a double header Wednesday against West Haven, and double headers Thursday and Friday against Bristol, a single game on Saturday against Bristol, and four straight double headers against West Haven.

"Please," Felske closed, "send me a box of pitchers."

To Gantner, though, the minor leagues were more than flooded fields, contentious umpires, and angry teammates (or, for that matter, a place where the Brewers would be spending $2.6 million annually in player development costs by 1982, trying to find his successor, and his successor's successor). The minors were a place to play regularly, and from which to look up to the major league roster and the men who stood in front of him there. By the end of his second Double A year, he had got more than comfortable at third, and at season's end he was brought up to Milwaukee for examination by the major league personnel. He played in 26 games, fielding credibly, but was flat at the plate. That next winter the Brewers signed Sal Bando to be their third baseman.

In 1977, Gantner went to Spokane, in the Pacific Coast League. Small parks in some cities, and thin air in others, make the PCL a joy for hitters and a constant irritation for pitchers. Gantner hit 15 home runs, with 80 RBIs, and batted .281. In 1978, while Yount held out and Molitor stepped immediately into the lineup, Gantner was kept on the major league roster as a substitute infielder. He appeared in 21 games as a second baseman, 15 at third, and 1 each at shortstop and first. As a reserve in 1979, he continued to play where he was needed, and in 1980, with both Molitor and Money suffering injuries, he became, as it were, a regular substitute. He played 69 games at third base and 66 at second (as well as 3 at short). He batted .282, and though his PCL power didn't survive the trip to Milwaukee, he stole 11 bases. George Bamberger, the manager that year, reveled in Gantner, as any manager would: he was always ready to fill in as needed, and ready as well to race to the scene of the action if a fight broke out on the field.

Mostly, though, Bamberger (and Dalton and Bob Rodgers) appreciated Gantner because he had learned, while sitting on major league benches and periodically substituting for the brittle Molitor, how to play a brilliant second base. Gantner had watched his old teammate, Sakata, often enough to think no one could, or ever would, pivot so quickly and adeptly on a double play. But in the Puerto Rican winter league, he had learned to turn and face the runner on his pivot, leaping *after* he released his throw, leaving it to the baserunner to get out of the way. Rodgers, for one, saw what Gantner didn't: he saw how Jim Gantner turned the double play, and he said, "He's even better than Sakata."

It was the unhappy fortuity of Molitor's rib cage injury that gave Rodgers and his colleagues the opportunity to see Gantner play second base. Yet the failure of the Milwaukee organization to test him there in his minor league years was understandable. Molitor, the natural shortstop, the prodigy, had demonstrated during Yount's walkabout that he had to find a place in the regular lineup, and Yount, after his return, by now a promising major league shortstop clearly on the way to greater accomplishments, was established at his position. Molitor was, at the end of the 1978 season, 22; Yount, the veteran, was 23. And Gantner (already 24 after laboring up the minor league ladder) was kept at third, as a backup.

By the end of 1980, though, after his .282 batting average, his 11 stolen bases, and his 66 outstanding games at second base, Gantner had won Rodgers' heart. While official Brewer pronouncements said Molitor was being moved to center field because of his vast athletic virtues — all of them real — everyone connected with the club knew Molitor was being moved because Gantner was, simply, a better second baseman. And if Molitor could use his great speed to cover more ground, and his shortstop's arm to make better throws than Gorman Thomas, so much the better.

For Gantner, it wasn't a question of whether he was a better second baseman than Molitor or of what was right for the team. He was unconcerned with the first issue, and though he cared about the second, his thoughts were focused on simply getting to play. No, not his thoughts — his urges. For Gantner was a man defined by his profession, and his profession was playing baseball. Athletic accomplishment had given him his identity, had taken him away from the insular life of tiny Eden and provided him with an opportunity for broadened horizons, a very healthy income. (During the 1981 strike, Gantner had helped a relative in his home-plumbing business, untrapping sinks. It was different from flying into Anaheim or Seattle — or even Cleveland, for that matter — sharing in the road life with his teammates, playing before the expectant eyes of thousands of people.) So many players said, "All I want is a chance to play"; after years in small minor league towns, playing on flooded fields, busing to even drearier places, it isn't an unreasonable request. More, though, than what was reasonable, what mattered to Gantner was what was *there,* the defining fact of his life: he was a baseball player.

In January of 1981, Gantner was one of the Brewers who participated in the club's annual winter promotional tour to the cities of Wisconsin. Dick Hackett, the marketing vice president, organized these tours, lining up sponsors in the Green Bays and Kenoshas who could turn out the town for a dinner, there to sell tickets for a special "night" in County Stadium the following season, when bus caravans would deposit much of the town's population in the County Stadium parking lot. The high school band would play; the mayor would throw out the first ball; prominent names would appear on the scoreboard.

On the 1981 tour, Hackett rented a small bus, equipped with lounge chairs and a bar, to take the Brewer party to the various towns. As Hackett read through a pocketful of clippings that contained an after-dinner speaker's chrestomathy of opening lines and other anecdotes, Gantner was already at the motel in Fond du Lac that would be the site of the evening's festivities. His wife, Sue, was with him, as were Sue's parents, stolid farmers from the Fond du Lac region. They waited in the hospitality room set up for the players, the press, and local dignitaries. Mrs. Gantner's father, a big man, his face creased, obviously uncomfortable in coat and tie, looked about with amazement. When Hackett's bus arrived, the room filled with familiar names and faces. Ben Oglivie sat grappling with a newspaper crossword puzzle. Bob Uecker told stories by the bar. Bob Rodgers glad-handed the local dignitaries. Gantner sat quietly with his wife and her parents.

Later, most of Fond du Lac appeared to be lined up around the motel's indoor pool, waiting to get autographs from the visiting Brewers. When they came to Gantner's seat, there were greetings from old friends and acquaintances, exhortations from people who had seen him play in high school. Later, after the dinner itself, when Hackett introduced the players present, the room filled with its biggest cheer for the local boy, whom Rodgers had announced would be his regular second baseman. Gantner rose, too shy to smile; he looked about with wonderment and disbelief in his eyes. He said a few nervous words about how he hoped to help the team, and how he hoped they'd go all the way. He believed his homilies, deeply; the audience found them thrilling. In another context, viewed dispassionately, the evening — Hackett's spiffy bus, the hospitality room, the autograph lines snaking around the pool, the dreary meal and the predictable speeches — was an achingly trite, disingenuous event. But Gantner's open face, his earnest mumbling, were real; so were the shouts of the crowd; so was the bond of hope and devotion and commitment that filled the room.

Fond du Lac poured into County Stadium the evening of June 9 and had to do without Jim Gantner, whom Kuenn had allowed to rest for the evening rather than have him bat against Baltimore's Mike Flanagan, a left-handed pitcher with whom Gantner had had trouble in the past. The high school band paraded around the field with the Fond du Lac Little League (the sort of privilege granted any group of 500 or more who bought tickets en masse). A sign in the parade, mounted on a boat on a trailer pulled around the infield, read DON'T FORGET WALLEYE WEEKEND, and another amplified this by proclaiming NATIONAL WALLEYE TOURNAMENT. Three city councilmen, the county executive, and a fan threw out first balls. The National Anthem was sung by a Fond du Lac tenor.

It was a homey evening, almost a parody of small-town America come to the big city. It was also evidence of the Brewers' marketing reach. The team could not survive on the population of metropolitan Milwaukee alone, and had consequently gone after an audience throughout Wisconsin and in contiguous parts of Illinois, Upper Michigan, and even Iowa.

Dick Hackett orchestrated the marketing efforts from his small office in the stadium, venturing out to solicit the support of corporate personnel departments, fraternal lodges, civic organizations, and the like. Hackett was a booster, a go-getter, a man who relished selling, and especially selling in the reflected light of ball-playing heroes. (Some players resisted Hackett's cheerleading involvement. Gorman Thomas once berated public relations director Tom Skibosh for giving his home phone number to Hackett, the third-ranking executive in the firm that employed Thomas.) When Bill Haig negotiated broadcasting contracts, he sought not only the best possible financial deal but the widest promotional reach as well. Hackett, in fact, participated in all decisions related to television and radio broadcasting because the club saw media exposure as more valuable for ticket sales than for the dollars generated from the broadcasters themselves.

Bud Selig pushed a willing Hackett into the civic life of Wisconsin, and though he made an occasional men's club speech or the like, Selig himself stayed largely in the background. His attention was riveted on the ball club, the financial control of the organization, and a network of social and business connections far removed from the civic club circuit. He'd travel for a dinner in Madison, site of his alma mater, and he'd welcome broadcasting executives to the club's dining room in the stadium. But during a game, there wouldn't be any councilmen from Fond du Lac in Selig's box. Selig's common touch was lavished only on those he could reach from a distance. Sure, any complaining fan who wrote him a letter — about bad ball players or parking lot security or the quality of the hot dogs — got a personal reply. But at a midwinter booster dinner in 1981, preceded by a high-ticket fund raiser for a charity the club supported, Selig stayed remote from the eager crowd, losing himself instead in the company of some of his partners; John Fetzer, the owner of the Tigers and Selig's primary mentor; and Commissioner Bowie Kuhn, who said at the banquet that he had come to Milwaukee to "see my friend Buddy."

Not only did Selig rarely mingle with the fans at the ball park, nor sit — ever — in the stands; he also stayed remote from that part of the baseball operation that didn't directly concern his 25 major league players. When Milwaukee scouts gathered for their annual September organizational meeting, Selig would drop in for a minute or two. In his thirteen years as club president, he had never seen a Brewer farm club game — not during the '81 strike, when other members of the organization took advantage of the hiatus and went on the road, not even during the 1982 season, when Milwaukee had a Class A club playing barely 70 miles away in Beloit.

Yet Selig was eternally riveted to what he cared about most. There was hardly a major league committee on which he did not sit. He was always available to a fellow owner who might call to chat, or to plan strategy concerning one or another of the initiatives owners became involved in. He swore by the common interest of the 26 clubs, and displayed a close-mouthed loyalty to that interest. He thought it was a mistake for baseball to keep its books closed to the players during the prestrike negotiations in '81 — the story revealed in the books, he insisted, could only help the owners' cause — but he'd never say so publicly. He was actively involved in the efforts to reorganize baseball but was never openly critical of the structure that needed revision. If his friend Bowie Kuhn erred in the public eye, Selig said, "He's a very complex man, and people just don't understand how capable he is, and what he's trying to do." Selig even abided the peculiar and byzantine ways in which baseball did its most important business: when the owners gathered for one of their periodic meetings, there was never even an agenda prepared beforehand. The ostensible reason was security; another owner, rather less entranced by the corporate aura of baseball than was Selig, felt it was for fear that the men who putatively ran the game actually might know what was going on.

By the top of the eighth inning on June 10, Selig had put an end to the day's jousting with the boys in the press box. He had settled into a folding chair, reserved for him by an attentive usher, at the first base end of the mezzanine catwalk. The chair was located almost directly beneath a ladder to the press box above, far removed from the intrusions of anything but the game itself.

Upstairs, Bob Uecker was taking over the play-by-play from Dwayne Mosley. In six National League seasons as a reserve catcher in the 1960s, Uecker had amassed a career batting average of .200; he was far better known, and far more accomplished, as a broadcaster than he had been as a player. "My pitch," he said, by way of self-analysis, "is to be ignorant." His flamboyant, self-deprecating, Rodney Dangerfield style had won Uecker a devoted following in Milwaukee and elsewhere, some of his fans wearing T-shirts emblazoned with UECKER'S PUKERS and the slogan BASEBALL, HOT DOGS, APPLE PIE, AND ALCOHOL. Off the air, he was genuinely funny, always original, usually profane. On bus rides from airports to hotels, Uecker would take the driver's hand mike and do impromptu tour guide impersonations, and the players would respond with cheers. He was extremely popular with the players, because he was one of them, albeit a retired and not very good one of them. Long baseball seasons demanded humor, and Uecker provided it. With the players, he was always charming; at other times, though, he could be brutally cold, as he was to his radio-booth partner from the year before, Lorn Brown. When Brown was doing the play-by-play, Uecker would turn off his mike, making himself inaccessible to a desperate Brown, a decent, earnest, and rather unimaginative man who couldn't easily make it through an inning without the help of a partner. Brown was stolid, plodding, hung up on statistics. He was also painfully ill at ease among ball players, and Uecker disdained him for it.

Down on the pitcher's mound, Rollie Fingers pondered the ineffective fastball that had enabled Baltimore to tie the game in the previous inning. Fingers thought his fastball, generally, was "a foot shorter" than the fastball of his professional youth. Like most pitchers, he had not been able, over the years, to retain the elasticity of arm and the drive of legs that give a pitch its speed (or rather "velocity," which for some reason has replaced "speed" as the descriptive word of choice). The development of his forkball had enabled him to use the fastball again with confidence, but when the fastball was off as much as it was today, the fork and the slider suffered, too. Major league hitters, by and large, expect every pitch to be a fastball and count on their reflexes to make the necessary adjustment if an off-speed pitch comes instead. That is careless thinking, of course, and it enables innumerable pitchers to disrupt timing and balance with well-placed curves and sliders. Yet the pitcher whose fastball lacks intimidating speed enables hitters to wait on the off-speed pitch; in Fingers' case on June 10, the fastball was so fat that Baltimore hitters were free to focus on the slider. His ineffectiveness in the seventh boded ill for the eighth. How he used the two off-speed pitches, how he would work one against the other while squeezing an occasional effective moment out of what he'd later call his "horseshit" fastball, would determine whether Milwaukee would stay in the game.

Hurled baseballs do, as countless batters and a few physicists can attest, curve; which is to say, they slice laterally across the plate while dropping down in the strike zone. Some fastballs, properly thrown, will rise, or "explode," when they reach the plate. Skeptics maintain this is impossible, claiming it defies the immutable laws of gravity. However, such skeptics have never looked at airplanes.

The point is that, like airplanes, pitched baseballs move through

the air in a fashion dictated by the force with which they are propelled forward and the action of air currents on their surface. The
"flaps" on a baseball are its seams, the slightly raised ridges of
thread and gathered leather that make its surface uneven. A pitch
thrown with fingers across the top of the ball, fingers that impart
backspin as the ball leaves the pitcher's hand, will — if thrown
hard enough, and especially if thrown with a full-overhand motion
and a high leg kick as a sort of lever — actually rise, as the ball
rotates bottom to top. Similarly, a pitch thrown with topspin, hurtling head over feet, as it were, will drop as the air through which
it soars pushes down on it. It is one of the essences of pitching.
Theorist Bob Shaw said, "The aim of pitching is to get the ball
to move in a vertical plane" — *any* vertical plane. Hence, Rollie
Fingers' forkball. With the index and middle fingers spread to either
side of the ball, the thumb supporting it beneath, he was unable
to impart backspin as the ball left his hand, and the thumb's motion,
pulling up at release, gave it topspin.

The threat of the forkball, as much as its reality, carried Fingers
through the eighth inning. In the seventh, he had thrown three
to Eddie Murray; each had approached the plate at knee level,
and each dropped precipitously as it reached the batter. Hour upon
hour of sideline and bullpen practice had made it behave this way,
and the three pitches to Murray had enabled Fingers to announce
the pitch to the Orioles. Fingers hadn't used the pitch on John
Lowenstein, but he felt Lowenstein was impossible to get out by
dint of strategy, and that simply moving the ball around, keeping
it out of the strike zone, would get him. It hadn't, of course.

Rick Dempsey, the first man up, jumped — rather surprisingly —
on the first pitch Fingers threw, a fastball just out of the strike
zone, wide. It traveled on a looping line to right center field, and
Gorman Thomas raced in for it, catching the ball at hip level. In
the radio booth, Bob Uecker called it "a fine running catch"; in
the press box, one writer cited a phrase used twenty-five years earlier
to describe a very different outfielder, Willie Mays: "He makes the
hard ones look hard." Charlie Moore, now in right, arrived at the
ball barely a moment later than Thomas. In Texas in late April,
Sam Suplizio had "scored" the Brewer outfielders on how quickly
they got the jump on hit balls, and the novice Moore had done
the best.

Rich Dauer followed Dempsey. He had three hits already, including his home run, and yet he had also been the goat on one of the costliest plays of the game, the missed hit-and-run that had caught Dempsey at second base in the sixth inning. With Dauer, Fingers' goal was to keep the pitch low, where Dauer couldn't slap it over the infield. A whistling slider on the first pitch forced Dauer to hit a ground ball to shortstop, where Yount handled it with ease.

Sometimes, Harvey Kuenn acknowledged, a pitcher who is getting batters to swing at the first pitch may not be cutting the strike zone carefully enough. Fingers hadn't been wild, though, so it wasn't a matter of Baltimore's hitters' figuring that he would be extra careful with the first pitch each at-bat. He was, simply, doing what good pitchers do: throwing strikes, but not throwing the kind of strike that was too easy to hit. Pitching, Cal McLish said, is throwing strikes when you want to and balls that *look* like strikes when you want to. Fingers, in the eighth, was working for strikes, not trying to engage in elaborate setups when he didn't have a good fastball to drive his point home.

With two out, Lenn Sakata saw a first-pitch strike, too, but he let it pass; it was a near perfect slider, at the lowest edge of the outside corner. Sakata, despite his barrel chest and muscular arms, was not the type of hitter who could often hurt a pitcher with a long ball. Fingers followed the slider with a fastball, which Simmons had asked him to send in tight. Sakata was looking to the outside again, and met the ball on the handle of his bat. The ball skipped on the ground toward the right side; Don Money was unable to reach it in time to get it on an up-bounce and unable to bend far enough to get it on its way down. It rolled into right for a single.

Cal Ripken followed. He was 2 for 4 on the day, including his seventh-inning single off Fingers. That was the first time the 21-year-old hitter and the 35-year-old pitcher had ever faced each other, and Ripken had won: fair enough. But Fingers was not notably enlightened by knowledge gleaned from their first encounter; he had seen a strong, quick hitter whose confidence was building with each day in the major leagues, and the fastball he had hit was a weak pitch. The pitcher thus didn't know whether it was his pitch selection or the pitch itself that Ripken had triumphed over.

Fingers, apparently willing to try anything, started Ripken off with a slider — but with a slider he threw from a full-sidearm position, something he did maybe four or five times a season. With his long arm snaking toward third, the pitch did not come from the spot Ripken would have been focusing on. It was a ball, low and away, but it froze Ripken, and Fingers hoped it would put him off stride a bit: "Nobody told me he could do that," Ripken might think. Fingers took the throw back from Simmons, glanced briefly at Sakata leading off first, placed his foot on the pitching rubber, and suddenly spun to his left, firing a pickoff throw almost underhand.

Pickoff motions are often clues to a pitcher's character. Pete Vuckovich often engaged in a strange little game, twitching his head rapidly toward first and back to its normal position again and again, as if he had a violent tic (or, as if he had — as Vuckovich did have — a streak of calculated weirdness running through him). Bob McClure developed his outstanding pickoff motion in hours of practicing it before mirrors, and it was consistent with the sneaky-clever style of pitching McClure, not blessed with the greatest physical gifts, had had to develop to stay in the major leagues. And Fingers' surprising move, quick and decisive, reflected yet more about him: how his whole game was predicated on keeping the opposition off balance. The less he was getting from his arm on a given day, the more he would turn to his head, like an experienced general whose troops are outnumbered.

Getting the ball back from Money, Fingers looked in at Simmons. Fingers was a supremely confident athlete, and he generally asked little of a catcher. He preferred to call his own game, agreeing with a catcher only up to the point where the catcher's call led to a hit. Then he'd shake his catcher off until the right signal was flashed. Simmons, though, was in Fingers' mind a stubborn catcher, and a cerebral one, who often would give the same signal over and over until Fingers, exasperated, was forced to throw the indicated pitch. Pete Vuckovich, for one, appreciated Simmons' single-mindedness. "If I miss two sliders," Vuckovich said, "he'll still call the third. A lot of catchers won't call the third to save your dick."

At 1 and 0, with Sakata on first and Ripken ready for the pitch, Simmons signaled for a fastball. Fingers wanted to throw a fastball, with a man on first and the batter ahead in the count, but he didn't want Ripken to be sitting in wait for it. By shaking off Simmons, Fingers hoped to indicate to Ripken that he, Fingers, knew (as the Baltimore dugout knew) that his fastball wasn't up to par today, that despite the situation he was fearful of throwing a weak fastball that Ripken could pounce on. Fingers' very visible shake-off of the signal, he hoped, could place Ripken on the defensive.

So when Simmons picked up Fingers' cue, and signaled again for a fastball, the pitcher was exactly where he wished to be. But the fastball limped to the plate, and Ripken lined it through the shortstop–third base hole. Paul Molitor, playing near the line for the pull-hitting Ripken, could only wave at it. Lenn Sakata moved up to second, the go-ahead Baltimore run.

Jim Dwyer was up, to be followed by Eddie Murray, Al Bumbry, and John Lowenstein. Four straight left-handed hitters, the game tied, a man in scoring position, and a bullpen depleted by the wear and tear of three straight losses. The best alternative to Fingers was Jamie Easterly, but Easterly had pitched the day before. Besides, rookie managers didn't use relief pitchers to come in for The Relief Pitcher. Rookie managers especially didn't do it less than two weeks after another manager, Bob Rodgers, had gone with Mike Caldwell in place of Fingers in Seattle. In the dugout, Kuenn never so much as motioned to the bullpen; Fingers had obviously been made rusty by his long layoff, but it was a must-win game, and Fingers was the must-win pitcher on the Milwaukee staff.

Jim Dwyer had endured an 0-for-21 stretch earlier in the season, an exceedingly rare occurrence for a contact hitter who slapped the ball to all fields. His luck had returned of late, though, and now he was facing a struggling pitcher. But Fingers retained one, indelible edge: his reputation. As Ben Oglivie put it, "The better you are, the better you can be. A pitcher's reputation can affect a batter's attitude, make him think twice, and cut down his aggressiveness." Fingers had to maintain his composure, his self-confidence, as Dwyer came up. These qualities, now, would count as much as his physical skills.

Kuenn watched Fingers pitch to Dwyer without resorting to the tricks and ploys that had failed him against Ripken. Fingers determined, finally, to give up his fastball and to beat Baltimore with his two other pitches. He threw a slider, inside and low, for a ball. He worked quickly now, not stepping off the mound between pitches, and threw another inside slider, this one in the dirt; it bounced off Simmons' pads and caromed some 30 feet toward the Milwaukee dugout. Simmons chased it down, and on second Sakata took only a step or two down the line. With two out, there was no great advantage in trying to move to third. A single would put Baltimore ahead as it was. Simmons found the ball and came up with his arm cocked, his eyes scanning the infield rapidly. He tossed the ball back to Fingers. The count was 2 and 0.

Then came Fingers' third straight slider, but this one was in the lower half of the strike zone, and the count went to 2 and 1. Had he possessed today a working fastball, this was the spot for it, but Fingers chose to abide by his catcher's analysis of the situation, and he threw a forkball, which Dwyer missed by six inches: 2 and 2.

Now Fingers had a tiny luxury, and he consumed it by throwing a slider so far outside that Dwyer didn't even move his bat. But Fingers had reason to hope the pitch had moved Dwyer's mind, had made him think that the outside part of the plate was where he was going. The first two pitches in the sequence had both been sliders tight, and both had been balls.

At 3 and 2, with two runners on, with the most frightening of Baltimore's batters, Eddie Murray, on deck, with no fastball, and facing a batter who had twice seen his inability to throw an inside slider for a strike, Rollie Fingers lifted his leg, reached back, grunted loudly as he released the ball, and threw a slider that headed for the middle of the plate and then broke in so tight that when Dwyer swung at it, he nearly brushed the ball with his hands. The bat came no closer, though, and the Baltimore threat was over.

	1	*2*	*3*	*4*	*5*	*6*	*7*	*8*	*9*		*R*	*H*	*E*
Baltimore	1	2	0	0	0	2	2	0			7	17	2
Milwaukee	2	0	4	0	1	0	0				7	12	0

The slider: it, as much as anything else, defined the nature of the offense-defense balance that had evolved by the 1980s. Ted Simmons spoke of looking for "the little red dot" made by the whirling seams on a slider as it approaches the plate. It is as good a way as any to detect the pitch, if you have the eyesight to pick up the seams on a speeding missile; if you have reflexes that can make the needed adjustments in your swing; and if seeing it and reacting to it helps you hit it as it skids across a corner of the strike zone. Even Simmons, in the deep frustration of his first season and a half in the American League, had reason to curse the pitch. He invoked the old saw that the National League was a fastball league and the American a breaking ball league, and for a while attributed his poor performance to the time it had taken for him to adjust. The sliders kept coming, though — as they did more and more in the National League, and the minor leagues, and even in the high schools. The pitch was ubiquitous, except in the lower reaches of the Los Angeles Dodgers farm system, where young pitchers were discouraged from throwing it lest they hurt their arms. Moose Haas's father, once an aspiring pitcher himself, had forbidden his son to submit his arm to the wrenching wrist turn required by the slider until he signed his first professional contract.

What makes the slider such an effective pitch, the "red dot" notwithstanding, is its resemblance to a fastball as it approaches the plate and its sudden passage into another horizontal plane as it gets there. Disdained at its inception — and for many years thereafter — as a "nickel curve," the pitch is also hard enough to hit even if the batter knows it's coming. Sparky Lyle, who shone as a relief pitcher for the New York Yankees in the 1970s, threw virtually nothing else. At his prime, he would come into a game in the eighth inning, throw slider, slider, slider, and watch with his own particular profane glee as batter after batter failed to hit it successfully.

The slider came into use the way all new pitches do, as the result of the evolutionary efforts of one species (pitchers) to overcome the depredations of an opposing species (hitters). From the game's very beginnings, the rules were forever being changed to help the hitters, and the pitchers were forever forced to improvise the means of their survival. When it was decreed in the nineteenth century that batters could no longer request a pitcher to throw the ball to a particular spot, the pitchers had been granted their last favor.

In 1884, the American Association instituted the rule that a hit batsman was entitled to first base; it was a change made expressly to curb the assaults of Will "Whoop-La" White, a Cincinnati pitcher who didn't like batters crowding the plate and who threw at any who did. Yet other pitchers of a less obstreperous nature than White continued to dominate — until 1893, when the pitcher's rubber was moved from 50 feet from home plate to 60 feet 6 inches away. This radical change — it effectively gave batters 20 percent more time in which to react to a pitch — forced the pitchers to adapt, and they turned to the development of various doctored pitches. There were shineballs, mudballs, scuffballs — anything that would affect the course of a pitch's path toward the plate.

The most popular, and enduring, of the trick pitches was the spitball, brought to the big leagues by Elmer Stricklett in 1904, made popular by Jack Chesbro the same year (he won 41 games with it, the modern record), and perfected by Ed Walsh of the White Sox. The idea of the spitter was — and is — similar to that of Rollie Fingers' forkball. The secret is topspin instead of backspin. In the spitter's case, wet index and middle fingers, lightly holding a wet spot on the ball, will slip off the ball virtually frictionless at the moment of release, and the thumb will "push" the ball plateward. Topspin thus imparted, the ball will drop sharply as it reaches home plate.

But the spitter was outlawed in 1920, coincident with the onset of the lively ball and the home run era. Ed Rommel of Philadelphia added a weapon to the pitcher's arsenal by refining the knuckleball in the early '20s, but the knuckler was a pitch that only a few men could control at all. Then George Uhle, with Detroit in 1930, came up with the first version of what became the slider, a pitch that Waite Hoyt said "skidded, almost at right angles, like an auto on ice." And in the mid-1930s, George Blaeholder put more bite and sweep into the pitch, giving it the general shape it has enjoyed since. (Blaeholder had strong reason to work on the pitch, as he played for the woeful St. Louis Browns. He also could work on it in virtual privacy, as the Browns in 1935 drew only 80,922 fans — fewer than 1,100 per home game.)

The slider didn't become widely popular until after World War II, and it didn't earn its present ubiquity until the '60s. Eventually, though, it became so firmly and effectively established in pitching strategy that by 1968 pitching was utterly dominant. That season, 21 percent of all games were shutouts; the American League batting championship was won on a .301 average; the *overall* batting average for the AL was .230 (in the National League it was .243); and the composite earned run average for both leagues was 2.98. Once again, rule changes: the pitcher's mound was lowered 5 inches, and the upper reach of the strike zone was dropped from the shoulders to the armpits.

These might seem to be minor changes, but they involved the most critical inches in the game. Five inches represent fully one third of the mound's height, and of the consequent leverage afforded a pitcher over the 60-plus feet he is required to throw the ball. And taking away the high strike at the same time effectively meant that the pitcher had a target 10 to 12 percent smaller to aim at. In 1969, the major league earned run average jumped to 3.60.

In the years after the last assault on the pitchers' prerogatives, the game settled into a semblance of balance. Pitchers had the slider, and managers completed the conversion to strategies that made bullpen specialists as critical to success as starting pitching. The swing-for-the-fences game that had dominated the '50s and '60s was modified somewhat, abetted by the construction of death-on-homers ball parks. As power hitting stabilized, the reintroduction of the running game, initiated by Luis Aparicio in the 1950s and given impetus by Maury Wills and Lou Brock in the years that followed, placed baseball offense in the closest thing to equilibrium it has known since the game's inception. If anything, some runners — Willie Wilson of Kansas City, Rickey Henderson of Oakland, and Montreal's Tim Raines — threatened to make the stolen base dominant in baseball offense.

Some teams, though — Milwaukee and Baltimore among them — saw that a stolen-base-dominated offense was an illusion: the number of runs scored simply did not increase in proportion to the risk that constant running entailed. Earl Weaver viewed the steal much as he did the bunt: the risk of losing an out was costlier than the potential advantage of picking up an extra base. In his younger years, Al Bumbry stole bases with relative frequency, but the Orioles by and large eschewed hyperaggressive basepath tactics.

Harvey Kuenn held no particular brief for the running game, having reached his baseball maturity in those dead days of the '50s, when the home run was everything (even if Kuenn himself, a slap hitter, made small contribution to the profligate power hitting of the era: in his fifteen-year career, he hit only 87 of them). Though the Brewers might lose a game or two because of their caution on the bases, Kuenn felt they'd win more than that at the plate. The Brewers had become the San Diego Chargers of baseball, an offensive machine capable of scoring sufficient runs to overcome whatever weaknesses there were in the starting pitching — capable of building a lead for Rollie Fingers to hold.

*

On June 10, though, Fingers had not held the lead, and despite a characteristically strong offensive performance, the Brewers found themselves tied in the bottom of the eighth. Yet there was a new spirit on the team, Kuenn felt, and it was showing itself on the Milwaukee bench. He was too modest a man to take direct credit for it, but it was clear that this group of grown men, earning salaries that averaged more than $250,000 annually, had simply been too unhappy, too fractious and bumptious, to continue to win under Rodgers. He let the lineup stay generally set. He continued to play cards with the players. He eliminated the off-limits status of the hotel bars. He stood awkwardly on his artificial leg, a benign Ahab, his cheek distended with his tobacco wad, and said, "Oh, shit, just go play your game." And as they took their seats in the dugout for the bottom of the eighth, they were surprisingly lively for a team that had lost three in a row and had just blown a four-run lead. Howell and Edwards, who had come out of the game, stayed on the bench. Cooper, in uniform, had left the whirlpool for the day. Starter Bob McClure had returned to the dugout, too. There was no one in the clubhouse listening on the radio and playing cards today; they believed, Kuenn thought, they'd win this game.

Weaver, for his part, had every reason to be confident. His bats had been noisy of late, whereas Milwaukee's had quieted down. Fingers was off his game; the Brewer bullpen and the offensive bench were all but bare. Tippy Martinez had had no trouble in the seventh, and if today were one of the days when the erratic Martinez lost his control, Tim Stoddard, the 6'7", 250-pound giant who had pitched in more games than any other Oriole over the preceding three seasons, was fresh and ready. "I love those complete games," George Bamberger said, just as often as he said "I hate those bases-on-balls." Bamberger's old boss, Weaver, for whom he had been pitching coach for ten years, had just enjoyed three of those complete games. With Fingers, Milwaukee had the better bullpen under normal circumstances, but three straight relieverless days for Baltimore, and the innings accumulated by Fingers' backups this week, had turned those tables.

The nine men in the Milwaukee lineup as they entered the bottom of the eighth were Molitor, Yount, Money, Oglivie, Thomas, Brouhard, Moore, Simmons and Gantner — two lefties (Oglivie and Gantner), a switch hitter (Simmons), and six righties. Gantner was leading off the eighth, and if Martinez could get past him, and later Oglivie, Weaver would surely turn to Stoddard, who had begun to warm up at the end of the seventh, to finish things off.

But Martinez could not get past Gantner. His first pitch was a good one, in on Gantner's hands, but the batter was able to punch it into right field for a single. Now there were three straight righties coming: Molitor, Yount, and Money. They were, collectively, 3 for 33 over their careers against Stoddard.

But Weaver, whose index cards told him that Molitor was 0 for 13 lifetime against Stoddard, left Martinez in. It was an obvious situation: tie game, home team at bat, no one out, an excellent bunter in Molitor at the plate, a capable runner in Gantner on base. Martinez was quick on his feet, a good fielder, while the huge Stoddard lumbered about rather ineffectively afield. Stoddard knew what was up, and began to pump his warmup pitches harder in the bullpen.

Molitor took his time coming to the plate, staring down at Harry Warner in the third base coaching box who in turn had just finished watching Kuenn touch his fingers to various parts of his face and head to signal the bunt. Warner went through rather broader gestures to pass on the strategy to Molitor and to Gantner. Kuenn might as well have yelled out "Bunt!" — so clear was it to everyone on the field what was afoot.

Rick Dempsey, on his knees behind the plate, went through a signaling routine, too, aimed at Martinez and the infielders, reminding his teammates who had responsibility for what part of the sacrifice play that was coming. The assignments — Murray to charge from first and Ripken from third, Dauer to cover for Murray, Sakata to go to second, Martinez to take the middle — were standard issue. One baseball thinker, former National League outfielder and longtime college coach Danny Litwhiler, argued that the better strategy had the second baseman charging from the right side and the first baseman holding his position. Litwhiler, a tireless diamond Johnny Appleseed, had also compiled a glossary of baseball terms in five languages, the better to enable an itinerant coach to know that the Yugoslavian for "guess hitter" was *udarac kojeg ne ocekuje bacac.*

Yet Litwhiler's bunt play had not been translated into general usage, where certain tactics had, over the years, become immutable. These were inscribed in all the basic strategy books, and also in the board-bound organization instructional manual first prepared by Dalton and company in Baltimore, and now in use as well in Milwaukee. This volume was presented to every player in the organization, so that there was consistency in defensive practice. A second baseman called up from Rochester for an emergency would cover a bunt, or position himself for a relay, or execute a cutoff in the prescribed fashion. Spring training drills were given over to the same routines. Today, Dempsey was simply invoking a sort of defensive reflex, reminding everyone of his lessons.

Martinez threw a curve that Molitor had no difficulty handling, dropping it between first base and the pitcher's mound. Martinez fielded it cleanly, but had no chance of getting Gantner at second; he flipped the ball to Dauer, covering first.

When the players returned to their positions, and Robin Yount stepped in to hit, Weaver made a gesture to Dauer from his station near the dugout runway. The second baseman left his position and joined Martinez on the mound. Umpire Dan Morrison waited about twenty seconds, then came out to tell the two Orioles there was a game to be played. Dauer walked slowly back to his position, Martinez stepped on the rubber, and Yount stepped into the batter's box — whereupon Weaver called time and walked slowly out to the mound himself. Dempsey joined him there, Morrison followed, and when the umpire reached the group, Weaver lifted his right hand, the signal for Tim Stoddard. The whole routine took about a minute and a half, long enough for Stoddard to pop some more capillaries and stretch out his arm.

While Stoddard walked in from the bullpen, Weaver and Dempsey chatted on the mound. Theirs was almost as colorful a relationship as the one Weaver shared with Palmer. When Dempsey first joined the Orioles, Weaver was a bit chagrined. He had a strong arm and was otherwise defensively sound, but he didn't have the power Weaver wanted from a catcher: a classicist when it came to structuring his basic lineup, Weaver wanted home runs from catcher, first, third, left, and right; he wanted singles and speed and hitting behind the runner from short, second, and center. Too, Dempsey hadn't quite mastered the role of field captain that Weaver wanted from a catcher. On throws from the outfield with men on base, it is the job of the catcher, with the action in front of him, to shout out the proper play, to tell the cutoff man whether to intercept the throw, and if so to tell him where to throw it. Dempsey shouted his "Cut!" quickly enough, but he failed to follow the shout with a "Two!" or "Three!" to indicate the base to which the cutoff man should throw. Weaver was caustic about it, and Dempsey brooded. He was an intense man, who concentrated mightily on the game. For relief from baseball pressures, he would take it upon himself to be the club entertainer. The son of two former vaudevillians, he had a knack for performance, and was particularly renowned for his "Baseball Soliloquy in Pantomime." It was a comic turn he'd occasionally perform during rain delays, stuffing his uniform with padding and prancing around a soggy tarpaulin performing exaggerated parodies of hitters, pitchers, umpires. It was genuinely funny, and while impatient fans waited for the rains to end, they'd applaud Dempsey lustily. His teammates and members of the opposing team would stand in the dugouts and applaud with the fans, especially when Dempsey concluded his routine with a mammoth belly-flop slide into home plate, a grand gesture he would contrive to execute in the largest puddle on the infield tarp, his momentum carrying him for yards, a rooster tail of rainwater behind him.

Weaver enjoyed the "Soliloquy" and came to enjoy even more the defensive skills Dempsey developed. He had the best record in the league at throwing out base stealers, and had mastered the rest of a catcher's defensive repertory as well. At the 1980 winter meetings, while Harry Dalton was trying to sort out the complexities of his big trade with St. Louis, Baltimore general manager Hank Peters told Whitey Herzog, "We wouldn't trade Dempsey and [then backup] Dan Graham for Simmons even up." Meanwhile, the rest of the Oriole offense was generating enough runs to let Weaver, after platooning Dempsey with Graham in 1980, learn to live with Dempsey's mild bat (Dempsey knew Graham was a good hitter, but also felt "Danny couldn't catch his own butt with both hands"). He called a good game, too, even if not good enough for the headstrong Palmer, who insisted on calling his own, using the signs only as a medium that would guarantee both pitcher and catcher knew what the next pitch was.

But still there was a conflict with Weaver. The manager not only seemed constantly to be searching for a catcher who could hit home runs (ideally from the left side of the plate); he also, until 1981, pulled Dempsey for pinch hitters rather more frequently than Dempsey preferred. They quarreled over how to pitch to batters and over virtually any other subject.

Weaver didn't really care about his catcher's contentiousness. In fact, he didn't care if all his players hated him. Unlike every other manager in the game, he knew — riskily, perhaps, but he knew nonetheless — that *he*, Weaver, was the constant on the Orioles, and the players came and went. Save for Palmer, he had been there longer than any of them, and had performed so ably, and to such delight among the Oriole fans, that he was secure. Occasionally, he would play at humility and say it was the players who made all the difference, that managers only lost games, they never won them. But his listeners never believed it, and never believed Weaver believed it either.

Standing on the County Stadium mound as Stoddard walked in, Weaver took the ball wordlessly from Martinez, who walked off the field head down. The manager waited for his new pitcher, hand on his hip, and chatted with Dempsey. His team had 17 hits, and wasn't leading. For a decade and a half he had watched good Baltimore teams play like great teams, mediocre teams play like good ones. He had also watched the men he relied on come up short despite their best efforts. All passed, in retrospect, with equanimity. What he could not abide was a team that played over its head but still lost. That implied there was something the manager had done wrong. When Stoddard arrived at the mound, Weaver gave him the ball, not greeting him with an exhortation, a pat on the butt, a hello, or even a look in Stoddard's eyes. The game, he seemed to imply by the very absence of gesture, was in his new pitcher's hands.

Stoddard took his eight warmup pitches, on each one looking as if he were throwing from somewhere in the upper deck. He had first achieved athletic prominence as a member of the 1974 North Carolina State University basketball team that won the national collegiate championships. He had been signed originally by the Chicago White Sox, who picked him in the January 1975 free-agent draft. Chicago gave up on him after three minor league seasons, and the Orioles signed him less than two weeks later. After two more minor league seasons, he joined the Orioles for good in 1979 and quickly became the mainstay of their relief staff.

As befit a man his size and strength, Stoddard threw exceedingly hard, usually with a full-overhand motion. He had a hard slider as well — a so-called white-dot slider, which presented itself with less break than most and with, consequently, less opportunity for the batter to discern its nature. He also threw generally high, at generally the same pace, without the confounding variations in speed that can throw a hitter's timing off. He was utterly straightforward, a huge, strong man who could throw a ball very, very hard and who relied little on guile or cunning. As a straight-ahead power pitcher, Stoddard was effective when he had his control; without it, he could be woeful. Baseball is full of big, strong men who throw hard, but the long careers belong to those who throw intelligently as well. That there have been relatively few long careers of distinction is testimony to the virtue, and rarity, of true intelligence among pitchers. It was no accident that the best long-tenure pitchers of the era — Palmer, Steve Carlton, Tom Seaver, Tommy John — were also men of notable intellect.

Against Robin Yount, Stoddard, whose career was still too young to appraise fully, looked terrific. He started with a slider, high, for a ball, but then came back with three straight low outside pitches, slider, fastball, slider. Yount was way out ahead on the first one, fouled off the second, and committed himself too soon on the third, striking out on a pitch that dropped heavily, ending up virtually in the dirt.

Stoddard had managed to keep the ball down against Yount, and he worked the same way against Don Money. But Money was more patient than Yount. He stood in his deathly still pose, leaning over the plate, seemingly daring Stoddard to come inside on him. After three straight balls, all of them outside, Ross Grimsley got up in the bullpen. He was an old Weaver favorite who had come to the Baltimore camp as a non-roster player in the spring; he had last played for the Orioles in 1977, and when he had reached the end of his string with Montreal and then Cleveland, Weaver had picked him up.

Stoddard finally threw a strike to Money, a cripple pitch in a take situation. It came inside, where Money liked it; he tried to crouch a bit more as it approached, to shrink the upper limits of the strike zone, but a strike it clearly was. On the next pitch, a low fastball, Money walked.

Two outs, Money on first, Gantner on second, tie game, bottom of the eighth. Ben Oglivie was the hitter. Grimsley, a lefty, was available, but there would be a ninth inning to play as well, with two righties and a switch hitter scheduled, and possibly innings after that. Stoddard was, Weaver said later, "our Fingers." He wasn't, of course, but he was the best they had.

The Baltimore outfielders shifted to the right when Oglivie came to bat, as they had all day. Sakata, the shortstop, stationed himself almost directly behind second. In the dugout, coach Jimmy Williams, whose responsibility it was to position the outfielders, jumped from his seat on the bench and made exaggerated gestures to Lowenstein in left and Bumbry in center, waving both arms over his head in grand rightward sweeps, as if he were actually trying to push his fielders into even more radical a shift. He rose to the top step and swept his arms to the right again. They were playing Oglivie to pull, and one could presume they would therefore pitch him to pull.

Oglivie, though, was concentrating on Stoddard, on the moment, on the cosmic music that coursed through his quirky and independent mind. He said he often shut out the action around him, and that he was doing his job best if he didn't even notice where the defense was playing — or, for that matter, if there *was* a defense.

Stoddard checked Dempsey for his sign. The catcher asked for a fastball, and Stoddard came in high. On the next pitch, Dempsey set himself up toward third base, way on the outside edge of the plate. Stoddard's fastball came in low and inside, out of control. It was ball two.

The usually free-swinging Oglivie had now remained immobile for 19 of the 22 pitches he had seen in the game. Three times he had swung, singling in the third, then fouling off a pitch and flying out in the sixth. He had walked twice. A disciplined batter like Ken Singleton, himself a power hitter, walked 90, 100 times a year; Oglivie had walked as much as 50 times in a season only twice. He had stretches when he'd chase bad balls as much as anyone in the league, lashing out with his bat at pitches he couldn't hope to reach. Today, though, he had determined in the first inning that he'd be selective, and would force Baltimore's pitchers to come low and inside, where his power was. If they kept the ball outside, he'd walk; if they managed to hit the outside corner, he'd adjust when the count registered two strikes.

Again Dempsey set up on the outside, and it seemed as if Jimmy Williams' continued dugout histrionics were designed precisely so Oglivie *would* notice them, and expect to be pitched inside. But the batter was still concentrating on Stoddard, on the spot above the pitcher's shoulder where the ball would first appear. The public address system blared forth a bar of exhortatory organ music. The immense scoreboard in right center provided an accompanying lyric for the inattentive in the stands: "Charge!"

Stoddard's arm came swooping up and over, and a slider came hooking in, outside to inside. Oglivie strode and swung, a furious gesture that concluded with his feet actually leaving the ground as he tried to maintain his balance, and he landed astride the plate, facing Stoddard, as Dempsey rose from his crouch to toss the ball back.

It was 2 and 1, and then the same pitch, which Oglivie watched, made it 2 and 2. Again Dempsey squatted away from Oglivie, almost behind the right-handed batter's box. Oglivie prepared himself for a fastball, guessing that Dempsey would want Stoddard to blow it past him. But again it was a slider — only Stoddard released it a millisecond too late, a fraction of a fraction of an inch too far in front, and this one hooked in right over the center of the plate.

Oglivie swung, and the ball jumped off his bat on a line into right field. Jim Dwyer, already playing near the foul line, had no time to get in front of the ball, so sharply was it hit. It caromed off the wall, bouncing in toward center, skidding past him. He chased it down, spun, and threw toward Dauer, his cutoff man. Dauer caught the ball chest high, duplicated Dwyer's pirouette, and fired the ball to Dempsey. It was well aimed but a quarter second too late to catch Don Money — with his bad knees, his bad back, his repaired hernia — who had chugged into home behind Gantner. In the stands, fans made desultory by the long afternoon and the frittered lead exploded in cheers. Up on the terrace, sitting alone in his chair beneath the ladder, Bud Selig jumped to his feet, thrust a fist in the air, and just as quickly sat down and stuck his Cherry Tipalet back in his teeth.

Gorman Thomas finished the eighth for Milwaukee. His at-bat had a neat symmetry: Stoddard would throw a slider for a ball, then follow it with a fastball that Thomas would start lunging for before attempting, futilely, to check his swing. The count thus worked its way, alternate balls and Thomas lunges, to 3-2, when Thomas fouled a fastball back. Finally, Stoddard threw a high slider, and Thomas took another incomplete swing and turned to jog to first.

But umpire Morrison pronounced it strike three, and Thomas tossed his bat in the air. He couldn't believe it; the pitch was chin high. Morrison didn't disagree. He simply told Thomas he had gone around on his swing. Thomas was still expressing his incredulity when Harry Warner, the third base coach, ran by, grabbing Thomas and dragging him with him lest Morrison eject him for arguing a third strike call. Kuenn said, "I was almost out there myself. We didn't have anyone left to play center field."

9

	1	*2*	*3*	*4*	*5*	*6*	*7*	*8*	*9*	*R*	*H*	*E*
Baltimore	1	2	0	0	0	2	2	0		7	17	2
Milwaukee	2	0	4	0	1	0	0	2		9	14	0

Rollie Fingers had had a lead when he came in in the seventh, lost it, and then he had it again after the eighth. If he could hold on here in the ninth inning, he'd undoubtedly get some clubhouse ribbing about "vulturing a win," about giving up just enough runs to make certain he and not Slaton would be credited with a victory if the Brewers emerged triumphant. The condition of his fastball and the inscrutable success of John Lowenstein made him feel grateful he had managed to scrape by even moderately well thus far. The scheduled Baltimore hitters were Murray, Bumbry — and Lowenstein. All three would hit from the left side of the plate. Bumbry had never posed much of a problem for Fingers — his lifetime batting average against him was beneath .100 — but Murray and Lowenstein were murder. Fingers knew he was good, but he knew it only in that part of him that didn't need gallons of milk to soothe the knots and sores of doubt. Fortunately, if those doubts were part of his permanent baggage, so was the ineffable determination that enabled him to triumph over them.

At the other end of the pitcher-catcher line — a tightrope on which this half inning, this game, would now balance — crouched Ted Simmons. He was unused to the role of "relief catcher," but he had told Kuenn, less than two weeks earlier, that he was willing to do whatever the new manager wanted, that he simply wished to know where he stood. He had come to the Brewers in the over-heated atmosphere of the big trade and the reports of the big contract, and when he first showed up for spring training in Sun City in 1981, he was aloof from his new teammates. He seemed to be outside himself, watching to make sure he behaved in the right fashion, conscious he was the subject of attention. A few weeks into that spring, Simmons had posted a sheet on the clubhouse wall inviting everyone in camp to participate in a pool on the NCAA basketball tournament. Promoting the pool opened him up to his teammates, and his teammates began to open up to him. Then he performed dreadfully at the plate that season, and again at the start of '82. He was booed in Milwaukee. He and his manager hissed at each other from a distance. If his bat could not make him the hero he wished to be, or expected to be, life with the Brewers would be painful. He knew his arm was questionable, and he had heard too often that he was otherwise defensively deficient. Even Harcourt, his agent, said the Brewers had got in Simmons "close to an outstanding catcher," an appraisal that, from an agent, was comparable to a less partial commentator's saying "an overrated dud." Simmons had lived by his skills too long, and suddenly to find that they were unappreciated hurt. If Simmons allowed doubt to invade his playing persona, he would be signing a coda to his distinguished career.

At the home plate end of the Milwaukee dugout, Harvey Kuenn bore the on-field worries for Simmons, for Fingers, for all his players. In the end, after the roster-choosing, the daily lineup-making, the strategizing and thinking and cheerleading a manager provides, what he can also do for his team is serve as the receptacle of the doubts that each of the players, individually, dare not harbor. It is constantly said that a manager can't hit or pitch or field for his team. What is equally true is that he doesn't *have* to. The players bear the burden of performing while the manager bears the burden of worrying whether they will perform well enough to win. The players guess at the next pitch, what and where it will be. The manager guesses whether the man he has selected to perform a certain task in a certain situation is up to it. Managers ache. Critically, this enables players to *act*. What a team sees in its manager determines, in many ways, how free they are to play their best.

Thus, this team's apparent rebirth under Kuenn wasn't nearly so critical as the *opportunity* for rebirth that his appointment had given them. Because the team had played poorly this year for Rodgers and had since played well for Kuenn, there were those who thought that proved Rodgers was a bad manager. But the exiled

Rodgers wasn't a bad manager at all, unless one felt it was a sign of functional weakness for a man to become the object of a team's anger, and for the team to allow that anger to interfere with their on-the-field performance. Bruce Bochte's killing hit off Mike Caldwell in Seattle was the direct result of a move Rodgers made — but up until that point, even in that one game, the hitting and fielding and pitching that had kept the Brewers from building a safer lead were not. There is no evidence at all that happy teams win more games than grumpy teams; the egg of success usually precedes the chicken of contentment, and not the other way around. But Rodgers had become a focus of discontent, and Harry Dalton had correctly perceived that replacing the focus would immediately dissipate the discontent, and that eliminating the discontent could get his team's mind back on playing the game.

True, the day Kuenn walked into the clubhouse as the new manager and said, "Have fun," all Milwaukee's excuses evaporated. But — a crucial but — it could have been the same if Rodgers had succeeded Kuenn and said "Quit having so much fun and get down to *work.*" Change for its own sake, in the dynamic of the long season, was what this team needed. They needed, in a manager, someone on whom they could lay off their doubts.

Dalton, the general manager, never invoked the cliché "You can't fire the players, so you've got to fire the manager." First, he *could* fire the players, disperse them through trade and sale to other teams. It wouldn't have to have been wholesale, either: one or two personnel changes can capture a club's attention, and that's what was needed here. But Dalton had been too painstaking in the assembly of this team, and was generally too conservative to take radical action. What he needed, he knew, was controlled change. Another clubhouse speech, like the one he had delivered in '81, wouldn't do the trick, for that wasn't change at all: he had used that weapon, and by its familiarity it would have been ineffective if he employed it again. He also could've painted the clubhouse walls a different color or taken to wearing an electric beanie, but concentrated attention on his team was focused in only one place, and if that attention were to be galvanized, it would have to be by action in that place: this team was staring at the manager, and by changing the object of attention, Dalton could perhaps stun them out of their reverie. Players, like Paul Molitor, who had defended Rodgers before his dismissal later felt at ease placing ex post facto blame on him.

Harry Dalton had relieved all of them of a responsibility by making the move. He dismissed his friend Rodgers, tacitly admitting he had been wrong to hire him in the first place. (He didn't believe it — Rodgers had directed them well enough in 1981 — but the implication was unavoidable.) This admission excused the players; it left them free to play.

Bud Selig had once been something more of a meddler in the team's affairs, though he steadfastly denied it. Players, agents, and former employees, though, said that Selig in his earlier years had become involved in contract negotiations, in personnel decisions, and had even offered instructions to his managers about the lineups they were employing. But he had stopped that when Dalton arrived. His previous expeditions into baseball matters were born of his frustration, his overweening desire to see his team become competitive. Being the president of a baseball club was too sweet for Selig, too much a seat for pride and, at times, for the pain we sometimes enjoy visiting upon ourselves. When Selig's divorce from his first wife was heard in court in 1976, Donna Selig testified, "From the day Bud became involved in baseball, he divorced me and married baseball. Baseball came first. Donna came second." When the Brewers were doing badly, she testified, "Bud would be sullen and morose; he wouldn't speak to me; he wouldn't show me love or affection." The *Milwaukee Journal* reported, "Selig said her testimony was substantially true."

Selig didn't withdraw from baseball when he hired Dalton in 1978, but when the team turned around so quickly after Dalton's arrival, Selig could for once bask in success, not consume himself in failure. Much to his credit, he was content to know he had made the right decision in hiring Dalton and giving him freedom; some other owners would — many had — take the correctness of the decision to hire Dalton as evidence that they needed, and deserved, to be *more* involved in the team's affairs. Selig, agonized as he was by the team's poor performance through the first two months of the 1982 season, and by the dreadful midwestern weather that had had a brutal effect on the gate receipts, had learned to stand back, to chew his Tipalets and his nails and his doubts in the solitude of his seat on the terrace.

His worries, too, gave the players freedom. With Hackett and Haig he worked to produce the revenues that would meet his substantial payroll. Hiring Dalton, he placed the team's development processes in an orderly trust. All told, he provided the players with all they could ask: the opportunity to win or to lose. In 1887, John Montgomery Ward, the shortstop-pitcher-lawyer who organized the first players' union, said, "We are hired men, skilled in a particular employment, who work not only for profit, but for the amusement of our employers." Selig's amusement came in unpredictable increments, postponed by the countless daggers of disappointment and anxiety: valuable players suddenly injured, victories followed by losses, leads overcome, relief pitchers allowing tying runs to score. When the ninth inning began, a companion asked, "Do you think you might need Fingers to win tomorrow or this weekend? Isn't three innings too many for him?" Selig gazed at the field, his nerves taut, and said, "We need to win this one first."

And they did. Eddie Murray hit a fly ball to center, and Al Bumbry followed with a ground ball up the middle. Fingers reached for it and deflected it toward Gantner, who instantly reversed direction, charged in, fielded the ball bare-handed, and scooped it to Money at first for the out. Fingers fell after knocking the ball down, and as John Lowenstein came to the plate, Freddie Frederico came out to check on the pitcher's condition. He had bruised his knee slightly, but he brushed it off and assured Frederico he was fine. Paul Molitor had come over from third to witness Frederico's brief examination. As the trainer ran off the field, Molitor shook his fist at Fingers, who was staring at the unknowable Lowenstein, and said, "You owe this guy one."

Rollie Fingers saw Ted Simmons thrust one finger downward. He rocked back on his right foot, and threw his fastball — the bad pitch, the one they had been hitting, the one Lowenstein could sit on — right down the middle. The batter swung, and the ball soared high into center field. Gorman Thomas waited underneath it, and when he caught the ball, he thrust his arms into the air in relief as much as in exultation. The ball game was over.

	1	*2*	*3*	*4*	*5*	*6*	*7*	*8*	*9*	*R*	*H*	*E*
Baltimore	1	2	0	0	0	2	2	0	0	7	17	2
Milwaukee	2	0	4	0	1	0	0	2		9	14	0

As the players filed off the field and the fans deserted their seats, Harry Gill's grounds crew pulled the tarp over the batters' boxes and the pitching mound, and turned on the sprinkler system. A cleanup crew fanned out through the stands collecting the refuse left behind by nearly thirty thousand people. The *Sentinel's* Vic Feuerherd, who had been writing his story for the paper's first edition throughout the last three innings, abandoned his Texas Instruments Silent 700 Electronic Data Terminal in the press box and raced downstairs with the other reporters.

In the Baltimore clubhouse, Earl Weaver told the gathered writers, "Stoddard's the man; he's our Fingers. He hasn't been doing the job lately, so he might not be our Fingers much longer." He said he would rather have had Tippy Martinez pitch to Oglivie in the eighth. "But Tippy couldn't get Gantner, could he?" He said of the abortive hit-and-run in the sixth, when Dauer swung and missed as Dempsey dashed vainly toward second, "That's what's wrong with the goddamn hit-and-run." Finally, sucking a beer as he stripped down in the visitors' clubhouse, his usually engaging charm utterly absent, he said, "When you're giving it up, you might as well just shit in your pants. There ain't much else to do. Any time you get 17 hits and 4 home runs, you should win the goddamn ball game — any time on this fucking club, anyway."

Across the way, in the Milwaukee clubhouse, Kuenn sat in his office and spoke in homilies. "Fingers proved in the last inning he's as good as he was last year," he said. "There was no question about Rollie staying in in the ninth." An out-of-town reporter asked if Kuenn's first nine days on the job had been all he had expected. Kuenn looked at Dalton, sitting in a nearby chair, and took a long drag on his cigar. "Sure they have," he said, "except for the three days we lost."

The clubhouse emptied quickly as it usually does after a day game, so the players can get home to their families. (A few, though, loitered in the trainer's room even longer than usual: day games also mean huge crowds of kids waiting hungrily outside for autographs.) Forty minutes after the last out, the main room of the clubhouse contained only a clutch of eight or nine reporters, huddled around Ben Oglivie's locker, and the coaches, slowly getting dressed. Someone said to Pat Dobson, "I don't think you'd want to win 'em all this way," and Dobson replied, "If we could win 'em all, this way would be just fine." Oglivie was still in the trainer's room, the sanctuary. Deadlines were racing forward, but Oglivie was the game's star, the critical interview. Finally, after almost an hour, he emerged, in long underpants and shower clogs, his chiseled upper body black and gleaming.

"I didn't know I was keeping you guys here," the star said in all ingenuousness. "In the future, I'll be here — if I contribute."

The Brewers continued to play well through the season under Kuenn, reaching a tie for first place on July 3, fluttering at or near the top for a while, then assuming first for good on July 31. Kuenn stayed with his set lineup, playing Moore yet more frequently in right, proceeding in predictable and stately fashion, leading the team to a 72–43 record under his direction. Simmons' bat began to wake up, and with outstanding years being assembled by Molitor, Yount, and Cooper, the men who usually hit in front of him, he collected nearly 100 RBIs. Cooper, Thomas, Oglivie, and Yount all exceeded that number. Yount, especially, shone throughout the season, and was the near-unanimous selection of the baseball writers as the Most Valuable Player in the American League.

Rollie Fingers continued to be the burden bearer, closing down opposing teams until early September, when a muscle tear in his right forearm ended his season. Dalton acquired pitchers Doc Medich and Don Sutton late in the summer to help the club down the stretch. Sutton had negotiated with the Brewers in 1980, when he was a free agent, but Dalton and Selig thought his price — more than $700,000 a year — was too high. However, in 1982, as the Milwaukee club stood on the lip of a month-long race to the wire, what would have been a foolish investment suddenly looked sensible. Besides, the half-million-dollar signing bonus, the front-end money of Sutton's contract with the Houston Astros, from whom he was acquired, had been paid. Dalton felt he got Sutton when he needed him, and at a manageable price.

Indeed, down through the last month of the season, Sutton pitched brilliantly. It was fortunate, too, for as the last weeks of the season played out, the Brewers barely clung to their lead. The Boston Red Sox fell out of the race first, leaving the Baltimore Orioles as Milwaukee's sole challenger. As schedule-making fortuity would have it, Milwaukee approached the season's last weekend with a four-game series in Baltimore, leading the Orioles by three games.

Earl Weaver had announced his retirement effective the end of the season, and the Milwaukee series was potentially his last managerial appearance in Baltimore's Memorial Stadium. The Orioles won the first game, and then the second (on a complete game pitched by Storm Davis). When they took the Saturday game, the two teams were tied for the league lead. On Sunday, with Don Sutton pitching, the Brewers came out of their fog and won the pennant. Ben Oglivie's double on June 10 suddenly loomed very large.

But pennants are not won by one hit, or even one game, despite what the standings say. The roots of the Milwaukee success in 1982 (they went on to win the American League pennant playoffs against the California Angels, then lost the World Series in seven games to the St. Louis Cardinals, who had a young outfielder named David Green in the lineup) stretched back months and years, in countless directions: to Jim Gantner's fortuitous twelfth-round selection in the 1974 draft, to Bud Selig's support of Harvey Kuenn during his physical tribulations in the late 1970s, to Harry Dalton's apprenticeship with the Orioles in the 1950s. Ray Poitevint had scouted and signed David Green out of Nicaragua. Ray Scarborough (who died of a heart attack early in July) had lobbied hard for the trade that sent Green to St. Louis and had brought Fingers and company to Milwaukee. After his eventually wasted efforts with Paul Molitor, Sam Suplizio had taught Charlie Moore the fundamentals of outfield play. George Bamberger had insisted that Dalton retrieve Gorman Thomas from the Texas Rangers. George Blaeholder of St. Louis had perfected in the 1930s the pitch that Rollie Fingers had built his success upon.

And Bud Selig had devoted most of his adult life to baseball in Milwaukee. He had begun, he said, with Steve Hovley and Jerry McNertney, and had finally attained success with an outstanding collection of genuine stars. He had once needed to sell a million tickets to make a profit; in 1982, he said the 1,978,896 the club drew enabled it only to break even.

Meanwhile, baseball in Milwaukee was pumping over $100 million annually into the local economy. It was providing a city devastated by a faltering economy with spiritual health as well. It gave Selig himself something more than an auto dealership on which to center his professional life. And it gave all those who took part — players, ownership, fans — an arresting focus for an afternoon, a season, a lifetime.

EPILOGUE

The delicate scaffolding that enabled the Milwaukee Brewers to defeat Baltimore on June 10, 1982, and go on to win the American League pennant took much less time to crumble than to build. Less than two years after Bud Selig's team had reached the pinnacle of baseball, it plummeted to the very bottom. The 1984 Brewers finished with the worst record in the entire American League.

The powerful team that Harry Dalton had assembled came apart in the only fashion that these things happen: suddenly. It is hard to imagine the best team so quickly becoming the worst team, but Dalton and his associates had put together a fragile juggernaut, as too many players in too many key positions reached the age of fragility or decay. Indeed, everyone over 30 on the championship team was ineffective by 1984, and of the younger players, only Gantner continued to perform at peak efficiency. At the same time, of those players who made up Milwaukee's second string in 1982, not one had emerged as an everyday player, and no new talent of note had yet bubbled up from the farm system.

In the meantime, pitcher Frank DiPino, who had gone to Houston in the Don Sutton deal, collected fourteen saves in 1984. Of the two young players who went to St. Louis in the Simmons trade, Dave LaPoint had become a regular rotation starter and David Green, though retarded in his progress toward stardom by an acknowledged drinking problem, had become the Cardinals' regular first baseman. Perhaps most dismaying of all, players Dalton had rejected in trades — pitcher Joaquin Andujar and infielder Ryne Sandberg — had joined the major leagues' very best players: in 1984,

Andujar won more games than any other National League pitcher, and Sandberg was the NL's Most Valuable Player. For the inconsequential price of Dick Davis in the winter of 1980–81, Dalton could have had Andujar; the following year, for Mike Caldwell, he could have had Sandberg. The trades Dalton did make won Milwaukee a pennant in 1982; those he didn't make might have saved his team from ignominy two years later.

This is what happened to the members of Milwaukee's June 10, 1982, batting order in the two years following:

• Third baseman Paul Molitor suffered yet another major injury at the start of the 1984 season — this time, it was his elbow — and did not get back in uniform all year.
• Shortstop Robin Yount, who was elected the league's Most Valuable Player in 1982, endured back problems. His 16 home runs in 1984 led the team; indeed, Milwaukee, which had paced the league with 216 homers in the pennant year, managed a league-worst 95 in 1984.
• Don Money, the first baseman, in short order got his release from Milwaukee, went to play in Japan, and, unhappy there, returned home to a permanent retirement. The man he had replaced in the batting order on June 10, Cecil Cooper, in 1984 suffered his worst season in ten years, batting only .275, with 67 runs batted in.
• Ben Oglivie's power deserted him almost as suddenly as he had discovered it in 1978. He hit 13 home runs in 1983, 12 in 1984.
• Gorman Thomas was gone from County Stadium's center field by midsummer of 1983, traded to the Cleveland Indians. His bitterness about the trade was exceeded only by the decline of his skills. The following season, when he was shunted along to the Seattle Mariners, a crippling arm injury placed Thomas's career in jeopardy.
• Roy Howell remained a fifth wheel, coming to bat but 358 times in 1983 and '84; at the close of the second year, he was granted his unconditional release. The regular designated hitter, Ted Simmons, saw his batting prowess return for one last season in 1983 and then abandon him again in 1984. Simmons also fired LaRue Harcourt, the agent who had engineered his lucrative transfer from St. Louis to Milwaukee.

- Charlie Moore, who caught for Simmons on June 10, soon moved permanently to the outfield and fairly soon after that to the bench. Third-string catcher Ned Yost was traded to Texas, where he proved to be the weakest hitting regular in the league; more surprising, he was virtually incapable of throwing out opposition base stealers.
- By Opening Day, 1984, outfielder Marshall Edwards was back in the minor leagues, where he would remain.
- Jim Gantner, alone among the offensive players, continued to perform to expectations; in 1984 he batted .282, with 56 runs batted in.

The pitching staff became equally unglued. Bob McClure won nine games in 1983, only four the following year. Jim Slaton was traded to California for Bobby Clark, an outfielder whom Dalton had signed to his first contract in 1975 but who distinguished himself little thereafter. Age and its companion, injury, caused Rollie Fingers to miss the last month of 1982 and all of 1983. He came back strong in '84, but his season ended in midsummer, near his thirty-eighth birthday, when he developed a severe back ailment. Mike Caldwell simply declined into ineffectiveness. Of all Milwaukee's pitchers, Pete Vuckovich experienced the most thudding crash to earth. Though he won the Cy Young Award in 1982, his peculiar variety of motions finally caught up with him. In all of 1983 and 1984, Vuckovich managed to appear in but three games.

Off the field, talk of money was the greatest distraction. The Brewer payroll continued to escalate as both Yount and Molitor signed contracts guaranteeing them each more than $1 million annually, and Gantner signed after the 1984 season for more than $900,000 a year. A home attendance record was set in the post-pennant year, but 1984 saw paid admissions decline to 1,608,509, the club's lowest full-season level since 1978. Still, Bud Selig could no longer cite the slow upward progress of franchise prices to justify baseball's cries of economic catastrophe. At the end of 1983, the Detroit Tigers were sold for more than $50 million; a far weaker franchise in a much smaller market, the Minnesota Twins, changed hands for more than $30 million in 1984.

On the labor front, the chief owners' negotiator Ray Grebey was dumped in '83, as was Kenneth Moffett, whom the players had hired to replace Marvin Miller at the end of 1982. Commissioner Bowie Kuhn failed to gather the necessary votes for his own reelection in 1983, and he stayed on the job through the '84 season only to keep the chair warm for his successor, Peter Ueberroth, who had shepherded the 1984 Los Angeles Olympics to financial success. As Ueberroth assumed his post, he said he wished to be the commissioner for "all of baseball." Just ahead as he spoke was the expiration of the Basic Agreement that had emerged from the 1981 strike.

Among the managers, Earl Weaver retired at the close of 1982 and spent the next two years playing golf, doing some occasional broadcasting, and watching his name pop up in print whenever a managerial vacancy occurred. Harvey Kuenn was fired after guiding the Brewers to a fifth-place finish in 1983. His immediate successor, Rene Lachemann, was bounced at the close of the catastrophic 1984 season. Bob Rodgers, who had stayed out of baseball for slightly more than a year following his own dismissal, returned in 1984 to manage the Montreal Expos' Indianapolis farm club in the American Association to the best record in minor league baseball; he was rewarded after the season with a promotion to the manager's job in Montreal.

And back in Milwaukee, on the last weekend of the 1984 season, Harry Dalton announced the appointment of a new manager who, he thought, might lead his team up from the basement and into the realm of American League respectability: George Bamberger.

MILWAUKEE (AP), June 10 — A two-run, two-out double by Ben Oglivie snapped a 7–7 tie in the eighth inning and carried Milwaukee past Baltimore, 9–7.

Jim Gantner opened the inning with a single and Paul Molitor sacrificed. Tim Stoddard relieved Tippy Martinez and walked Don Money to put runners on first and second with two out. Oglivie followed with his double to the right-field corner.

The Orioles and the Brewers engaged in a long-ball hitting contest in the first two innings. Lenn Sakata led off the first with his second homer of the season for Baltimore, but Money followed a single by Molitor with his eighth homer in the bottom of the first to give Milwaukee a 2–1 lead.

Baltimore regained the lead at 3–2 in the second when Rick Dempsey and Rich Dauer slammed consecutive homers.

The Brewers chased Sammy Stewart, the Oriole starter, in the third. Singles by Money, Oglivie and Gorman Thomas loaded the bases before Roy Howell drilled a two-run double to left.

Brewers 9, Orioles 7

BALTIMORE	AB	R	H	BI	MILWAUKEE	AB	R	H	BI
Sakata, ss	5	1	2	1	Molitor, 3b	4	1	2	1
Ripken, 3b	5	1	3	0	Yount, ss	5	0	1	0
Ford, rf	4	1	2	0	Money, 1b	4	3	2	2
Dwyer, rf	1	0	0	0	Oglivie, lf	3	1	2	2
E. Murray, 1b	5	0	2	1	Thomas, cf	5	1	1	0
Ayala, lf	1	0	0	0	Howell, dh	3	1	1	2
Bumbry, cf	4	1	1	0	Brouhard, ph	1	0	0	0
Roenicke, cf	3	0	0	0	Moore, c	4	0	0	1
Lowenstein, lf	2	0	1	1	Edwards, rf	3	1	2	1
Singleton, dh	4	1	1	2	Simmons, c	1	0	0	0
Dempsey, c	4	1	2	1	Gantner, 2b	4	1	3	0
Dauer, 2b	4	1	3	1					
TOTALS	42	7	17	7	TOTALS	37	9	14	9

Baltimore   120 002 200–7
Milwaukee   204 010 02x–9

E–Roenicke, Dempsey. DP–Baltimore 1, Milwaukee 1. LOB–Baltimore 8, Milwaukee 8. 2B–Howell, Molitor, Oglivie. HR–Sakata (2), Money (8), Dempsey (4), Dauer (5), Singleton (5). SB–Edwards. S–Molitor.

BALTIMORE	IP	H	R	ER	BB	SO
Stewart	2⅓	7	6	6	1	1
Davis	3⅔	5	1	1	1	2
T. Martinez						
(L, 1–4)	1⅓	1	1	1	0	0
Stoddard	⅔	1	1	1	1	2
MILWAUKEE						
McClure	2⅓	6	3	3	0	1
Slaton	3⅔	6	2	2	0	3
Fingers						
(W, 3–5)	3	5	2	2	0	2

WP–Stewart. T–3:04. A–22,013.

Source: *New York Times,* June 11, 1982

INDEX